Shakti

Aum Sri Ganeshaya Namaha!

Sarva vigna haram devam,
Sarva vigna vivarjitam,
Sarva siddhi pradhadaram,
Vandeham Gananayakam

I bow to Lord Ganesha,
Who removes all obstacles,
And gives all knowledge.

Ambikahridayanandam
Mathrubi paripalitam,
Bhaktapriyam madonmatham,
Vandeham Gananayakam

I bow to Lord Ganesha of supreme intellect,
Who is the delight of his mother Ambika,
And beloved by his devotees.

Shakti

Realm of the Divine Mother

VANAMALI

Inner Traditions
Rochester, Vermont

Inner Traditions
One Park Street
Rochester, Vermont 05767
www.InnerTraditions.com

Originally published in India in 2006 by Aryan Books International under the title *Sri Devi Lila: The Play of the Divine Mother*

Library of Congress Cataloging-in-Publication Data

Vanamali, 1935–
  [Sri Devi Lila]
Shakti : realm of the Divine Mother / Vanamali.
  p. cm.
Originally published: Sri Devi Lila. Aryan Books International, 2006.
Includes bibliographical references and index.
ISBN 978-1-59477-199-6 (pbk.)
1. Goddesses, Hindu. I. Title.
BL1216.V34 2008
294.5'2114—dc22

2008017988

Printed and bound in the United States

10 9 8 7 6 5 4

Text design and layout by Priscilla Baker
This book was typeset in Garamond Premier Pro, with Kingsbury used as a display typeface

To send correspondence to the author of this book, mail a first-class letter to the author c/o Inner Traditions • Bear & Company, One Park Street, Rochester, VT 05767, and we will forward the communication.

Aum Sri Adbhutacharitrayai Namaha!

Amale Kamalasana sahide,
Adbuda charithe,
Palayamam.

O Amala! Who sits on a lotus,
Whose stories fill us with wonder,
Pray protect me.

◆

Dedicated to my beloved daughter Amala

Aum Brahmanyai Namaha!

I meditate on the beginningless Brahmavidya,
who is of the nature of All Consciousness (Satchidananda Swarupini).
May She stimulate our intelligence to the realization of THAT.

Contents

Aum Ambayai Namaha!

Foreword

Mata Devi Vanamali—Mataji, as I shall refer to her hereinafter—is a fit person to write about the Divine Mother of the universe. Mataji is a deep devotee who is also filled with India's ancient concept of wisdom or *jnana*. Because my own devotion to God finds particular expression to the Divine Mother, I was deeply touched when Mataji asked me if I would write a few words of introduction to this beautiful book.

There are two aspects of the important subject of the cosmic mother: the scriptural and the experiential. Mataji has rightly given us the scriptural slant on the subject. In this age, when most of us think of God as "He," it is necessary to point out, as Mataji has done, that God is neither He nor She, and at the same time God is both! In the words of a great Kaali *bhakta* (devotee) of Bengal, Ram Prasad, "A thousand Vedas declare my Tara [a name for the Divine Mother] is *nirakara* [without form]."

Yet religion in these times has become too rationally formal and therefore too rational altogether. Years ago in America, the inspiration came to me to spread the concept of God as mother and not only as father. I wasn't thinking of the Virgin Mother only, as is more common in the West, but of the formless infinite in its motherly aspect. I went to many Western shrines dedicated to the Divine Mother and worshipped in them. I received in each of them great inspiration and love. And I say now, is it not time for dogmatic religion to be replaced by devotion and love? There has been too much *thinking* about God. Mankind must learn to love Him, to talk with Him, and to experience Him. And that "Him" needs to be understood first in its higher impersonal aspect and then brought down to earth in its more truly personal aspect as the Divine Mother.

For God is inherent in "His" different aspects, though each in essence is different from every other aspect. It matters not only how we ourselves look upon God and define Him in our minds; it is also a question of how God views us. If we invoke God as the Divine Mother, She comes closer to us. The infinite—which is beyond all sexual differences, comprising the maternal as well as the paternal principle—opens its heart to us when we appeal to it as mother.

There is a story from the life of that same poet, singer, and saint Ram Prasad. He was mending the fence in front of his house. At one point, his daughter came up to him and offered to help with his job. He had been singing. She said to him, "Whom have you been singing to, Papa?"

"I've been singing to my Divine Mother," he replied. "But she's very naughty. I keep calling and calling her but she won't answer!"

"If she doesn't answer, Papa, why do you waste your time calling to her?" The little girl then ran off with a childish laugh.

When Ram Prasad came indoors later on, he told his wife how their daughter had come and helped him with the fence and talked to him playfully.

"But that's not possible," answered his wife. "Today she's visiting on the other side of our village."

"But I know it was her," he exclaimed. Later on when their daughter returned home, he pressed her, "Wasn't it you helping me with our fence today?"

"Why no, Papa. You can ask anybody. I was with friends on the other side of our village."

Thus did Ram Prasad come to know that the Divine Mother herself had come to him and teased him.

"O my Mother!" he cried. "What a naughty dear you are! Though you pretend to be inaccessible, you are ever near me and, Mother, ever dearest to me."

All aspects of God hear us when we pray, but the Divine Mother listens to us—I don't say more so but more particularly. For we are her children. She cares for each one of us specially. When we err, she spanks us through the law of karma. But when we love her, she also forgives. For she is ever anxious for us to understand that we may return with outstretched arms to her lap of infinity!

SWAMI KRIYANANDA (J. DONALD WALTERS),
FOUNDER OF THE ANANDA COMMUNITY
AND AUTHOR OF *THE HINDU WAY OF AWAKENING*

Aum Aim Hreem Kleem

Aum Devyayai Namaha!

ॐ

How do I love thee,
Countless are the ways.
From the glistening locks on thy forehead,
To the tips of thy lotus feet,
Drenched am I in the radiance of thy form.
Thy arched brows, thy shell-like ears,
Thy upper lip of exquisite beauty,
The lower one a treasure trove of desire,
Soft and sweet like the petals of a rose.
Thy determined chin,
Thy slender neck,
O queen of desire, Kameswari,
Accept this gift of love.
Filled with the wondrous tales of thy glory,
I lay this book at thy golden feet,
This holy book,
Timidly—my offering of love.

—Vanamali

Aum Paramatmikayai Namaha!

Introduction

Ya Devi sarvabhuteshu, Vishnumayethi shabdita,
Namasthasyai, namasthasyai, namasthasyai namo namaha!

O Goddess who is known as Vishnu Maya in all creatures,
Hail to thee, hail to thee, all hail to thee!

The ancient sages of India looked at our amazing world, filled with beauty, filled with fascinating and horrifying forms, and wondered what it is all about. Is this the only face of the creator, or is there something beyond this? Somehow they were sure that this extraordinary universe with its myriad structures is only the mask that hides the visage behind.

A Rig Veda hymn says,

> *By a golden lid*
> *Is hidden the face of Truth,*
> *Uncover it O Sustainer!*
> *Let the seeker behold it!*

The scriptures describe many paths for discovering the truth underlying the phenomenal world as well as the truth of one's own self, and

1

these paths are known as *yogas*. But what we should remember is that all the paths of *yoga* are only different methods by which this golden lid can be removed.

Hindu philosophy asserts that the Brahman is the supreme reality underlying both the manifest and unmanifest states of being. It is an integrated state that is changeless, indivisible, without distinctions, and utterly beyond human comprehension. It can be known only by the direct experience of penetrating and transcending the levels of the mind on the material plane. In this way consciousness becomes aware of its own real, undying nature, which is also the nature of the supreme unmanifest.

The individual spirit or *atman* is a centralized or contracted expression of the Brahman. It contains the whole in a potential form. Though it is nothing but an expression of the supreme consciousness, it is obscured by the limited psychological world of the individual. When pure consciousness descends to the individual frame, it begins to relate to its limited body and displays itself in different ways according to its inherent nature, and thus it plays its own distinct role in the drama of manifestation. Although the centers of consciousness in the individual frames appear to be many, they are actually not separate. In the manifest realm they function separately through the agency of their separate minds. In the realm of the unmanifest, however, they cannot be considered as separate since they have emanated from the one supreme consciousness. This divine mystery can be comprehended only by the direct realization of the source from which the *atmans* have sprung. Thus a reverse process is possible in which the *jivatman* (embodied soul) is capable of withdrawing inward to its central source through *yoga* and contemplation and developing to its full divine status. Cosmic evolution proceeds from the superconscious, unmoving, unknowable, and unmanifest absolute to the conscious, moving, knowable, and manifest microcosm. Human evolution is a return journey from the gross physical plane of the microcosm back to the absolute. In one case the force is centrifugal and in the other centripetal. Thus all embodied souls represent different expressions of the ultimate reality of the Brahman, which is whole, indivisible, and integrated through different centers of consciousness.

Brahman is the uncaused cause of everything, the one source of all qualities and forms, though in itself it has no qualities and no forms. From this basic standpoint, Hinduism gives us the freedom to worship God in whatever shape appeals to us. We are each given liberty to accept any form of the divine that appeals to us as our personal aspect of reality, dearest to our heart. The logic behind this stance is that that which is formless can take on any form. This is the basis of the great tolerance found in the Hindu religion. Since the Brahman is formless and qualityless, any form can be worshipped as "its" form. As the Vayu Purana asserts, "He who fanatically affirms the superiority of one deity or incarnation over another is a sinner."

According to Hinduism, the purpose of life is to return to the source from which we have come. The embodied soul (*jivatman*) comes from the Brahman, goes through the dramas of its many lives, and then at last desires to return to its origin. All Hindu scriptures, epics, ceremonies, and festivals are charged with this spiritual connotation. They have a far-reaching esoteric significance that is not always readily apparent. All rituals, even those that we perform automatically, are a spiritual dedication of the soul for that single aspiration it has been enshrining within itself from eternity. All Hindu scriptures likewise are dedicated to this aspiration, but unfortunately, the casual reader will not understand this.

Ancient India saw no contradiction between science and religion. The ancient *rishis* or philosophers were both scientists and spiritualists. They understood that the basis of all matter is spiritual. Their investigations into the material world took them to the spiritual world, since they did not hold any preconceived notions about a world that existed apart from its spiritual foundations. Modern Western scientists, however, started from the unfortunate hypothesis that nature, man, and God are totally unconnected, so that it took a very long time for them to understand this truth. Even now they have not fully grasped it; it was only in the twentieth century that they began to glimpse this connection.

Not long ago advanced thinkers believed that science would ultimately overthrow all the age-old spiritual concepts and reconstruct human society on a purely materialistic basis. But now we see that a totally different picture is emerging. Einstein himself said,

> The most beautiful and the most profound emotion we can experience is the sensation of the mystical. It is the source of all true art and science. He to whom this emotion is a stranger—who can no longer pause to wonder and stand rapt in awe, is as good as dead; his mind and eyes are closed. The insight into the mystery of life coupled though it may be with fear has given rise to religion. To know that, what is impenetrable to us, really exists, manifesting itself as the highest wisdom and most radiant beauty which our dull faculties can comprehend only in their most primitive forms—this knowledge, this feeling is at the centre of true religiousness.

The *rishis* of ancient India were able to experience this knowledge through deep personal understanding brought about by intense austerity and meditation.

Indian philosophy is famous for its symbolism, and from ancient times Indian pictorial representations of God took both male and female forms. Over time, the universal form of the motionless absolute came to be associated with the male form and the manifested energy of nature with the female form. The absolute and nature are therefore not two but two-in-one; they are necessary to each other as complementary manifestations of the one.

In the Skanda Purana, Indra, the king of the gods, asks Vishnu how the Brahman is able to project itself as both male and female. Vishnu replies, "Listen, O Indra, the male and female are eternal principles involved in the projection of the universe. They are never separate.

Fundamentally they are one, as gold and ornaments made of it are one."

This two-in-one existence came to be known as Purusha and Prakriti or Shiva and Shakti. It is something like the dynamo and the force that charges it; one is powerless without the other. Shiva and Shakti are polar opposites, inseparable but having a varying relative predominance under different directions. But in the unmanifest, each aspect of the one reality is only a potential. It is merged in the pure consciousness with the other and is indistinguishable from it.

So we find that in Hindu mythology Prakriti and Purusha or Shiva and Shakti are always found together, though when they are manifest in an organism one or the other predominates according to the organism's stage of evolution. If the *jivatman* wants to realize its own divine nature, it has to extricate itself from the illusory haze created by *maya shakti*, penetrate through its own center, and emerge on the other side of the point, as it were. It is then in the realm of pure consciousness and is able to have a direct experience of that consciousness that is both Shiva and Shakti. (This process is explained in detail in chapter 31.)

Shakti, or Devi, presupposes all forms of existing knowledge—past, present, and future. She is the female creative aspect of the Brahman. It is through her that the one becomes the many. She is Adi Shakti, the primeval force, and the first emanation of power from the absolute, Brahman. She is the womb of the universe.

Creation and dissolution follow each other. It is a cyclical process, not the linear one described in Western philosophy. During the period of dissolution, Shakti lies quiescent. Just as the tree lies latent in the seed, so this universe of names and forms lies enfolded in Shakti. In fact, Shakti is a mass of latent, undifferentiated energy that rests in the Brahman and contains the seed power of many universes. During the period of creation this energy flowers into the manifest, evolved cosmos, and during dissolution it withdraws everything into itself and remains in the latent state till the next period of evolution and creation. This expansion and contraction continues throughout eternity. Like day and night the universe alternately expands into matter and recedes into primal energy or Mula Prakriti. From Shakti comes this entire manifestation of myriad forms, from the stars to the earthworms, from the oceans to the dewdrops! Shakti *is* cosmic energy, the physical ultimate of all forms of matter. Matter is nothing but energy in motion, as modern physics has come to acknowledge. Spirit and energy are inseparable. They are essentially one. They are like fire and heat.

In the Bhagavad Gita, Lord Krishna tells Arjuna, "Earth, water, fire, air, ether, mind, intellect, and ego—these constitute the eightfold division of my nature. Know this to be my lower nature. My higher nature, O Arjuna, is that spiritual being that sustains the entire universe. That is quite different from this. These two natures form the womb of all beings. I am thus the origin and the dissolution of the entire universe." This spiritual being of which Krishna speaks is what the Devi Bhagavatam describes as Devi or Adi Shakti or Mula Prakriti.

Shakti, the mother power or divine energy, has many forms and symbols. All beauty and all ugliness flow from her. She is Lakshmi, the auspicious, bestower of boons and beauty. She is Saraswati, the giver of all wisdom and art. She is Tripurasundari, the most beauteous in the three worlds. But she is also Kaali, the destroyer, whose wrath ignites the storm, the thunder, and the lightning. She is Mahishasuramardini, killer of the demon Mahisha. She is Chandika, the terrible, who lets loose the typhoon, the flood, and the tidal wave.

The Shakta cult is one of many in which the divine is worshipped in the form of the Divine Mother. Such mother worship has fascinated humankind through all time, since the mother is one with whom everyone can have an intimate relationship. In fact, this is a primary relationship. The devotee has greater freedom when he conceives of God as mother. The great sage of Bengal, Sri Ramakrishna, said, "Just as a child can force his demands on his mother, so a devotee can force his demands on God as mother."

Goddess worship is said to have begun in ages long past among the ancient hunter-gatherer tribes of prehistoric India. Archaeologists have unearthed goddess figures in the earliest strata of Indian settlements. Goddess worship kept on growing and growing until today it is a full-fledged sect with adherents among all the cults that exist in India. The goddess might have begun as a simple divinity of one universal goddess representing the earth deity, but she has slowly assumed different forms and different names until at last we have a whole pantheon of female goddesses with different functions. But we must understand that all of them are merely powers of the one universal Shakti—Adi Shakti or Parashakti.

Some savants assert that Shaktism is an intrusion of non-Aryan thought into the mainstream of Aryanism. They affirm that the mother-worship cult is pre-Aryan and originally belonged to the Sumerian and other cultures. Whatever the truth may be, we can only assert that the worship of the mother aspect of God is as deeply rooted in human nature as the worship of the father aspect. Today it is an integral part of the Hindu culture. It has been practiced and elaborated by millions of seekers during the ages. Poor and rich alike can approach the Divine Mother, some with wisdom and some out of despair, but all have love in their hearts. Shaktism has inspired saints and yogis, artists and poets.

The worship of God as mother is found in all civilizations. In Egypt she was known as Isis, in Babylon and Assyria as Ishtar, in Greece as Demeter, and in Phrygia as Cybele. Judaism and later on Islam put an end to mother worship in the Middle East. Christianity repressed it at first but later came to venerate the Virgin Mary as the mother of God.

Our first relationship with the world is through our mother. The earliest memory of any person is that of lying on his or her mother's lap and gazing into her love-filled eyes. In the mother is centered a whole world of tenderness, love, nourishment, and care. She is the embodiment of security. She personifies the ideal of love, from which the child draws sustenance, comfort, protection, and nourishment. To transfer this concept to a cosmic being is a natural step, which the ancients took. Therefore we can understand that the concept of the Divine Mother is as old as life itself. It is only natural to think of the divine as the cosmic mother, who lov all, nourishes all, cares for all, and protects all. Devi is the Divine Mother, the eternal womb of all creatures, human and animal. She cradles her children in her loving arms, suckles them, and nurtures them with her infinite love in all forms. Wherever you see maternal love, in a bird or an animal or a human being, know that to be but an aspect of Devi's love for the universe, for she is the universal mother.

The wonder is that this modern age seems to have forgotten the Divine Mother's very existence. This is the Dark Age, Kali Yuga, in which our increasing engrossment with the physical side of life has torn us away from our metaphysical roots and alienated us from our Divine Mother. The ancients were nurtured by the milk of kindness that is always oozing from the breasts of our Divine Mother, and that is why they had a sense of the higher purpose of human life, a sensibility that seems to be lost in this age.

In terms of power the Divine Mother has a dual aspect: one as *avidya,* or cosmic delusion, and one as *vidya,* or cosmic deliverance. She binds us with her bewildering *maya* (cosmic illusion) in this worldplay of birth, death, and enjoyment. On the other hand, it is she who releases us from this wheel of existence. Artists have depicted her as holding a noose in one hand, with which she binds us, and a sword in the other, with which she cuts the knot.

Another beautiful image of the Divine Mother is that of the Indian kite, which children play with. The Divine Mother also plays this game. The thread that holds her kite has sharp bits of glass in it, and as the kites soar up into the sky, she cuts the thread of some of them and releases them from their bondage. The kites stand for souls in bondage. In both aspects, as the deluder and the releaser, the Divine Mother has set up this cosmic drama. She deludes us by her *maya* and makes us keep on playing the game endlessly. But when she sees that we are no longer interested in this game and wish to discover the controller of the game, she releases us by cutting the string.

Sri Ramakrishna gives another beautiful allegory of the Divine Mother. As long as the child is playing with his toys, the mother busies herself with household chores, but when the child throws away the toys and cries for its mother, she puts down the cooking pot and runs to the child. This analogy illustrates the strong bond that exists between the divine conceived as the mother and the devotee.

One who has become fed up with the vain and futile running about in the game of the world has only to turn to the Divine Mother and beg her to release him from it. She will do so if his desire is strong enough. Her grace is infinite. Her compassion and love for all human beings and especially for true seekers is indescribable. The Divine Mother is ever ready to take back the straying child into her arms. It is true that she is the one who has set about this momentary play of duality, this divine drama upon the stage of the physical universe. But she is ever ready to take back into her loving bosom those children who have lost interest in the play and have had enough. The child who has wandered far from the Divine Mother one day realizes that she is the only source of security and runs back to her and begs her to take her back into her arms. The Divine Mother opens her arms wide, and the errant child jumps into them and regains her original bliss.

Purusha is that which we cannot know or conceive. It is the supreme being, the transcendental Para Brahman. That which we know through our mind and senses is nothing but the manifestation of the Divine Mother. Everything that we can think of or know is the form of the goddess. But she has a transcendental aspect as well. She is not contained in this little universe of which the earth is a part, with its sun and moon and countless stars and solar systems. All this is but an infinitesimal speck in the vastness and infinity of the Divine Mother. Innumerable such universes have their rise and fall within her ample bosom. She is all-power and all-manifestation through eternity and infinity.

The Devi Bhagavatam describes the Divine Mother as the mother of the trinity—Brahma, Vishnu, and Maheswara (Shiva). These three dynamic manifestations of the absolute are all manifestations of Adi Shakti, or the first force. As Brahma Shakti, she manifests in the form of Saraswati. As Vishnu Shakti, she manifests in the form of Lakshmi.

And as Shiva Shakti, she manifests in the form of Durga or Kaali. These are not three distinct devis but the one energy of the Brahman worshipped in three different manifestations. She is the creator of many worlds and universes; numerous Brahmas, Vishnus, and Shivas have emanated from her.

In her transcendental aspect she is Prakriti or Para Brahma Swarupini, the form of the absolute Brahman. Therefore, when we worship the Divine Mother, we are not only offering adorations to the supreme in its aspect of motherhood but also adoring the supreme absolute. She is that aspect of the supreme power by whose grace alone we shall be ultimately released from the darkness of ignorance and the bondage of *maya* and taken to the abode of immortal knowledge, immortality, and bliss.

The problem with writing about the Divine Mother is that there is no complete story about her. She has taken many manifestations in order to help her devotees and especially the gods. All these are described in various Puranas, so her stories will not have a consecutive order but will be chosen at random from various sources. May she bless this poor scribe with the power to write about her mysterious *lilas* (cosmic plays).

> *For One was there Supreme behind the God,*
> *A Mother Might brooded upon the world.*
> *A consciousness revealed its marvellous front.*
> *Transcending all that is, denying none,*
> *Imperishable above our fallen heads,*
> *The undying truth appeared, the enduring power,*
> *Of all that here is made and then destroyed,*
> *The Mother of all godheads, and all strength*
> *Who, mediatrix, binds earth to the Supreme.*
>
> —*SAVITRI* BY SRI AUROBINDO

Aum Aim Hreem Kleem

Aum Prakrityai Namaha!

1

Prakriti

Sarvamangala maangalye
Shive sarvartha sadhike,
Sharanye tryambake Gauri,
Narayani namosthuthe!

Salutations to Devi Narayani, who is blessed with every
    felicity,
Filled with auspiciousness, able to accomplish everything,
Who is the protectress, the three-eyed Gauri.

The Sanskrit word *pra* means "exalted," "superior," or "excellent," and
the word *kriti* means "creation." So the Divine Mother is known as
Mula Prakriti, since she is the supreme creator of the world. Prakriti
is the eternal matrix from which all the components of reality have
sprung. She is the point in the center of the ocean of energy that is the
ultimate source of all the energetic fields that Western science knows,
like gravity, the electromagnetic field, and so on. Tantric philosophy
calls this point the Divine Mother, Devi Prakriti, or Parashakti. She
is the very source of the subtle dimensions of reality that our physical
senses can never perceive.

All creation is made up of combinations and permutations of the

11

three *gunas*, or essential qualities of Prakriti: *sattva, rajas, and tamas*. Her name correlates directly to these qualities, with *pra* denoting *sattva, kri* denoting *rajas,* and *ti* denoting *tamas.* These *gunas* are found in all aspects of creation; they are the qualitative building blocks of creation. Without them the universe and its inhabitants would have no qualities. *Tamas* has the ability to distort reality, *rajas* to veil reality, and *sattva* to allow it to be seen, though dimly. If we employ the terms used in physics, we can say that *tamas* is the quality of inertia, *rajas* of kinesis, and *sattva* of equilibrium. *Tamas, rajas,* and *sattva* correspond to different colors, according to Indian thought. *Tamas* is black, *rajas* red, and *sattva* white. These are the colors of the Divine Mother herself: Kaali is black, Lakshmi red, and Saraswati white.

Prakriti is known as Maha Maya or the great deluder. But her *maya,* or power of illusion, has two aspects: *vidya maya* and *avidya maya. Vidya maya* is the power of the goddess to dispel illusion by illumining our intellect through knowledge of reality; it is omnipotent and omniscient and is capable of revealing the Brahman, which is Prakriti's receptacle. (Remember she is known as Para Brahma Swarupini, or the very form of the Brahman.) *Avidya maya* is the goddess's power to veil, by which she binds the immortal soul to the mortal frame of the body. The three *gunas* form the very essence of the Divine Mother's *avidya maya.* Through *avidya maya* the supreme self is reflected in the individual as the *jiva* or *jivatman*—the embodied soul that has forgotten its original, pristine state. The *jivatman* is said to have three bodies: the gross body (or physical body), the subtle body (consisting of the mind, ego, and intellect), and the causal body (the astral body, which transmigrates to the spiritual plane). Prakriti resides in the subtle body in two different forms as *vidya maya* and *avidya maya.*

Avidya maya conceals the supreme, and thus the *jivatman* experiences all types of sorrows. In actuality the self or inner spirit, the *atman,* is self-luminous; it is the eternal and blissful fountain of love. *Jnana* or knowledge is the very nature of the *atman.* It is the basis of the knowledge of "I am" that every *jiva* possesses. It is also the source of all love. Though they are in essence nothing but the one supreme self, the *jivas* thus appear to be many, as each is contained in a mortal frame, and they appear to differ from each other due to the different composition of the three *gunas* in them.

When Himavan, king of the mountains, practiced *tapas* (meditation) to Maha Devi in order to procure her as his daughter, she appeared to him in her most spectacular form and promised to incarnate as his daughter. After this she proceeded to enlighten him as to her true nature, since he was eager to know her secret essence. This discourse by Devi to Himavan is known as the Devi Gita:

Hear this, O Himavan, by knowing which all *jivas* will become liberated. Before creation I alone exist—eternal, immutable. My real self is no different from the Para Brahman. In that state I am pure *sat* (existence), *chid* (consciousness), *samvit* (intelligence), and *ananda* (bliss). At that time I am beyond all attributes or transformations. *Maya* is my power of illusion, and it is inherent in me. It is co-eternal with me. It arises out of me like heat from fire and rays from the sun. Though it has no beginning, it is possible to end it with the attainment of supreme knowledge. *Maya* can be called neither existent nor nonexistent. If it existed eternally, there would be no liberation for the *jiva*. But if it were not present at all, the practical world would not exist, so it cannot be nonexistent. It can be destroyed with the knowledge of Brahman, so it cannot be called existent either. It is thus my mysterious power of delusion, and it can be overcome only through my grace.

In essence I am *nirguna* (without qualities), but when I relate myself to *avidya maya*, I become *saguna* (endowed with qualities). Then do I become the cause of the universe of names and forms. Thus *avidya maya* is the cause of this whole creation. From the point of view of the Brahman, there is no *maya* and no creation. Therefore I am ever pure even though involved in creation, just as the sun's rays are not defiled by illumining dirty objects.

When *maya* unites with *chid* or consciousness, it becomes the instigating cause of the universe, and when it unites with the five original elements, it becomes the material cause. *Avidya maya* is what creates the delusion of time, space, and causality, and its characteristic is to hide my true nature, but *vidya maya* has the ability to liberate the *jiva* from this illusion.

Infinite and endless creations are threaded on me as pearls on a string. I myself am the lord that resides in the causal and subtle bodies of the *jivas*. I am Brahma, Vishnu, and Shiva. I am the sun, moon, and stars. I am the beasts and the birds, the Brahmin and the untouchable. I am the noble soul as well as the hunter and the thief. I am male, female, and hermaphrodite. Wherever there is anything to be seen or heard, I am to be found there, within and without. There is nothing moving or unmoving that can exist without me. This world cannot appear without a substratum, and I am that substratum.

The world is composed of twenty-five *tattvas* or elements. The first five—*akasa* (ether), *vayu* (air), *agni* (fire), *apas* (water), and *prithvi* (earth)—are known as the *maha tattvas*. When the Para Brahman relates to my *avidya maya,* the sound *hreem,* which is my seed sound, is produced. Within this sound are contained my three *shaktis* (powers), known as *iccha shakti* (the *tamasic* power of will), *jnana shakti* (the *sattvic* power of intelligence), and *kriya shakti* (the *rajasic* power of action). These three are absolutely essential for creation. The sound *hreem,* which denotes me—the Adi Shakti or the first force, who is of the nature of the Brahman and is known as Para Brahma Swarupini—is the twenty-fifth *tattva.* The rest of the twenty-four *tattvas* come out of it.

The five qualities of sound, touch, form, taste, and odor are known as *tanmatras* or subtle elements. The subtle quality of sound is the first *tanmatra* to manifest from *hreem.* Then come the subtle elements of touch, form, taste, and odor. Out of the subtle *tanmatra* of sound is manifested the gross element (*tattva*) of *akasa* or ether, the vast field of energy that comprises the universe. Vibrations in the ether cause the movement of air. Thus from *akasa* appears *vayu* or air, which has its own subtle feature of touch plus the added quality of sound, which it incorporates from the previous *tattva* of *akasa*. Friction caused by the continuous movement of the air principle creates heat, which we call fire. Thus from *vayu* comes *agni* or fire, which has its own subtle feature of form plus touch and sound. Condensation of the density of these forces results in the formation of liquid or water. So the next to manifest is *apas* or water, which has its own subtle quality of taste plus those of form, touch, and sound. The solidified form of all this is earth, so the last to appear is *prithvi* or earth, which has its basic subtle feature of odor plus the qualities of the other four elements of taste, form, touch, and sound.

What we come to understand from this teaching is that creation proceeds from the subtle to the gross and not the other way around, as we might suppose. The subtle elements (*tanmatras*) are sound, touch, form, taste, and odor. The gross elements (*tattvas*) are ether, air, fire, water, and earth, which are all derivatives of the subtle elements. These five gross elements represent the entire gamut of our advanced modern physics. But from the Shakta point of view, physical matter and its fields represent only a tiny fraction of reality.

The five subtle elements all have *sattvic, rajasic,* and *tamasic* qualities. The five *jnanendriyas* or sense organs of knowledge are created out of the *sattvic* portion of the first five subtle elements. These are the ears, skin, eyes, tongue, and nose, and they are the instruments through which the mind can interact with these elements in the material world.

The *karmendriyas* or organs of action come from the *rajasic* portion of the *tanmatras*. These are the organs of speech, the hands, the feet, the organs of procreation, and the anus or organ of excretion. The subtle element of sound gives rise to space and ends in speech. The subtle element of touch projects as air, which is felt by the skin, especially the skin of the hands. The subtle element of form gives rise to fire, which eventually takes the form of the feet. The subtle element of taste gives rise to water, which in turn produces the organ of procreation. The subtle element of odor produces the earth, which results in the production of the anus.

The five *pranas* or subtle breaths, which control the involuntary functions of the body, arise from the *tamasic* portion of the *tanmatras*. They are the *prana vayu,* which resides in the heart and controls blood circulation; the *apana vayu,* which resides in the lower portion of the body and controls the expulsion of waste matter; the *samana vayu,* which resides in the navel and controls digestion; the *udana vayu,* which resides in the throat and controls speech; and the *vyana vayu,* which pervades the whole body.

The sensations of sound, touch, form, taste, and odor are important components of our experience of life. Indian philosophy claims that these elements exist in intangible and subtle forms. They are visible to our inner eye and are the very stuff of our dreams. However, the gross body is not able to experience them.

The seventeen *tattvas* that make up the *jivatman* are the five gross elements, the five sense organs that correspond to these, the five *pranas* (or vital breaths), and the mind and the ego. The *linga sarira* or subtle body of the *jiva* is made up of these seventeen *tattvas* in their subtle forms. Yogis who perfected the ability to leave their physical bodies at will realized that their subtle or astral bodies were able to travel unhampered through space and gross matter. However, they could still hear, touch, smell, and feel in this state, so they concluded that the actual experience of these five sensations lies in the subtle body and not in its physical counterpart.

The mind is a psychic organ that operates through a physical nervous system in this life, allowing it to interact easily with physical matter. While in the physical body it has three functions with separate names. The part that receives information through the *jnanendriyas* (sense organs) and then processes and stores that information is called *manas* or mind. The part that relates to a particular individual, giving him a strong sense of individuality, the feeling of "my" and "mine," is called *ahamkara* or ego. The part that weighs alternatives and makes decisions is called *buddhi* or intellect.

However, the mind has another aspect that is most subtle, called *chitta.* It has no equivalent English name, though it is sometimes called the superconscious, which is not quite an accurate translation. It is capable of obtaining data from our inner dimensions of reality and is a storehouse of information. It is in direct contact with *akasa,* or the energy field or ether of the universe. After death—or, for *yogis,* during astral travels—the mind separates from the physical organism and operates in the realm of the *tanmatras* or subtle elements. Then it is pure *chitta* alone. The *chitta* is very close to pure spirit (or *atman*). The difference is that the chitta is still individualized. It carries all the information of the individual and is carried to another body. The *atman* on the other hand is ever pure. It carries nothing and goes nowhere since it is ever full. It is not born and thus never dies. It is not affected by the changes of the mind—ego, intellect, and chitta.

This brings us to another important point of Indian philosophy. The first three aspects of the mind (*manas, buddhi,* and *ahamkara*), which are the basis of our personality, are all material constituents and not spiritual entities. They have their roots in Prakriti or primordial matter and not in the spirit or *atman.* The mind changes every moment and eventually perishes with the body, but the *atman* or spirit remains. This is the eternal self that never perishes, that is the undying witness and never the doer.

Indian philosophy is slowly coming to find an ally in evolving Western science. The Newtonian world was a law-abiding but desolate place from which we were totally unconnected. Next came Darwin, who stripped life of all its spiritual potential and left us bereft. Our only purpose was survival. The pinnacle of humanity appeared to be the terrorist who could efficiently dispose of all weak links. Life was not about sharing and interdependence but about winning and, if need be, warring. These theories produced the modern psyche and have led to some of the world's greatest technological advancement. Unfortunately, such advancement has been at the cost of our humanity and of our divinity. No wonder suicides claim as many lives as homicides and wars.* Science tore the human being from his roots and left him with a sense of brutal isolation.

*_The Injury Chartbook_ (World Health Organization, 2002.)

With the advent of quantum physics in the early part of the twentieth century, many scientists underwent a dramatic reversal in their views of man and the universe. Modern science is slowly coming to understand that underlying every aspect of the universe is a field of energy that connects every thing to every other thing. Scientists call this the zero-point field. They have found that the tiniest bit of matter isn't matter at all but energy in motion. As Lynne McTaggart has said in her book *The Field,* "Living beings are a coalescence of energy." Even more interestingly, scientists have discovered that subatomic particles have no meaning by themselves but function only in relation to everything else! This astonishing finding is slowly replacing the old Newtonian physics wherein everything had a set pattern and was totally predictable by the human mind.

Lynne McTaggart goes on to say that the pulsating energy field that underlies existence is the central engine of our being and our consciousness—our alpha and omega. There is no duality between the universe and us. We are connected to every single thing in the cosmos by this one underlying energy field. In *The Field* she says, "This field [of energy] is responsible for our mind's highest functions, the information source guiding the growth of our bodies. It is our brain, our heart, our memory—indeed a blueprint of the world for all time. The field is the force, rather than germs or genes, that finally determines whether we are healthy or ill, the force which must be tapped in order to heal. . . . 'The field,' as Einstein once succinctly put it, 'is the only reality.'"

The Puranas depict this energy field of Prakriti as the ocean of primeval waters on which Vishnu lies, in which the Island of Jewels or the Mani Dwipa floats. Maha Devi's throne on the Island of Jewels (see chapter 4) is the *bindu* or point from which all energy eddies in circles to create the expanding universe. Maha Devi or Para Prakriti or Para Shakti is actually nothing but the Brahman. They are a two-in-one reality. In the unmanifest state there is no difference between them. However, when the urge to create occurs, this Para Prakriti pierces through the *bindu* in the form of the sound *hreem,* from which the entire world of manifestation arises. Prakriti is the energy of the Brahman. This energy remains latent during the period of dissolution when the cosmos is in a latent state within her. But during the time of evolution and creation she comes to the forefront and carries out the work of manifesting creation.

The universe's underlying energy field is *akasa,* the ether that is the twenty-third *tattva*. It is a timeless, spaceless quantum that provides the ultimate blueprint of the world for all time—past, present, and future. Any person who desires or professes to see the past or future has to tap this source. Quantum physics has come to realize that pure energy as it exists on the quantum level is not bound by the ordinary laws of time and space. It exists in a vast continuum of fluctuating charge. When we bring this energy to our conscious awareness through the act of perception, we create the separate objects of our world that exist in time and space. In fact we create our own worlds in time and space and thereby create our separate individualities. This brain-boggling theory, which Western science has only recently become aware of and is still wary of accepting, is something that has been recognized by Indian philosophy from ancient times. In fact it is what the Devi told Himavan in the Devi Gita. Of course the words she used were different, but the meaning is the same.

All the Puranic stories point out this amazing truth. For instance, in the story of the churning of the milky ocean (see chapter 21), the *devas* (gods) and *asuras* (demons) represent the positive and negative sides of each person's personality. This personality churns the ocean of all possibilities (the zero-point field), using the churn of space (Mandara) and the rope of time (Ananta), and thus draws out for himself many wondrous things, including the nectar of immortality if he so wishes it. Thus each creates his own separate world.

Time has generally been considered a primary, independent, and universally applicable order both in physics and in common experience. It is one of the fundamental orders known to us. Now modern scientific research is slowly coming to accept the fact that it is a secondary order that is, like space, derived from a higher dimensional ground. Both time and space depend on another multidimensional reality that cannot be comprehended fully through common experience; for human consciousness to operate on this quantum level, it must reside outside space and time. In theory such a state of consciousness would mean that we would be able to access information of both the past and the future, and that every moment of our lives could be made to influence every other moment, both forward and backward. These are breathtaking ideas that science is loath to accept. But Indian *yogis* have known them from time immemorial.

In every *puja* or ritual there is a particular step called *sankalpa* or intention in which the gods are invoked. This intention is the reason the priest undertakes the ritual. It may be for some physical purpose, like the curing of a disease or passing an exam, or anything else. The intention is said to be so important that it can actually change the chain of events and make manifest the desire of the one who performs the ritual. Such reasoning is now backed by modern science; the quantum age has shown that the intention of the experimenter has a lot to do with the final result to be achieved from the experiment. The human factor influences the end result of any experiment!

The individual is not an isolated phenomenon, a piece of flotsam floating aimlessly in the sea of the world, totally unconnected with everything else, with freedom to pursue his own selfish ends. He is part of an interconnected whole in which all of us are deeply involved. Human consciousness is absolutely essential to the making of some objective sense out of the constant flux of subatomic particles. This is the amazing discovery of quantum physics that many scientists are still unable to accept.

In the Devi Gita, Devi says,

I am the intelligence from which the universe emanates and in which it abides. The ignorant believe me to be nothing more than Nature or Prakriti, but the wise experience me as the true self within. They glimpse me in their own hearts when their minds become as still and clear as an ocean without waves. The supreme wisdom is that which ends the delusion that anything exists apart from me. The fruit of this realization is a total lack of fear and the end of sorrow. When one understands that all the limitless universes are but a fraction of an atom in the unity of my being, that all the numberless lives in the universes are the wisps of vapor in one of my breaths, that all triumphs and tragedies, the good and the evil in all the worlds, are merely games I play for my own amusement, then life and death stand still and the drama of individual life evaporates like a shallow pond on a warm day.

This world that you are experiencing now is nothing but my power. The only remedy for your ignorance is to worship me as your innermost self. Surrender yourself to me with one-pointed devotion and I will help you discover your true being. Abide in me as I abide in you. Know that even now at this very moment there is absolutely no difference between us. Realize and be fulfilled this instant.

> *Its mind of error was stripped off from things,*
> *And the dull moods of its perverted will.*
> *Illumined by Her all-seeing identity,*
> *Knowledge and Ignorance could strive no more.*
> *No longer could the titan opposites,*
> *Antagonist poles of the world's artifice,*
> *Impose the illusion of their twofold screen,*
> *Throwing their figures between us and Her!*

> —*SAVITRI* BY SRI AUROBINDO

Thus ends the first chapter of *Shakti*, known as "Prakriti," describing the process and nature of creation and the relationship between Brahman and Prakriti.

Aum Aim Hreem Kleem

ॐ

Aum Ambikayai Namaha!

2

Parameswari

Ya Devi sarvabhuteshu chetanethyabhidiyathe,
Namasthasyai, namasthasyai, namasthasyai namo namaha!

O Goddess who is designated as consciousness in all
   creatures,
Hail to thee, hail to thee, all hail to thee!

The central concept of Hindu philosophy is the belief that wisdom is something to be recovered rather than discovered. Absolute truth is not something to be discussed as an intellectual concept but is something to be lived. It is a way of life—the Sanatana Dharma. In fact, Sanatana Dharma is the original name of the Hindu religion. This way gets lost or diluted through the process of time, but great incarnations appear from time to time in order to uplift this eternal *dharma* (law of righteousness), as Lord Krishna tells Arjuna in the Bhagavad Gita.

The Vedas are the most ancient source of Indian wisdom. They are the heritage of the world. They were revealed to, or recovered by, ancient *rishis* in a state of superconsciousness. The Puranas, on the other hand, are of human origin. The Puranas are epics; the literal meaning of *purana* is "narrative from ancient times." Indians as a whole did not believe in writing down history, but the Puranas give us a good view of the different

22

phases and aspects of the life of the diverse ages of this land. These books allow us a glimpse into ancient religion, philosophy, history, sociology, politics, and other subjects. The Puranas are normally recited by a class of people called Sutas during periods of rest between the various rituals of a Vedic sacrifice. They are divided into two classes: the Maha Puranas and the Upa Puranas. Each class contains eighteen books. Thus the total number of Puranas is thirty-six. The Maha Puranas are classified into different categories—Vaishnava, Braahma, Shaiva, and so on—depending on the preferential treatment they give to each of the three primary deities, Vishnu, Brahma, and Shiva.

The Puranas are intimately related to the Vedas. They interpret and adapt the metaphysical truths of the Vedas so that they can be understood and appreciated by the common man. The Puranas do not proclaim any new truths but only make the Vedic truths available in a contemporary and relevant way. The Vedas are revealed truth, known as *sruti*. The Puranas reveal the same truth in a modern setting; this is known as *smrti*, and *smrti* is in complete harmony with *sruti*. The Vedas are reserved for the Brahmin caste and the initiates and may not be taught to all. All, on the other hand, may hear the Puranas. Recitations are done in public to audiences of all classes. With its usual flexible approach to spirituality, the Hindu tradition believes that each generation must make the Vedic truth its very own in its own way, as must each individual. Thus, though the Vedic truths remained fixed and unalterable, the Puranas could and did change with the changing times, incorporating the devotional teachings of numerous cults and saintly teachers that arose from time to time in this holy land.

Time, according to the Puranas, is changeless and without beginning or end. Though it is by nature insubstantial, it takes form when it causes the stirring of the three *gunas* of Prakriti at the beginning of each creative cycle. The sun is the visible form of the supreme absolute as time. The shortest period of time is called a *paramanukala,* and this is the period of time it takes for the light of the sun to pass one *paramanu,* which is the tiniest particle of matter. The time taken for the light of the sun to pass through the twelve *rasis* or constellations around the earth, which is a huge amount of matter, is known as a year. One human year is only one day for the gods. The six months from January fourteenth to June fourteenth comprise a divine day, and from June fifteenth to January thirteenth is a divine night. The years cycle through four *yugas* or epochs of three thousand years each: Krita Yuga, Treta Yuga, Dwapara Yuga, and Kali Yuga. These four together are known as one *chaturyuga*.

A thousand *chaturyuga*s is only one day in the world of Brahma, the creator. His night is another thousand *chaturyugas*. The life span of each Brahma is a hundred such years and is known as a *kalpa,* which is an astronomical period of time as can be seen. We are now living in the dawn of the first day of the present Brahma, who is in his fifty-first year. Each day of Brahma is divided into fourteen ages or *manvantaras* of approximately seventy-one *chaturyugas*. The lawgiver Manu, who rules for one *manvantara,* is in charge of each *manvantara*. He is the one who makes the laws for that particular *manvantara*. It must be remembered that the name Manu only denotes a status and does not refer to just one person. All the lesser gods, including Indra, the seven sages, and various other celestial beings, exist in each *manvantara*. Lord Vishnu and Maha Devi incarnate themselves in each *manvantara* in order to maintain the balance of righteousness.

According to the Puranas, creation is cyclic in nature. A vast period of creation is followed by a vast period of *pralaya* or dissolution. At the time of *pralaya,* everything in the cosmos is taken back into the primeval essence. After the passage of eons, when the time is ripe for another creation, the one eternal Brahman takes on the form of duality, just as one face becomes two when reflected in the mirror, allowing again the illusion of differentiation that creates time, space, and causality. This is all the play or *lila* of the supreme.

There are three different types of *pralaya* based on time, substance, and the attributes of Prakriti. The first, called Nitya Pralaya, is dissolution based on time alone, which all of us experience when we go to sleep. Each night is a *pralaya* for the *jiva* (embodied soul). When we sleep we have no world and no individuality. We have not totally disappeared but are merely in a state of latency, submerged in the total consciousness. The moment we awake, the world springs into being and individuality asserts itself.

The next type of dissolution is Maha Pralaya or Naimittika Pralaya, which is the night of Brahma, the creator. After one day of Brahma, which lasts for a thousand *chaturyugas,* one night of Brahma or Maha Pralaya occurs, lasting another thousand *chaturyugas*. During this time the whole universe, up to Satyaloka (the world of Brahma), goes into a state of involution. At the end of this vast period of time, Maha Maya employs her power as time and causality to evoke another period of creation and evolution.

In the third type of dissolution, called Prakritika Pralaya, all the qualities and attributes of Prakriti dissolve into their ultimate cause, which is Maha Prakriti or Mula Prakriti. This in turn reverts to its ultimate cause—the Brahman. This *pralaya* lasts for eons. But it is to be noted that even during this dissolution, nothing is destroyed; everything merely remains in its latent state.

As each *manvantara* proceeds through its *yugas,* humankind's memory and intellect become poorer, and they have more difficulty memorizing the vast *mantras* (mystical incantations) of the Vedas. For this reason, in every Dwapara Yuga (third *yuga*), Lord Vishnu himself takes on the incarnation known as the sage Veda Vyasa. Vyasa's duty is to divide the Vedas into four parts so that they become easier to memorize.

The original Purana is said to have emanated from the fifth mouth of the creator Brahma and comprises a billion *slokas* (verses). This original exists only in the world of the gods, however. In order to reach out to the common people, Veda Vyasa also compiles the Puranas that exist in the mortal world, an abridgment of the original divine Purana. These Puranas are an outpouring of his compassion for the masses, allowing them to understand the mystical truths of the Vedas. In the present *manvantara,* known as Vaivasvata, we are now living in the

Kali Yuga or the Iron Age. The Veda Vyasa of this *manvantara* was known as Krishna Dwaipayana.

It is to be noted that though Vyasa is the author of all the Puranas, in each of them he extols the uniqueness of the particular deity addressed. There are two reasons for this. The first is to show people that all deities are only aspects of the supreme truth and that sincere devotion to any of them will give us liberation from our mortal coils. The second reason is to convince the votaries of each particular deity of the greatness of their own personal god. In general Hindus can be classified as one of five types of votaries. The worshippers of the supreme in its aspect as Shiva are known as Shaivites. The worshippers of Vishnu are known as Vaishnavites, and those who worship the supreme as Devi are known as Shaktas. There are also two lesser-known sects: the Ganapatyas, who worship the supreme as Ganesha, and the Souryas, who worship the sun as the supreme. Of course there are also the Advaitins, who worship the supreme as the formless, nondual Brahman. The Upanishads, which come at the end of the Vedas, deal with the nondual Brahman, while the Puranas deal with all other deities.

The Devi Bhagavatam, classified as one of the Maha Puranas, focuses on the supreme in its aspect as Devi; indeed, it is sometimes called the Devi Purana. It is said that Veda Vyasa narrated this Purana to his son Shuka, who then taught it to various others. It has eighteen thousand *slokas* and is divided into twelve books. This Purana depicts the ultimate reality as feminine. It is the earliest literary work in which the character of the goddess stands fully revealed; even today Hindus conceive of her as she is pictured in this scripture. In the Devi Bhagavatam we find that all the gods and the great kings have recourse to Maha Devi in order to get her blessings. This Purana deals with all her different incarnations and forms, from the river Ganga to the plant *tulasi* and so on.

Each Purana must deal with at least five topics: creation or *sarga*, secondary creation or *visarga*, the ages of Manu or *manvantaras*, genealogies of various kings, and a description of their heroic deeds. The Devi Bhagavatam describes creation thus: Devi is beyond attributes, eternal and omnipresent. She is formless and immutable. But for the sake of the world she assumes the form of three *shaktis* (powers) based on the attributes of her three *gunas*. Her *sattvic shakti* takes the name of Maha Lakshmi, her *rajasic shakti* is known as Maha Saraswati, and her *tamasic shakti* is called Durga or Maha Kaali. In the *sarga* portion of the Devi Bhagavatam, these three *shaktis* of Devi assume different forms for the creation of this universe of diverse forms. In the *visarga* portion, these *shaktis* take on male counterparts known as Vishnu, Brahma, and Shiva for the preservation, creation, and dissolution of the universe. Thus all male gods have *shaktis* or inherent powers that enable them to create.

The Devi Bhagavatam's description of the origin of the world differs from that of other Puranas in that Devi is named the supreme power and creator of the cosmos.* She herself describes the process of creation to the creator Brahma. She is Maha Devi, Maha Maya, Maha Prakriti, and Maha Shakti. She is also Lakshmi, Saraswati, Parvati, Durga, Kaali, Chandika, and a host of other powers that are depicted in the Purana as goddesses.

The book begins with a request by the sages to the narrator, known as Suta, to describe the qualities and glories of Devi. Suta responds,

> I bow at the lotus feet of Devi—Bhagavati, who is worshipped by
> Brahma, Vishnu, and Shiva and who is the sole source of liberation
> to all. This is the best of all Puranas and contains all the sentiments
> that a human being can conceive. It is known as the Srimad Devi
> Bhagavatam. May that highest primal Shakti, who is known as Vidya
> in the Vedas, who is omniscient, who controls all, and who is skilled
> in cutting the knot of the world, give me the intelligence to describe

---

*Each Purana is about one god, for example, the Shaiva Purana is about Shiva and Vaishnava Purana about Vishnu. The Supreme power and the origin of the world would be credited to whichever deity is extolled in the Purana in question.

her glories. I meditate on that Divine Mother who creates this universe, whose nature is both real and unreal, who creates, preserves, and destroys everything in her *rajasic, sattvic,* and *tamasic* aspects, and who in the end dissolves everything back into herself and remains alone during the period of universal dissolution.

The Devi Bhagavatam goes on to describe the basic formation of the universe and the forms—human and otherwise—that comprise it. It introduces the idea that Brahman, the supreme absolute from which everything emanates, has a dual aspect of male and female, personified as Shakti and Shiva or Prakriti and Purusha. The Devi herself is both Shakti and Prakriti. She is known by various names as Parashakti and Parameswari—the Absolute force as well as the Absolute God. However, as mentioned in the introduction, neither male nor female can exist in isolation. Each is inherent in and dependent on the other; each completes the other. The whole of creation is at first only an idea in the mind of the supreme Brahman. The idea is given a concrete reality and expression in the world by Shakti or Prakriti, the feminine force that underlies and impels creation. But to make a difference between the "force" and the "receptacle of force" is an error. Prakriti or Parameswari is the inherent tendency of Purusha to express himself in concrete forms and individual beings. However, she has to be set in motion by the will of Purusha and acts according to his force and design. It is only through Shakti or Prakriti that the male aspect is able to express himself in creation. Though the male and female aspects are one in essence, differences are conceived during creation; when everything melts back to its original causal state of *pralaya,* then there is no distinction between Purusha and Prakriti, Shiva and Shakti, and Brahman. There is neither male nor female. There is only Brahman, with Devi (Maha Maya) or Parameswari latent in it.

Brahman is the ocean of pure consciousness. It can never be known and it is always one, never two. But when it wants to become conscious of itself, a desire bubbles to the surface of this ocean and this bubble is Prakriti or Maha Devi or Parashakti or Parameswari, which develops itself into this variegated universe in the method described above. Even though Maha Shakti appears outwardly in numerous forms, this creative force is always emanating from the Brahman so it has all the qualifications of the Brahman. When it manifests itself in the human being it is called the *atman,* which is nothing other than the Brahman. However, when it puts on the clothing and personality of a human being, it is called the *jivatman,* which is the *atman* that thinks itself to be a bound and unhappy creature always on the seesaw of sorrow and joy, pleasure and pain, swimming—and sometimes drowning—in the sea of duality. In actuality, its abode is the ocean of pure consciousness, which is also an ocean of bliss.

Many beautiful allegories are given in the Puranas to give us an idea of this interdependence of Purusha and Prakriti. He is the supreme subject and she is the essence of all objects; he is the ocean and she the waves. He is the sun and she the light; he is the sky and she the earth. She is all qualities and he the enjoyer of all qualities; she is all activity and he the sole witness of all activity. She is the form of everything in the cosmos and he the thinker of the forms. She is speech and he the meaning. In other words, she is creation and he the creator.

Prakriti and Purusha have no beginning and no end. They exist in everything. Purusha is the universal consciousness that exists in everything; he is the highest self. Prakriti is the energy that is felt in all beings. Both are *nirguna* or without qualities. No human being can know the essence of their union even by the study of the scriptures or the Vedas, for the *jivas* are all *saguna* or endowed with the qualities of the three *gunas*—*sattva, rajas,* and *tamas.* How then can we ever know that which is *nirguna* or beyond all *gunas?*

The *gunas* are the agents of Prakriti by which the immortal and imperishable *atman,* though it is nothing but pure consciousness, imagines itself to be the mortal and perishable body. Maha Maya weaves a net of these three strands (*guna* means "thread") to catch the *atman* and trap it in this delusion. Once caught in the net of *maya,* the immortal self delights in its mortality and frailty. This is the wonder of the work of *maya*. The mind has a predilection to enjoy the limitations of its body. It is happy to shrink into the cocoon of its small, prejudiced individuality and refuses to believe in its universality. *Moksha* or enlightenment is liberation from the shackles of this puny individuality—from the limitations of particularized existence. The only way out of this web of delusion, as Krishna tells Arjuna in the Bhagavad Gita, is to go beyond the three *gunas*.

Sattva is the source of pleasure and happiness. It induces a person to all types of good thoughts and activities. *Rajas* is the source of hyperactivity, leading to pain and unhappiness. *Tamas* leads to laziness, sloth, and sleep. The path to liberation lies in encouraging *sattvic* qualities, controlling *rajasic* qualities, and destroying *tamasic* qualities. However, it is not enough to strive to become purely *sattvic*. After all, none of these qualities can exist by itself. Though at different times and in different people one or the other might become prominent, they are always intermingled and dependent on one another. And so long as we are in their power we will always live in dread of a fall. Only a *gunatita* or one who has gone beyond the *gunas* can have no fear of a fall. Such a person comes to realize his own divine nature as pure consciousness and is thus freed from the bondage of *maya*. Such realization, however, can come only with the grace of Maha Maya herself, since she is the one who has caught us in this net of delusion. Therefore those who desire *moksha* have to pray to her to remove the veil of illusion from their eyes.

The Devi Bhagavatam teaches us that the Brahman is the undecaying principle of fullness—the ultimate substratum of everything. It is totally without desire or qualities. Therefore it is not able to create or accomplish any action without the help of its inherent force or Shakti—Maha Maya, the feminine principle, the great goddess—Parameswari. All the gods—Brahma, Vishnu, Shiva, Ganesha, Indra, and so on—can do their respective work only if they are united with Shakti. So Maha Maya can be considered the sole cause of this entire universe of movable and immovable objects. She is the cause of all causes and manifests as Maha Lakshmi, Maha Saraswati, and Maha Kaali. We should worship her with all adoration. Even the gods worship her in order to do their allotted tasks.

> *Infinity turned its gaze on finite shapes.*
> *Observer of the silent steps of the hours,*
> *And the passing scenes of the Everlasting's play,*
> *In the mystery of its selecting will,*
> *In the divine comedy a participant.*
> *The Spirit's conscious representative.*
> *God's delegate in our humanity,*
> *Comrade of the universe. Transcendent's ray.*
> *She had come into the mortal body's room,*
> *To play at ball with time and circumstance.*

—*SAVITRI* BY SRI AUROBINDO

Thus ends the second chapter of *Shakti,* known as "Parameswari," describing the Devi Bhagavatam and its view of creation.

Aum Aim Hreem Kleem

Aum Sarvabhuteshwaryai Namaha!

3

Maha Devi

Ya Devi sarvabhuteshu, buddhi rupena samsthita,
Namasthasyai, namasthasyai, namasthasyai namo namaha!

O Goddess who resides in all creatures in the form of
   intelligence,
Hail to thee, hail to thee, all hail to thee!

It was the dawn of the first day of the present Brahma—the very first dawn of this present cycle of creation. There was nothing but water everywhere. Brahma, the creator in the Hindu trinity, opened his eyes to find himself seated in the center of a lotus in the middle of a vast expanse of water. The stalk of the lotus moved forlornly to and fro in the waves of a mighty ocean. The whole scene was bleak and lonely. There was no sun or moon or stars or earth. Brahma looked around for something that would give him a clue as to how he got there and what was the purpose of his existence, but he could find nothing. After some thought he decided to try and find the source of the lotus. For a thousand years he searched in the water but could find nothing. The stalk of the lotus seemed to thrust endlessly down into the water. Exhausted with his futile search, he came back up to the surface and sat on the lotus, wondering what he should do. Then came a celestial voice asking him to practice *tapas* (meditation). Content with this, he took his seat on the lotus and meditated for another thousand years. At the end of this period of time he heard the voice again, commanding him to create. He was perplexed as to how to proceed with this command and was wondering what to do when out of the waters appeared two gigantic demons, named Madhu and Kaitabha, who challenged him to fight.

Brahma was dreadfully frightened and hurriedly climbed down the stalk of the lotus, seeking some help. When he reached the end of the stalk, he saw a blissful vision. A most beautiful being appeared to be sleeping on the coiled-up body of a serpent. He was the color of a dark blue rain cloud. He wore a luminous yellow garment and had four arms, which held a conch, a discus, a mace, and a lotus. Around his neck was a garland of wildflowers. He was fascinating, and Brahma instinctively knew that he was looking at Narayana (Lord Vishnu), the lord of the universe. The lotus flower on which he had been sitting appeared to grow from the navel of this wonderful being. But unfortunately he appeared to be in deep sleep, and Brahma did not dare to awaken him. The demons were thrashing about the ocean and intimidating him with their baleful looks, so Brahma decided to take recourse to the goddess Bhuvaneswari.

He praised her thus,

O Maha Maya! Bhuvaneswari! You are the imperishable one. You are the nectar of the gods. By you alone is the universe created, by you supported, and by you consumed at the end of time. At its emanation, you take the form of the creator; for its protection, you take the form of steadfastness; and at the end of this epoch, you take the form of destruction. You are Maha Vidya (the great knowledge), Maha Maya (the great illusion), and Maha Medha (the great memory). You are the primordial material (Mula Prakriti) of everything, manifesting as the three *gunas*. You are Kalaratri, the great night of destruction, as well as Moharatri, the terrible night of delusion. You are all auspiciousness, modesty, intelligence, tranquility, and forbearance. You are terrible with your sword and spear, cudgel and discus, conch and bow, sling and mace. Yet you are gentle, gentler than other gentle ones, exceedingly beautiful, the supreme queen! Whatever and wherever anything exists, whether it be real or unreal, you alone are the power. How then can I adequately praise you?

By you, Vishnu, the sustainer of the world, the protector of the world, has been brought under the influence of sleep. Kindly condescend to awaken him, the lord of lords, so that he may slay these two great *asuras*.

Pray remove yourself from the form of Lord Vishnu so that he can kill the two demons who are threatening me.

Hail to thee, hail to thee, all hail to thee!

Pleased with Brahma's hymn, the goddess in the form of sleep left the body of Vishnu from all quarters. It is said that in this episode it was Maha Lakshmi who had taken on the form of Yoga Nidra, goddess of the mystic sleep, and it was she who now condescended to leave the body of Lord Vishnu. One by one she left his eyes, his mind, his hands, and every limb.

As soon as she had left his body, the great lord of the world woke up and revealed himself in all his inexpressible grandeur. He fought with Madhu and Kaitabha and killed the two mighty titans by pulling them onto his thighs and cutting off their heads.

The goddess was still in the sky, and it was her *shakti* that had enabled Vishnu to kill these mighty demons. As Brahma and Vishnu gazed at her, they were joined by Shiva, and all three of them hymned her. Pleased with their hymn, she cast her benign glance over them and told them to go ahead with their respective duties of creation, preservation, and destruction.

Brahma looked at her in distress and said, "O Mother! There is nothing here except this wide expanse of water. With what am I to create?"

Hearing this, the goddess smiled and told them, "Beyond the ken of the material world there lies an island made of priceless gems, resting on a sea of bliss. In the center of that island is a temple of light, where I sit on my throne of limitless dimensions, made of numberless universes both material and nonmaterial. If you draw your awareness up your spine into my antechamber, I will take you to that island and admit you into my throne room."

So saying, she beckoned them into an aerial chariot, which had just appeared. The car was decorated with jewels and pearls and tinkling bells. The three gods got into the vehicle and were transported to the Island of Jewels or Mani Dwipa. On the way they passed the worlds of other gods and even saw themselves sporting in their own worlds. There was Brahma in Satyaloka, and Vishnu lying on the celestial serpent in Vaikunta, and Shiva in deep meditation on the icy peak of Kailasa. The three gods were totally bewildered when they saw this and asked each other, "Who is this Brahma and who this Vishnu and Shiva?" None of them could think of a satisfactory explanation.

Before they could make further conjectures, the chariot reached the Island of Jewels. They saw all the glorious features of this island and were taken to the *chintamani griha,* the sanctum sanctorum of Maha Devi. They were struck with wonder to see the form of the goddess Tripurasundari (most beautiful in all the three worlds). She was the color of the rising sun, and her beauty was indescribable. Even the birds in that place chanted her *mantras.* While they gazed at her in wonder they saw that her four arms had become a thousand. She was thousand-eyed and thousand-footed. Her form filled the entire universe. As they gazed in astonishment, she regained her original form and smiled at them.

Vishnu was the first to recognize her and spoke to the others.

She is Maha Maya, Maha Vidya, and Mula Prakriti. She is the cause of all causes. She is the eternal Brahman as well as that which is non-eternal. She is the power of will of the supreme. It is she who creates the cosmos and displays it to the Paramatman (the supreme soul or Brahman). O Brahma! O Shiva! Today we are indeed fortunate that we have received this blessed vision of the Divine Mother. I recall how I was once in the form of an infant, lying in the cosmic waters on a *peepul* leaf. At that time it was she who rocked me lovingly in her tender arms. Let us bow down to her and receive her blessings.

As the three gods came closer to her they were amazed to find that the entire universe of movable and immovable things was reflected in her toenails. They themselves were there, as were the two demons Vishnu had just killed.

They extolled Devi with beautiful hymns.

O Mother, we realize that this whole universe rests in you. It rises from you and folds back into you. It is you who creates the elements at the time of creation and, through them, this manifest universe, in order to beguile Purusha, who is the sole enjoyer. His nature is pure consciousness, and he is untainted by any desire to create. You alone have the power to create. Without you there would be no objects and no universe. You alone have the knowledge to create (*jnana shakti*), the will to create (*iccha shakti*), and the ability to create (*kriya shakti*). Even we cannot fathom your inconceivable glory, let alone those who are steeped in ignorance. You have created countless universes by your power. On our way here we saw many such, with other Vishnus, Shivas, and Brahmas. Such is your divine power and majesty. We—Brahma, Vishnu, and Shiva—create, preserve, and destroy only through your command and grace. It is your endless might that supports this entire universe. You are in essence one with Purusha, the attributeless self, but by the power of your *maya*, you appear in the form of this universe of attributes. You alone are the ancient, eternal Prakriti and the mother of the universe. The three of us are products of your creation and thus we also come under the power of the *gunas*. *Rajas* is predominant in Brahma, *sattva* in Vishnu, and *tamas* in Shiva. It is because of this that we are able to carry out our work of creation, preservation, and destruction.

O Devi! You are the intelligence of the intelligent, the fame of the famous, the beauty of the lustrous, and the wealth of the wealthy. You are the source of both desire and dispassion, leading to bondage and liberation. You have expanded and manifested this whole phenomenon of the visible cosmos for the liberation of the *jivas*. When the *jiva* comes to realize fully that all this is your work and your *lila* (play), then it understands that it is only a participant in this divine drama. With the dawn of this understanding it comes to the end of its role in the cosmic comedy.

O Divine Mother! Help us overcome your *maya* and continue our work according to your commands.

Thus saying, the gods bowed before her and begged her to explain everything to them. The goddess then described her divine nature to them.

This entire universe that appears so real to the finite intelligence is no more real than a reflection in a mirror. All the entities in all the worlds, from the gods to the barely conscious creatures, are but fragments of my glory. I am worshipped by all beings in many such universes. Though many worship me, few know me in truth. Creatures imagine that they exist apart from me, but this is not true. The realization that they are integral parts of my being comes only through deep, sustained devotion to me. When the mind is directed solely toward me, the *jiva* discovers its unity with me. When obstructions limiting the *jiva* fall away, it recognizes that it is not limited by the body and has never been and will never be anything but my very self. The devotee who cleanses the mind with tranquility, concentration, and loving devotion will discover me at the root of all things, self-luminous, transparent, and perfect. With this realization, all doubts will vanish. Such a person will go beyond suffering and will not know the meaning of fear.

There is no difference between Brahman and me. We are the same. Without Brahman there would be no *maya,* and without *maya* there would be no creation. At the beginning of creation Brahman and *maya* must appear to have difference between them, or else there would be no creation. Out of this apparent duality, all the differences visible and invisible have come forth. Nevertheless, there is nothing in the universe that is not a part of me. When you perform the act of creation, O Brahma, it is my *shakti* that will enable you to create. It is my *shakti* that will enable Vishnu to take care of the universe and Shiva to destroy.

Sattva is prominent in Vishnu, so he is superior to Brahma, in whom *rajas* is prominent. If any difficulty arises in the world of Brahma's creation, Vishnu will take an incarnation and go down to the earth in order to uplift the Sanatana Dharma, which is the eternal Law of Righteousness that is imprinted in the consciousness of all human beings, but which decays and fades from the mind in the course of time. Vishnu, being the sustainer in the Trinity, is always the one who chooses to go to Earth in many forms in order to uphold that cosmic law. He will take birth in the wombs of women and sometimes in the wombs of birds and animals in order to destroy the demons and uphold *dharma.* There is no difference between Hara (Shiva) and Hari (Vishnu). He who worships one worships the other, and he who makes a difference between them is ignorant of the truth.

Everything springs from the supreme reality of the Brahman. He is neither cause nor effect. I am his *maya,* the power of illusion that creates this world of duality. From me come the three illusory powers of time, space, and causality. The first to come out of me is *avyakta* and then *ahamkara* (this is the cosmic *ahamkara* or cosmic ego), which is the essence of the three *gunas,* without which no creation is possible. There is nothing in this world that is devoid of the three *gunas,* including the three of you. Everything that is visible is endowed with them. Whatever was or will be cannot exist without them. Only the supreme self or Purusha is without the *gunas,* and he is not visible. I myself am Adi Shakti or Mula Prakriti. At times I'm with *gunas* and at times without. I'm always the cause and never the effect. When I take on my causal nature I'm with *gunas*. When I am enfolded into the supreme essence I am without *gunas*. From this supreme essence comes the sound *hreem,* which is my seed mantra and which contains everything else. The whole manifested world comes from the vibrations of sound. The cosmic *ahamkara* proceeds from this. From this comes the five *tanmatras* (subtle elements), and then the five *tattvas* (gross elements), the five *jnanendriyas* (organs of knowledge), the five *karmendriyas* (organs of action), and the four aspects of the mind (*manas, buddhi, ahamkara,* and *chitta*). Out of these twenty-four *tattvas* the whole universe of forms is created. At the end of one cycle of creation this universe, including the three of you, will be dissolved and will fold back into me, Maha Maya, the primeval energy, and I myself into that supreme essence.

It is not possible for the embodied self or *jiva* to know me in my *nirguna* (without *gunas* or qualities) state, nor is it possible for the mind born out of the cosmic *ahamkara* to know the *nirguna* Brahman. Purusha and Prakriti pervade everything and exist in everything. Nothing in this universe can subsist without both of them. The universal consciousness that is felt in all beings is Purusha, the highest self. The energy that is felt in all beings is Prakriti, the universal Shakti. Both are *nirguna,* undecaying and without impurities. The *jivas* are all *saguna* or endowed with qualities. How can they ever see that which is *nirguna* or beyond all qualities? Purusha, Prakriti, Brahman, and myself can be realized through deep meditation, when the mind has transcended the three *gunas.*

This universe is both eternal and noneternal. It is noneternal inasmuch as it is always changing. But I am in all things and I am eternal, so in that respect the universe, even though ever changing, can still be considered as eternal. The unreal can never come into existence. The real can never cease to be. The forms change but I am that supreme reality that upholds these various forms. So do not confuse yourselves with questions about the reality and the unreality of this world. Plunge yourselves into your respective functions and have recourse to my name by which alone you will be able to discharge your duties.

Now I will give you my nine-syllabled *mantra* by which you will be able to realize me and carry on with your work.

So saying, Devi gave them the nine-syllabled *mantra*, which must be preceded by the *pranava* (the *mantra aum*) and followed by *namaha: Aum Aim Hreem Kleem Chamundayai Vicchai Namaha!* This supreme and most esoteric *mantra* of Maha Devi, she told them, could lead to liberation by being chanted constantly.

Devi blessed the three gods and told them to go to their own worlds and commence their work in this present cycle of creation. She also presented them with her *shaktis*. She gave the *shakti* known as Maha Saraswati to Brahma, whose predominant trait is *rajas*, since he is the one to undertake the task of creation as detailed by Maha Devi. He was to take Maha Saraswati and go to his abode of Satyaloka. To Vishnu, in whom *sattva* is preponderant, she gave the beauteous Maha Lakshmi, and she told him to go and live in the world known as Vaikunta. To Shiva, whose prominent *guna* is *tamas*, she gave Parvati and told him to go and live in Kailasa. She told him to use *rajas* and *tamas* in order to undertake the act of destruction but also to resort to *sattva* and perform austerities.

"All three of you are my *devas*, born of my *gunas*," Devi told gods. "You will undoubtedly be worshipped and respected by the whole world."

This parable tells us that the whole of creation is but a revelation and a manifestation of the sole divine essence. Advaita, the philosophy of a nondual Brahman, proclaims that Brahman alone is real and the world unreal—*Brahma satyam, jagat mitya*. But here we see that Maha Devi asserts something quite different. She seems to make a wholesale, indiscriminate sanctification of everything on the earthly plane so that there is no need to think that liberation can be gained only through an ascetic renunciation of the world. We are all in immediate contact with the divine here and now if we can only look upon everything as part and parcel of the divine's ever-changing, everlasting self-revelation. Here the popular picture of *maya* as the dreaded delusory power of the supreme, which is so difficult for even the sternest ascetic to overcome, takes on a surprising aspect. She, Maha Maya, is herself the revelation, the incarnation of the divine energy of the absolute. Life with all its dualities, its extremes of peace and strife, of dread and bliss, is holy and divine and is only a screen for the divine within it. Just beneath the veil of *maya*, the magic mirage of the universe, dwells the supreme spirit. The energy of *maya* is nothing but the energy emanating from that spirit. Maha Devi emerges in the forefront, masking the absolute but also displaying its inner potentialities.

As Devi herself tells the three gods, the process of creation is a conversion of the static repose of the absolute into a procreative power. First there is the absolute Purusha, which is complete inactivity, inertia, and void. From that we come to the infinite activity and dynamic differentiation of a universe with an abundance of creations and variety of forms, all seemingly bound by time, space, and causality. These three delusions are the very essence of *maya*. They are the most elementary frames of our limited human perceptions and conceptions. We view the world with this three-framed glass. But they do not apply to the transcendent absolute. The three are only aspects of a single, unique, and eternal essence. The truth is voidness and plenitude, everything and nothing.

The absolute rests in transcendental quietude, all-comprehensive and enigmatic. It is serenely unaffected by the tensions produced by the three *gunas*. It never feels the joys and agonies of their mutual interactions. The restless effects of the threefold play of creation, manifestation, and destruction are subsumed in its eternal repose. This glorious presence is indifferent to the processes of the universe and the dualities experienced by the individual. So also the *atman*, the self of the individual, rests unconcerned with the sufferings and delights of the personality, enshrouded within the various sheaths of the physical body, the astral body, and the mental and intellectual bodies.

When viewed against the background of eternity, the drama that is enacted on the stage of space and time is as insubstantial as the play of light and shade. It is all a creation of the mind that passes, flows, and vanishes into thin air. The true work of *maya* is the production of the phenomenal world, which has its basis in nescience or *avidya*. *Maya* is what produces this extraordinary universe that we experience within our limited, individualized consciousness. We experience it both when we are awake and asleep, remembering and forgetting, enjoying and suffering, always grasping for that which is ephemeral and unable to grasp the reality of its existence. This is the paradox of *maya*. The universe, like our own personalities, is as real or as unreal as the dualities that seem to emerge from the supreme center and are ignored by it. Brahman and *maya* coexist. *Maya* is the continuous self-manifestation and self-disguise of Brahman—its self-revelation as well as its concealing mask. Hence everything in the universe is divine. Nothing can be scorned or cast aside as unworthy. Maha Maya herself is the sum total of all and is worshipped as the mother and life energy of even the gods as well as of all creatures.

The *yogi* should concentrate on this truth and realize that the individual personality is one with the universal self, who is none other than Maha Maya. That which is mortal in us is also that which is imperishable. What is change and what is above change are one and the same. Thus the *yogi* should learn to accept the *maya* of his frail, transient existence as the dynamic radiation of the eternal, absolute self.

Brahma, Vishnu, and Shiva then took leave of Maha Devi and ascended the chariot, which took off into the ether. When they turned around to look at the island they found that there was no Mani Dwipa, no Devi, and no ocean of nectar!

Her look, Her smile awoke celestial sense,
Even in earth stuff and their intense delight,
Poured a supernal beauty on men's lives.
A wide self-giving was her native act.
A magnanimity as of sea or sky,
Enveloped with its greatness all that came
And gave a sense as of a greatened world,
Her kindly care was sweet temperate sun,
Her high passion a blue heaven's equipoise.

—*Savitri* by Sri Aurobindo

Thus ends the third chapter of *Shakti*, known as "Maha Devi," describing the nature of Devi and creation.

Aum Aim Hreem Kleem

Aum Rajnyai Namaha!

4

Rajarajeshwari

Ya Devi sarvabhuteshu, kshuda rupena samsthita,
Namasthasyai, namasthasyai, namasthasyai namo
namaha!

O Goddess who resides in all creatures in the form
of hunger,
Hail to thee, hail to thee, all hail to thee!

Mani Dwipa, the esoteric island to which Brahma, Vishnu, and Shiva were transported, is where Maha Devi resides with her attendant *shaktis,* which are numerous in number. It is situated somewhere in etheric space far above the worlds of the gods, so it is known as Sarvaloka (that world from which all other worlds emerge).

The Devi Bhagavatam gives a graphic description of the island. It is set in the middle of an ocean known as Sudha Samudra (Sea of Nectar). Many types of brilliantly hued fish play and leap about in this ocean. The shores of the island are made of the dust of millions of gems and that is how the island got its name: Mani Dwipa, or the Island of Jewels. (The Sanskrit word *mani* means "gem.") The trees that line the beach have clusters of jewels hanging from them, and the sand is made of jewel dust. An aerial view of this island shows that it is designed in the shape of a *yantra* (mystical mathematical figure). There are many enclosures, some circular and some square in shape. The squares cut into the circles and thus make the *yantra*.

A few yards away from the beach is an iron enclosure with four gates. Many guards are stationed here. All the gods who come to this mystic island must alight from their vehicles at this place to be taken forward through a series of enclosures by Devi's attendants.

The walls of the second enclosure are made of white copper. In this space are many trees laden with fruit and fragrant flowers. Forests, gardens, and lakes abound here, with cuckoos cooing sweetly and stately swans and other aquatic birds swimming in the lakes.

The third enclosure is square in shape and is made of copper. The forests here are filled with *kalpavrikshas* (wish-fulfilling trees), bearing golden leaves and flowers and fruits of gems. The lord of the spring season is the king of this place. His throne and ornaments are made of flowers, and a canopy of flowers is held above him. His food is the nectar of a thousand newly opened buds. The sweet perfume of full-blown blossoms drenches the air. Everywhere is the beauty of the vernal season.

The next enclosure is made of lead. Within it is the *santanaka* tree, whose flowers look like gold and have an intoxicating perfume that spreads to several miles around. This tree is always in full bloom, and its fruits are luscious and sweet. The king of the summer season lives here. It is very hot, and the inhabitants have to seek the shade of the trees and anoint themselves with sandal paste in order to remain cool. All of them carry flower fans in their hands. Many *yogis* can be seen practicing severe austerities in this place.

The walls of the fifth enclosure are made of brass. The prominent tree here is the sandalwood, and the ruler is the rainy season. Lightning flashes from his amber eyes and rain clouds are his armor; thunder is his voice and the rainbow his weapon. There is a constant drizzle here. The trees have new leaves all through the year and are entwined by tender buds and creepers. The rivers are ever full and flow swiftly and forcefully. The pools are filled with muddy water, like the minds of materialistic people!

The sixth enclosure is made of five types of iron. The gardens here are covered with beautiful trees, flowers, and creepers. The ruler is the king of the autumn season. Many *siddhas* or perfected souls live here.

The seventh enclosure is made of silver. The gardens here are filled with *parijata* trees, the flowers of which drench the air with their sweet perfume. The ruler is the king of the *hemanta* season, which comes immediately after autumn and is characterized by pearly mists and clouds.

The eighth enclosure is made of molten gold. In the center is a garden of *kadamba* trees. They are covered with fruits and flowers from which honey drips constantly. The ruler here is the king of winter season.

Next comes the ninth enclosure with walls of topaz. Even the drains and roads here are made of topaz. Various enclosures made of many types of gems connect to this space. The regents of the quarters reside in the different directions. Indra and his retinue live on the eastern side. The southeastern enclosure belongs to Agni, the god of fire. To the south is the abode of Yama, the god of death, and in the southwestern corner dwell the demons. In the west resides Varuna, the god of waters and drink; his vehicle is the king of fishes and his subjects are all aquatic animals. In the northwestern corner dwells Vayu, the wind god; *yogis* who have practiced *pranayama* or control of breath live with him. On the northern side resides Kubera, the corpulent king of the *yakshas,* the guardians of wealth.

The northeastern corner is the abode of the god Rudra. His eyes are always red with anger and his attendants have distorted faces. Around his neck is a garland of skulls, and tiny snakes are twined around his fingers. He wears a tiger skin and his body is anointed with the ashes of the dead. Bhadrakali is his mate. The sound of his *damaru* (drum) reverberates through the universe in the form of thunder, crashing waves, and furious storms. Spirits, ghouls, and phantoms surround him.

The walls of the tenth enclosure are made of coral that is deep red, the color of the rising sun. All the gates, temples, and arbors here are made of the same material. Here the sixty-four *kalas* or subsidiary powers of Devi reside, each with her separate vehicle and weapons. Fire falls from their lolling tongues, and their eyes are red with anger. Wherever there is war, death, and destruction, they will be present. They are ever ready to swallow the entire universe at the command of Maha Devi.

The eleventh enclosure is made of hessonite. The whole ground is covered with the dust of these gems. Here live the thirty-two *maha-shaktis* or super forces of Devi, adorned with many ornaments and holding weapons of destruction. They are always ready to fight, and any one of them could destroy a million universes if Devi so commands. They can never be defeated at any time. They will always be present at the time of universal destruction.

The twelfth enclosure is made of diamonds. The entrance gates are also of diamonds, and even the trees are resplendent with diamond drops. This is the residence of the maids of the Bhuvaneswari, the goddess of all the worlds. Her eight main ladies-in-waiting dwell on the eight sides of this enclosure.

The thirteenth enclosure is made of cat's-eye. The courtyards and houses here are all made of the same gem. This is the residence of the Sapta Matrikas or seven mothers, known as Brahmaani, Maheswari, Kaumari, Vaishnavi, Vaarahi, Indrani, and Nrisimhi. Their forms are similar to those of Brahma and Vishnu and his *avataras* (incarnations). They are fierce goddesses, always present at the time of wars. At the four gates of this enclosure the various vehicles of Maha Devi are stationed, always ready to start at her slightest command. These vehicles are not merely chariots but also include swans, lions, peacocks, and bulls.

The fourteenth enclosure is made of blue sapphire. In the center of this enclosure is a huge lotus with sixteen petals. On each petal resides one of the sixteen main *shaktis* of the great goddess. All are dark blue in color, like sapphire. They are in charge of all the other *shaktis*.

The fifteenth enclosure is made of pearls. Courtyards, roads, and houses here are all of pearls. Here again is a huge lotus; this one has eight petals on which reside the eight *shaktis* that are the ministers of Maha Devi and her *jnana shaktis* or powers of knowledge. They know everything that takes place in the entire universe, and it is their duty to keep her informed at all times.

The sixteenth enclosure is made of emeralds. It is a hexagonal *yantra*, and the goddesses Gayatri and Savitri, the Vedas and the Puranas live in every corner of the hexagon. Ganesha resides here in a special corner.

The seventeenth enclosure is made of opals. The goddesses of the five elements reside here. The body of each has the color of the elements over which they preside.

The eighteenth enclosure is made of the *navaratnas* or nine precious gems. Here dwell the different *avataras* of Maha Devi, the incarnations she has taken in order to kill various demons.

The nineteenth enclosure is known as the *chintamani griha,* which is made of the precious gem known as *chintamani* that is capable of fulfilling the wishes of all devotees. All the artifacts within this enclosure are made of the same gem.

The twentieth enclosure lies within this *chintamani griha* and is the crowning palace of the Rajarajeswari (the queen of queens). It is called the *ratnagriha* or house of gems. It is situated in the mathematical center of all the enclosures.

Rivers of gems and other precious metals stream from all sides of this palace and flow into the Sudha Samudra (Sea of Nectar). On all sides flow rivers of ghee, milk, curd, honey, nectar, pomegranate juice, and more. Different parts are lit up with the luster of the different jewels to be found in them, such as emeralds, sapphires, and diamonds.

Even the sky reflects the glory of these jewels. The mountains looming in the distance are made of gems and jewels. All the pools are filled with beautiful red lotuses.

The enclosure has four halls comprised of canopies that look like rainbows supported by pillars that shine like the sun, moon, stars, and lightning. These halls are known as the Hall of Beauty, the Hall of Liberation, the Hall of Wisdom, and the Hall of Solitude. They are surrounded by perfumed gardens overflowing with flowers. When she wants to listen to the songs of all the creatures of the universe, sung to her through the mouths of her maids, Maha Devi sits in the Hall of Beauty. When she wants to give liberation to her devotees, she sits in the Hall of Liberation, and when she expounds on the wisdom of the ages, she sits in the Hall of Wisdom. Seated in the Hall of Solitude, she gives commands to her ministers.

In the center of these halls is a dais in the shape of a *shatkona yantra* or mystical six-sided figure of two triangles intersecting each other. The throne of Maha Devi, which is made of *chintamani,* is placed in the center of the dais. The ten steps leading to this throne are made of the *tattvas* or primary qualities that make up the universe. Brahma, Vishnu, Rudra, and Shiva support the four legs of the throne.

Maha Devi sits here in all her glory. She is Rajarajeswari, the queen of queens. She is also Tripurasundari, the most beautiful in all the worlds, who is beyond the triple bonds of the physical, subtle, and causal dimensions. Though she is the ancient one, she appears to be in the full bloom of youth. Her face has the brilliance of a thousand suns. She has three lotus-petaled eyes. The third eye, known as the eye of wisdom, is located in the center of her pearly forehead and opens only when she wants to destroy something. Her other two eyes are filled with compassion and overflowing with love. Below the third eye is the red mark known as a *tilaka,* made of musk and saffron. Her nose ornaments are tiny crystal replicas of the planet Venus, which cast their rainbow lights over her rose-tinted cheeks.

Her lips are red as the *bimba* berry. Her lustrous locks are twined with jasmine flowers and crowned with a tiara, which has jewels in the shape of the sun and moon. Her earrings are shaped like the Sri Chakra (the mystic *yantra,* or mathematical figure, which denotes the Maha Devi) and enhance the beauty of her small, delicate ears. Her slender neck is adorned with necklaces of various shapes and wonderful hues. A jewel-studded bodice covers her full and enticing breasts. Her waist is adorned with a delicately wrought jeweled girdle with golden bells that tinkle as she moves. Her armlets are made of burnished gold, studded with rubies. Her wrists are heavy with bangles with tinkling bells. Her long, delicate fingers with pink-tipped nails have curiously carved rings set with precious gems. She has four hands, which hold the noose, the goad, the bow and arrow, and the *abhaya mudra* or the sign of grace and fearlessness. Her voice is sweeter than a lute.

We should now try to understand the esoteric significance of this island, the exalted and mysterious residence of Maha Devi as described in the Devi Bhagavatam. The deep blue tranquil waters that surround it are the same waters that surrounded Brahma when he first came to be, the same waters in which Lord Vishnu lay recumbent on the cosmic serpent (see chapter 3). This ocean is the Sudha Samudra, the Ocean of Nectar, whose waters are the elixir of immortality and endless life energy. Though it appears dormant, like the universe, which modern physics has only recently understood is not static, the ocean is full of infinite potential. It is the field of all possibilities and is capable of unlimited combinations and permutations. It contains the germs of all conflicting opposites, all the pairs of cooperating antagonisms. All these energies evolve and concentrate at the center, which is the Island of Jewels, the abode of Maha Devi. The ocean, which represents universal consciousness, is comparable to the subtle element of *akasa* or ether that constitutes all space and is the stage for all subsequent evolution and development.

The island is the metaphysical point of power. It is the *bindu* or point that spreads, unfolds, expands, and becomes transmuted into the tangible realm of our limited consciousness and this universe of myriad forms. This *bindu* is the first concentrated drop of the dynamic force of the universal divine substance. From it the creative process starts as a primeval sound or *nada* and spreads out in waves of beauty and bliss. Therefore the universe is nothing but the projection of Maha Devi's majesty and glory. The island, which is shaped in the form of a *yantra*, has to be visualized and meditated upon with great devotion before it yields its esoteric secrets.

Maha Devi is also Mula Prakriti, the power behind the Purusha, the original force that projects this phenomenal world. The weapons she carries have an esoteric meaning apart from the obvious one of being used to kill demons. The bow and arrow denote the power of her supreme will, known as *iccha shakti*. The noose is usually the lasso, which catches and fetters the enemy. This denotes *jnana shakti*, or the master force of the intellect that seizes and fixes with a firm hold on its objects. The goad, which is used for urging a beast to move, denotes action and thus *kriya shakti*. These are the three *shaktis* that Maha Devi uses for creating the objective world of duality; without them, creation would not be possible. The *abhaya mudra* is the sign of grace and fearlessness. One who surrenders to her will be given freedom from fear.

The modern mind might dismiss these descriptions as the wild imaginations of the ancient *rishis*, bound as they were to the infancy of the world. But when we see the consistency and uniformity of the descriptions in the various Puranas, we are able to accept the truth that these are recorded impressions created by the powerful impact of vivid and similar spiritual experiences. The portrayal is symbolic, and in inner worship the *sadhaka* (one who practices spiritual disciplines) will be able to unravel the truth represented by the symbols.

Every aspect of the Island of Jewels is meant for meditation and visualization in the innermost recesses of the heart. At first it appears to be a vindication of our hidden desire for the splendid and the beautiful. But in time we will come to realize that in its total acceptance of the beautiful life (which appears almost as if we were going against the usual norms of spirituality to extol a life of extreme pleasure), it is actually as stern as the total negation of life that is the way of the ascetic. In India this pendulum of thought has always existed. On one hand we find the pessimistic criticism of life that leads to practices of the severest ascetic, which will enable the devotee to shatter the nightmare of life by a great awakening into the reality. On the other hand we have certain Tantric practices that appear most hedonistic and immoral but actually lead to the same goal. Hinduism is a goal-oriented religion and thus it accepts all paths that lead to this goal of liberation for the *atman* from the hold of *maya,* and its realization that it is nothing but the Brahman. Human existence is but a springboard to help us in the bound into the suprahuman, supradivine sphere of being that is beyond the spell of *maya.* The literal meaning of *maya* is "that which measures the immeasurable." *Maya* sees limitation where none actually exists. But in the symbolism of the goddess on the Island of Jewels, we find the same *maya* in her most benign aspect. She is the very essence of the absolute, pure bliss and pure spirit.

She also displays the true feminine nature: the life-bearing, life-nourishing maternal principle. She is beneficent and bright. She exhibits only the positive aspect of *maya shakti* or the power of illusion. We have also to see how her negative aspect is depicted in the fearless world of Indian myth and folklore. Maha Devi's ever-destructive function, which takes back and swallows time and time again all that she has created, gives us a shock of horror if it is duly expressed. To this end we will have to see her as Kaali, the black one. *Kaali* is the feminine form of the word *kaala,* which means time, which is the all-producing and all-consuming principle. Time alone is the vanquisher and the killer. Everything that comes into existence vanishes again after the passing of its brief spell of allotted time.

A joy in the world her master movement here.
The passion of the game lighted her eyes.
A smile on her lips welcomed earth's bliss and grief,
A laugh was her return to pleasure and pain.
All things she saw as masquerades of Truth,
Disguised in the costumes of ignorance.
Crossing the years to Immortality.

—*SAVITRI* BY SRI AUROBINDO

Thus ends the fourth chapter of *Shakti,* known as "Rajarajeshwari," describing the Island of Jewels or Mani Dwipa.

Aum Aim Hreem Kleem

Aum Maheswaryai Namaha!

5

Maheswari

Ya Devi sarvabhuteshu, nidra rupena samsthita,
Namasthasyai, namasthasyai, namasthasyai namo
namaha!

O Goddess who resides in all creatures in the form
of sleep,
Hail to thee, hail to thee, all hail to thee!

The birth of the two terrible *asuras* or demons that Vishnu destroyed
at the beginning of this *kalpa* (cycle of creation), Madhu and
Kaitabha, is a curious phenomenon. At the end of the Maha Pralaya,
when the whole universe was dissolved in the cosmic waters, Lord
Vishnu lay sleeping on the cosmic serpent Ananta. At that time it
is said that a drop of honey (*madhu*) came out of his right ear, and
it transformed into the enormous demon known as Madhu. Out of
his left ear came a small pellet of wax, which turned into the mighty
demon Kaitabha. What is the esoteric meaning of this strange episode? Lord Vishnu is the preserver in the Hindu trinity, and he is
the one who is always aware of what goes on in the universe. The
Upanishads describe him as having many limbs, many eyes, and many
ears. This means that he hears all that happens in the world, both the

54

good and the evil. All the slanderous and ugly tales, lies, and false-hoods that are told by so many countless people collect as wax in his ears. The driving human passion for comfort, luxury, power, for-tune, and wealth is transformed into the drop of honey. The karmic effect of the uncontrollable desire for wealth and comfort and the accumulated amount of negative, self-destructive thoughts and talk transformed into two terrible demons who threatened to destroy the creator, Brahma. This happens at the beginning of every *kalpa,* and it demonstrates the power of collective negativity. It is this that erupts into world wars. The terror that we are facing now is nothing but the work of these two demons who have been brought to life out of our own negativity.

These two titans who had thus been borne out of Lord Vishnu's ears found themselves splashing about in the cosmic waters, pondering on the where and why of their existence. At last the idea came into their minds that the mighty goddess Maha Devi or Maheswari was their cause. They determined to discover her whereabouts. As they cogitated over the matter, they heard the celestial voice of the goddess Saraswati, who told them to meditate on her seed *mantra.* They decided to try this, and they proceeded to repeat the *mantra* and meditate on her for a thousand years.

At the end of this period of time they heard the celestial voice once again: "I'm very pleased with your *tapas,* and you can ask for any boon you like."

The *asuras* immediately asked for immortality. The divine voice said that no one could be granted that. So they opted for death only of their own volition. This was granted, and the demons became bloated with pride and thrashed about the mighty ocean searching for a suitable opponent on whom to try their valor. When they came upon Brahma, they did not think him a suitable candidate on whom to display their prowess. Nevertheless, they ordered him to give up his lotus seat and accept their suzerainty or fight. Brahma was frightened and desperately searched in the waters for some aid. At last he was given the vision of

Lord Narayana (Vishnu). But as described in chapter 3, Vishnu was in the thrall of Yoga Nidra, the goddess of sleep. It was only after she left him that he rose from his couch and saw Brahma.

Brahma bowed low before Vishnu, the lord of all lords, and begged him to deliver him from the threat of these two mighty demons. Vishnu pacified him and told him to retire to his own abode, leaving him to deal with the demons. At this point the bloodthirsty demons arrived on the scene, glad to have found a more worthy opponent.

They saw Lord Hari (Vishnu) of unspeakable beauty lying on his divine bed, the coil of a snake that was many leagues wide and many leagues long. He was clad in a yellow robe and had a diamond diadem on his head. On his chest flashed the enormous ruby known as the Kaustubham. He glowed with an ethereal splendor and beauty. From his navel sprouted a lotus with the luster of the sun, and within the lotus was seated Brahma, the four-faced one, the *guru* (spiritual teacher) of the world, with four arms holding the four Vedas.

The *asuras* were blinded by the brilliance emanating from Vishnu. They were astonished to see this sight, but undaunted, they roared and tried to intimidate the trembling Brahma. They cried:

> There is nothing greater than us in this world, O Great Sage! We are the ones who cover this whole universe with darkness (*tamas*) and passion (*rajas*). We, whose nature consists of *tamas* and *rajas*, are the main cause of *dukkha* (sorrow) to the world. We are deceitful among those of virtuous conduct and invincible among all embodied ones. We are born age after age and delude the world. We are made up of those objects that are desired by everyone: wealth, possessions, happiness, joy, and fortune.
>
> We will kill you first and then kill this one who seems to be sleeping on a serpent.

Brahma immediately disappeared from the lotus and took up a safe position behind Vishnu.

Lord Vishnu laughed and leisurely got up from his bed. He told the demons that he was ready to fight with them if that was what they desired. The brothers were delighted to put their might to use.

Madhu came first and challenged the lord. After some time, when he saw his brother getting tired, Kaitabha joined the fray. Vishnu used only his fists since the demons had no weapons. A tremendous battle ensued between the bloodthirsty demons and Lord Vishnu. Brahma and Adi Shakti from above witnessed this spectacle. After fighting for a thousand years the titans were still not tired. Lord Vishnu started wondering why this was so.

The *asuras* were elated at their success and taunted him: "If you are too tired to fight you can give up and become our slave!"

Vishnu replied, "O *danavas* (demons)! You are two in number and mighty in size, whereas I am single and puny when compared with you. Therefore let us rest awhile and then we will recommence our battle."

The *asuras* agreed with alacrity, since they were sure of the outcome and did not mind having a small rest themselves. While they rested Vishnu began to think of the reason for the apparent invincibility of the two brothers. He soon came to know of the boon of the goddess. He thought, "If this is the reason, they can never be slain, since no one ever wishes for their own death. So my only hope is to appeal to that *devi* herself who has granted them this boon."

So thinking, he looked up at Adi Shakti, who was shining in the sky, and extolled her: "O Maha Kaali! Bhuvaneswari! Chandika! You have given them these boons and puffed up their pride. Kindly help me destroy them, since they are threatening to kill Brahma."

Pleased with his hymn, Adi Shakti told him sweetly, "O Narayana! Do not fear. I will delude these two heroes by my *maya*, and then you will be able to kill them easily. Let it be a battle of wits between you and not just of fists." (It is to be noted that from the very commencement of this *yuga* or cycle of time, the gods have had to depend on the Maha Devi's power to help them in their tasks.)

In all his encounters with foes Lord Vishnu is noted for using his intelligence, showing the superiority of brains over brute strength. Once again he proceeded to challenge the *asuras*, who were still thirsty for battle. Fist for fist, arm for arm, thrust for thrust, the fight went on and on, interminably. At last Vishnu shot a desperate look at Adi Shakti or Maha Maya, who was shining with all her beauty in the sky. Seeing his look, the goddess came down to the ocean and cast her side-long glances enticingly at the two demons, who became quite bemused by her.

To those *asuras*, who were thus swollen and drunk with pride, Vishnu spoke: "O *danavas!* I'm pleased with your prowess in the art of wrestling and wish to give you a boon. Go ahead and ask for what you want."

The haughty demons were quite insulted by this and told him, "We are not beggars to accept boons from you. We are the ones who should be giving you boons. We are donors, not receivers! We are your benefactors, so you can go ahead and ask us for whatever you want!"

The lord smiled at the enormity of their egos and sweetly replied, "I accept your boon, O heroes! Indeed there is something I desire. I know you have great prowess. There is none equal to you. But for the good of the world I have to ask you for something. I wish that the two of you will allow yourselves to be killed by my hands."

The *asuras* realized that they had been neatly tricked by Vishnu's *maya*, which is a power of the Divine Mother. They thought for a minute and saw that there was nothing but water everywhere, so they swiftly hit upon a ruse to save their skins: "O mighty being! No one is equal to us in strength, beauty, bravery, generosity, might, and self-control. We will always keep our word. Yet we want to change our minds and ask you for the boon that we refused previously. You have our permission to kill us provided you do it on that which is not covered by water."

"So be it," said Vishnu, and he allowed them to set conditions on their commitment even though he could not see any space that was not covered with water. He then happened to glance at his own uncovered thighs, which had not a trace of water on them, and he expanded them so that they appeared like solid earth.

"O mighty *danavas!*" Vishnu said. "Place your heads on this solid foundation and keep your word, as I will keep mine!"

When they saw this, the demons were terrified and expanded their forms to double their size. Vishnu also expanded his thighs. This game went on until the demons realized that they were beaten. They laid their gargantuan heads on Vishnu's thighs and the lord took his discus—the Sudarshana Chakra—and used it to saw off their mighty heads. The marrow (*medhas*) from their bones filled the ocean and was sucked into the earth, and that is how the earth goddess got the name Medini. And after slaying Madhu and Kaitabha, Vishnu came to be called Madhusudana.

It should be noted that in this episode of the killing of Madhu and Kaitabha, the goddess did not take an active part. The episode establishes her cosmic, transcendental status. Adi Shakti is indeed Maha Maya, the great illusion who deludes the *asuras* into thinking that they could outwit the divine. How great was their opinion of themselves when they talked to Brahma! This is typical of the *asuric* ego that thinks itself to be superior to God. As they themselves proclaimed to Brahma, these *asuras* are born at the beginning of every cycle of time, and the earth is nourished by the fat of their enormous egos. Naturally they are at the root of all our desires for earthly pleasures. But behind all such desires is the power of Maha Maya, who leads human beings to believe that this life has an absolute reality of its own and that we are are the masters of our own life, and thus we make their own futile attempts to outwit the divine. These attempts will end in failure, for only the divine truly abides.

He who would save the world, must be one with the world,

All suffering things contain in his heart's space.
And bear the grief and joy of all that lives.
His soul must be wider than the universe,
And feel eternity as its very stuff.
Rejecting the moment's personality,
Know itself older than the birth of time.

—*SAVITRI* BY SRI AUROBINDO

Thus ends the fifth chapter of *Shakti,* known as "Maheswari," describing the defeat of the *asuras* Madhu and Kaitabha by Lord Vishnu.

Aum Aim Hreem Kleem

ॐ

Aum Bhavanyai Namaha!

6

Parashakti

Ya Devi sarvabhuteshu, chaaya rupena samsthita,
Namasthasyai, namasthasyai, namasthasyai namo namaha!

O Goddess who resides in all creatures in the form
   of shadow,
Hail to thee, hail to thee, all hail to thee!

Once the creator Brahma went to Vaikunta, the abode of Lord Vishnu,
and found him in deep meditation. When Vishnu came out of meditation, Brahma asked him a pertinent question:

O Janardana (Krishna, supreme incarnation of Vishnu)! You are the
lord of lords! The lord of the present, past, and future! Kindly tell me,
who or what is the object of your meditation? I myself have sprung
from the lotus that grew from your navel and have been ordered to
create. It is due to your will that I have been able to do this. By your
command the sun shines and the winds roam, fire heats and clouds
shower rain. Then what is the need for you to meditate, and on whom
are you meditating?

Hearing his words, Bhagavan Narayana (Vishnu) spoke:

O Brahma! Listen to me carefully. Though it is well known by every-one that you and I and Shiva are the cosmic triad for creation, preser-vation, and destruction, a little consideration will tell you that these three acts are actually performed by the *shaktis* or forces of creation, preservation, and destruction. Therefore this force that resides in you, Rudra (Shiva), and me is all-powerful. When these *shaktis* are absent, then you are powerless to create, Rudra to destroy, and I to preserve. Directly or indirectly we are always under that *shakti*. At the time of Maha Pralaya, I lie down on my bed—Ananta. At the time of creation I wake up, swayed by that Parashakti's power of time. It is on her that I meditate, O Lord of Creation! All of us are subservient to her!

O Brahma! Don't you remember that in one *kalpa,* the four Vedas were stolen from your mouth and you were searching for them in vain? At last you came to know that they had been stolen by the *asura* Hayagriva, and you begged me to restore them to you. At that time I had to take the form of a person with the head of a horse in order to kill the demon.

Brahma confessed that he had forgotten that episode and begged to be told the whole story, and Vishnu proceeded to do so.

In ancient days there was a demon called Hayagriva who practiced severe austerities on the banks of the river Saraswati. He repeated the *bija mantra* of the goddess in her *tamasic* aspect until she appeared to him, seated on her vehicle—the lion. On seeing her, the *asura* was greatly pleased and started to hymn her: "Obeisance to thee, O Devi! O Maha Maya! O Parashakti! You are the creator, preserver, and direc-tor of the universe. You are skilled in giving boons to your devotees. All things moving and unmoving are fashioned by you."

Parashakti was pleased with his devotion and asked him to choose a boon. He immediately asked for immortality.

She spoke, "Birth brings death in its wake and death brings birth. This is the inevitable law of life. Therefore, O *daitya* (demon), ask for some other boon."

"O Mother! If you do not want to grant me the boon of immortality, then grant me this: that I may be killed only by one who is horse-faced."

The Devi or Parashakti granted this boon and vanished. The demon then roamed the universe, destroying everything and troubling both gods and humans. He who stole the four Vedas from the mouth of Brahma so that all wisdom disappeared from the world. In despair the gods went to Brahma to ask him to intercede on their behalf and request Lord Vishnu to take an *avatara* (incarnation) in order to kill this demon who was harassing the world.

Lord Vishnu had to undertake a severe sacrifice in order to fulfill this prayer of the gods. But he is the Uttama Purusha—the supreme person. He is compassion incarnate. He has infinite love for creation and is ever ready to sacrifice himself, if need be, for the sake of the world. For this particular bit of work he would have to acquire a horse's head, but even this he was prepared to do for the sake of his devotees.

A cause must exist for everything, and therefore Vishnu created a cause. He seated himself in *padmasana* (the lotus posture) in a beautiful spot and rested his head on the front of his bow, which had been tautly strung. It appeared as if he was fast asleep. At this time the gods along with Brahma came to request his help. When they saw that he was resting, they feared to disturb him. They thought of a clever plan to wake him. Brahma created white ants and told them to eat the string of the bow so that it would break and disturb Vishnu's sleep. The white ants were not too happy at this order. To disturb someone who is sleeping is said to be a heinous crime, so they wanted to know what benefit they would get out of it. Brahma promised them that at the end of every fire sacrifice they could eat the ghee that had fallen from the sacrificial pit.

Satisfied with this, the insects ate through one end of the string. Immediately the string gave way and the bow flew up with a tremendous sound. The earth trembled, the ocean rose up in huge tidal waves, violent winds began to blow, the mountains shook, and ominous portents like comets and falling meteors were seen in the sky. All the quarters assumed a terrifying aspect. The sun sank down and the entire world was enveloped in darkness. The gods were petrified and did not know what to do. While they huddled together, the darkness slowly disappeared and they were horrified to see the decapitated body of Lord Vishnu lying on the ground. Of the head there was no sign.

They started crying and wailing, "O Lord of Lords! O Eternal One! You are incapable of being cut or pierced or wounded or burnt! How is it that now your head has been cut off? O Lord of Gods! Where are we to go now? Whom shall we approach for help? You have always been our only help and succor. What are we to do now?"

Seeing their plight, Brihaspati, the *guru* (spiritual preceptor) of the gods, said to them, "O *devas*! Instead of bewailing your bad luck, start thinking of how you can recoup yourselves and regain what you have lost. Remember that destiny is not all-powerful. It can be overcome by using your intelligence. So start thinking how this can be managed."

Brahma now said:

However auspicious or inauspicious it may be, that which is ordained by destiny has to be borne by everyone. When one takes up a body, one must experience both pain and pleasure. However, fate can be off-set by the grace of Maha Devi. She is Parashakti, the great force, the mother of all, the supporter of all, and ever ready to bless anyone who approaches her. So let us begin to chant her hymns.

Parashakti (the original force) is seated above the mind and will and sublimates them into wisdom. She is the wise one who opens to us the cosmic truths of infinity and eternity. She is ever calm and immutable, for she knows everything. She comprehends everything about creation. Nothing is hidden from her. Her strength is the power of knowledge coupled with the power of action, and thus none can go against her. She is equitable, patient, and unalterable in her will. To the wise she gives luminosity, to the wicked she imposes the consequences of their own wickedness, and with the ignorant and stupid she deals according to the levels of their understanding. She handles everyone and everything at its own level. She is bound by nothing and attached to nothing. But she has the heart of the universal mother, overflowing with a compassion that is limitless and unending. Every creature including the *asura* is her child. Her so-called punishments are part of her grace. Her sole mission is to build and mold our nature so that it merges into the divine.

Thus Brahma told the gods to approach Maheswari, for she alone was capable of helping them.

So all the gods started to hymn Maheswari: "O Devi! Thou art the merciful mother of the whole universe. No one is able to know your true form. You are the one who has created all of us, including, Brahma, Vishnu, and Shiva, so how can we ever know you, who are the cause of all? You are the knower of everything, so you should know the reason why Vishnu's head has fallen off. We don't know where his head has flown off. O thou who gives life to all creatures, kindly bring life to the headless body of Lord Vishnu."

At this, the gods heard an ethereal voice: "O gods, do not fear. You are all immortal. None of you can be killed, least of all Vishnu, the god of all gods! There is a cause for everything. The *asura* Hayagriva, who has been troubling all of you, has been given a boon by me, that only one who has the head of a horse can kill him. So go to the divine architect Vishvakarma and ask him to fit the head of a horse on the headless body of Vishnu. Then all your desires will be fulfilled."

Hearing these words, Vishvakarma cut off the head of a horse and fixed it on Lord Vishnu's trunk. Vishnu, who had been prepared to sacrifice himself for the sake of the world, now proceeded to destroy the demon Hayagriva, who had been creating havoc in all the three worlds. In this *avatara* Lord Vishnu took on the name of the *asura* and hence became known as Hayagriva.

Vishnu as Hayagriva advised the sage Agastya to worship Maha Devi in her form as Lalitha or Kameswari, the queen of desire. The thousand and one names of Lalitha, known as the Lalitha Sahasranama, were given to the sage by Vishnu and are revealed in the Brahmanda

Purana. It is one of the most famous poems to Maha Devi and is
recited by all Shakti worshippers to this day.

> She knew herself the beloved of the Supreme,
> These gods and goddesses were He and She,
> The Mother was she of beauty and delight,
> The word in Brahma's vast creating clasp,
> The world puissance in almighty Shiva's lap,
> The Master and the Mother of all lives.
> Watching the world their twin regard had made.

—SAVITRI BY SRI AUROBINDO

Thus ends the sixth chapter of *Shakti,* known as "Parashakti,"
describing the defeat of the *asura* Hayagriva by Lord Vishnu.

Aum Aim Hreem Kleem

7
Lalitha

Ya Devi sarvabhuteshu, shakti rupena samsthita,
Namasthasyai, namasthasyai, namasthasyai namo
namaha!

O Goddess who resides in all creatures in the form
of power,
Hail to thee, hail to thee, all hail to thee!

The Brahmanda Purana is one of the eighteen Maha Puranas. In it we find the story of the goddess known as Lalitha, Lalithambika, or Tripurasundari, which is the most pleasing and beautiful incarnation of Maha Devi. In fact, the very word *lalitha* means "lovely," "elegant," or "charming." Devi took this incarnation to destroy the demon known as Bhanda or Bhandasura. The Brahmanda Purana devotes practically the whole of its fourth book to the story of Lalitha. Of the forty-four chapters that make up this book, forty are devoted to Lalitha; together they are known as the Lalithopakhyana (the story of Lalitha). The Brahmanda Purana describes the origin of the goddess; the construction of her city, Sripura, which was modeled on the *yantra* known as Sri Chakra; the preparation for the war with Bhandasura; and the actual war and final triumph of the goddess over the demonic forces.

Lalitha's worship is most common among orthodox Hindus, since she represents the best of all feminine qualities. Her form evokes lofty spiritualism and philosophic calm. Adi Shankaracharya, the founder of Advaita, wrote a hymn to Lalitha, called the *Trisati,* and attached special significance to her worship. He addresses her with three hundred names in the *Trisati.* The *Tripura Rahasya* (a poem extolling Lalitha that appears in the Brahmanda Purana) says, "That which shines within as pure being is her majesty, the supreme empress, absolute consciousness. The universe and all the creatures that range within it are that one reality. Yes, all this is she alone."

The *Saundaryalahari,* also by Adi Shankaracharya, a poem whose name translates as "intoxication of beauty," emphasizes Lalitha's extraordinary beauty. It describes every detail of her physical body and claims that the great power of attraction of Kama, the god of love, was bestowed on him by just one glance from the goddess.

The Lalitha Sahasranama, the thousand and one names of Lalitha given in the Brahmanda Purana, describes her every feature in names thirteen to fifty-one. These names are intended to be an aid for concentration so that the devotee can visualize the goddess in all her beauty. The Lalitha Sahasranama gives her many epithets that identify her with sexual desire and points out that she is the one who manifests in all creatures as sexual attraction. She is called Ramya, the beautiful one; Kanta, the lovely one; Vamanayana, the one with beautiful eyes; Vamakesi, the one with beautiful hair; Kamya, the desirable one; Sringararasapurna, the one who is filled with amorous sentiments; Lolakshikamarupini, the one whose tremulous eyes are the desire of the world; Mohini, the enchantress; and Kamakelitarangita, the one who overflows with desire and pleasure. Each name mentioned in the Lalitha Sahasranama is a special *mantra;* the names were not randomly chosen but each have an esoteric significance.

Lalitha has all three *shaktis: iccha shakti,* or the power of desire, constitutes her head; *jnana shakti,* or the power of wisdom, constitutes her body; and *kriya shakti,* or the power of action, constitutes her feet.

The necessity for Lalitha's incarnation is told in the Brahmanda Purana. There was once a powerful *asura* (demon) called Taraka. Brahma had granted to him the boon that only a son of Shiva could kill him. Taraka knew Shiva to be a confirmed celibate who might never have a son, and he thought he could outwit Brahma by asking for such a boon. He then proceeded to destroy *dharma* (the law of righteousness) on earth and ousted the gods from the heavens. The defeated gods went to Brahma to beg for his help in their plight. Brahma was helpless, though, and so he accompanied them to Vaikunta (the abode of Vishnu) to get his advice. Lord Vishnu answered that since the *asura* could be killed only by a son of Shiva, the obvious thing would be to divert the mind of Shiva from his *tapas* (meditation) and make him fall in love and marry. At this time Parvati, the daughter of Himavan, king of the Himalayas, was doing severe penance in order to get Shiva as her husband. The gods decided to help her by sending Kama, the god of love, and his wife Rati to disturb Shiva's *tapas*.

Kama and Rati proceeded to the icy abode of Lord Shiva and carefully prepared their plan. As soon as Kama's feet touched the barren land, the snows melted and turned into gurgling rivulets. Spring spread her exquisite carpet of flowers and fruits and new shoots on the trees. The celestial damsels who had accompanied them danced in abandon, churning the minds of the severest ascetic. The full moon rose to shed its dazzling brilliance on a perfect setting for a lovers' tryst.

When Shiva opened his eyes, he noticed this untimely intrusion of spring into his wintry hermitage and wondered at it. However, he closed his eyes again and continued with his meditation. Then Kama took on his most beguiling form, and he and Rati started a wonderful dalliance filled with amorous gestures, calculated to rouse passion in the heart of even the sternest *yogi*. The celestial damsels played enticing music all the while. But Shiva seemed undisturbed, and Kama began to doubt his own ability to rouse him. Just at that moment Parvati appeared and started her morning *puja* (ritual) for Shiva. She was used to doing it even if he was in the deepest *samadhi* (superconscious state). At the end of the worship she stood shyly beside him, hoping that he would open his eyes. As luck would have it, Lord Shiva opened his eyes for a split second and turned his gaze on Parvati. Kama took the opportunity and shot his enchantment-filled flower arrow straight at the lord. Usually when Shiva happened to open his eyes, he would close them again even though Parvati stood before him. This time, thanks to Kama's intervention, he found that he could not tear his gaze away from Parvati's loveliness. But master *yogi* that he was, he realized immediately that something had happened to churn his mind. He looked around to find the cause and his gaze fell on Kama, who stood with Rati beside him, proud of his prowess in having brought the great *yogi* to heel. Kama was holding his bow taut and ready, and at Shiva's glance he loosed a second arrow. As the arrow sped from his bow he felt the full blast of Shiva's wrath sweep over him, and he cried out to the gods to help him. Before any of them could come to his aid, Lord Shiva opened his third eye and a great flame of fire shot up from his forehead like a fiery meteor. It dropped on Kama's hapless head and reduced him to a heap of ashes.

Seeing this piteous spectacle and hearing the wails of Rati, an inspired artist called Chitrakarma gathered up the ashes and shaped them into the figure of a human being. When Shiva's glance fell on this figure, it started to breathe and was filled with life and effulgence. Chitrakarma was enamored by his own creation and asked the creature to pray to Shiva by repeating the hymn to Rudra (Shiva's fiercest incarnation). Pleased with this, Shiva blessed the creature with unequaled overlordship of the world for six thousand years. He also gave him the power to drain half the energy of his enemy in any encounter. The creator Brahma was quite disgusted with Shiva's show of leniency and expressed his opinion with the expletive *"Bhand! Bhand!"* Thus the creature came to be known as Bhanda. Since he was born from the wrath of Shiva, he had all the most fearful aspects of the lord's nature and behaved like a veritable demon. Bhanda was a caricature of Kama, who represented pure love and was the sacred movement of nature to nurture and propagate; Bhanda symbolized distorted, aggressive, and selfish lust. He subdued the gods with his ferocity and forced Mayan, the principal engineer of the gods, to build a magnificent city called Sonitapura for his residence. Shukra, the preceptor of the demons, had him anointed as overlord of the whole world. Thus the *asura*'s position was firmly established, and he started to wield his iron hand over the gods.

The gods as usual were desperate, and they asked the sage Narada to help them. Narada asked Indra, the king of gods, to perform a great sacrifice to the goddess Parashakti, who alone would be able to conquer Bhanda. Thus the gods performed a wonderful fire sacrifice and propitiated the goddess by offering animal sacrifices. A circular mass of blazing light rose up over the fire. In the center was the shining wheel of time, on which sat the lovely form of the goddess, resplendent as the rising sun. She was the color of the pomegranate flower and the quintessence of beauty and desire. In her four hands she held a noose, a goad, a sugarcane bow, and five arrows tipped with flower petals. She was the manifestation of Lalitha, the embodiment of self-awareness. The gods were enchanted by this vision; they praised her as the universal mother and father and begged her to save them from the scourge of the demon Bhanda.

They extolled her thus:

Victory to the mother of the universe. You are greater than the greatest. You are the source of all prosperity and well-being. You are the holiness of the act of love!

Hail to the inexpressible beauty of consciousness, unparalleled in all the three worlds. Pervading unlimited space, yet fully manifest in every atom, it is you who in an act of overflowing love gave birth to all creatures.

The dawn is your robe. Past, present, and future are your body, and the scriptures are your words.

Hearing of the bewitching appearance of the goddess, the Trimurtis (the trinity of Brahma, Vishnu, and Shiva) came to offer their homage to her. Brahma in his role of the universal grandsire declared that a suitable spouse should be found for her. But who in the world would be worthy of this enchantress except Lord Shiva himself? But Shiva was standing beside him, clad in tiger skin, with matted locks and ash-covered body. Would she deign to look at him? Sensing the creator's thoughts, Shiva assumed the incredibly handsome aspect of Kameswara, the lord of desire, and turned to look at Lalitha. It is said that even Shiva, who had incinerated the god of love, found himself unable to withstand the extraordinary beauty of the mother of the universe. Lalitha returned his gaze and appeared to be totally captivated by his strikingly handsome form. He was indeed the lord of desire.

Lalitha agreed to marry Shiva, but she made certain conditions: "Remember that whatever I say or do is according to my own will alone. Whoever accepts me as his wife must also accept my complete independence."

Shiva agreed to this, since he knew her to be an incarnation of Parashakti, without whom he was powerless to act. She took the wedding garland that Lord Vishnu gave her in his role as her brother and tossed it high into the sky. The garland circled the heads of all the gods in turn and gently landed on the neck of Kameswara. Thus the couple were married and Lalitha came to be known as Kameswari, the queen of desire.

Kameswari grants all desires, from the hunger for sexual fulfilment to the yearning for union with the supreme. Lalitha is worshipped on full-moon days because its waxing phases represent the increasing light of the soul as it expands to its greatest stature, which is the desire for liberation.

Though married to Shiva, Lalitha was self-willed and independent. At the same time she was also the devoted consort of Kameswara. She existed in a state of harmony most of the time, but since the form she had taken was for the fulfilment of a certain purpose, she had to take up arms immediately in order to restore the balance of good and evil in the world. The sage Narada, who was at the wedding ceremony, took the opportunity to remind the goddess of the reason for her incarnation before he departed.

In order to keep her promise to the gods, Lalitha proceeded to make preparations for the great battle. The Brahmanda Purana enumerates the names of all her *shaktis* or demigoddesses, eager to free the world from evil, and the names of all their extraordinary chariots. These *shaktis* were the innate energies of the subtle body, and their chariots were in the shape of *yantras* (mystical mathematical figures) or *mandalas* (mystical designs) in which these energies embody themselves, so that they are available for worship.

Lalitha herself was in the chariot called Chakraraja, the king of chariots, seated in the foremost position. The chariot had nine partitions, in each of which were stationed various *shaktis,* all armed to the teeth. In the ninth partition were the *ashta shaktis* or eight powers. In the eighth part were the *gupta shaktis* or secret forces, armed with bows and arrows. In the seventh part were the two *shaktis* known as the embodied and the swift. In the sixth were the *ajna shaktis,* or those in charge of wisdom. In the fifth were the *shaktis* whose weapons were the plowshare, noose, mace, and bells. In the fourth came the ten goddesses whose arms were the thunderbolt, spear, and wheel. Warrior goddesses known as Vagadeeswarees took their stand in the third part. In the second were the secret police known as Atiguptarahasya ("extremely confidential"); they had the full confidence of the goddess.

Lalitha's two commanders-in-chief were Mantranayika, sometimes known as Mantrini, and Dandanatha, sometimes known as Dandanayika. Her chief attendants were Yantrini and Tantrini. Mantrini was mounted on the great chariot known as Geyachakra, which had seven partitions. She sat in the first part. In the second were the *shaktis* Rati, Preeti, and Manoja, who represented the different types of love. The fourth part had the five *shaktis* whose function

was to create delusion in the minds of the enemies. Another part held
Bhairavis (goddesses who were terrifying to behold).

The chariot occupied by Dandanatha was known as Kirichakra. Her
weapons were the plowshare and the pestle. The different parts of this
chariot also held many *shaktis*, all well armed. In the sixth joint of
this chariot were the Ashtadevis, guardians of the eight directions.

These three amazing chariots were drawn up in front of the army.
Many musical instruments were playing; drums were booming and
bugles blowing to announce the approach of the army. Lalitha's chariot, Chakraraja, had six charioteers including the goddess herself, while
the other two had only one each. Over every chariot were held satin
umbrellas in dazzling colors. Loud cries of "Hail to Lalitha! Victory to
Maha Devi!" rent the air as the expedition set out.

The terrific war cries from Lalitha's camp were heard far away in
Bhanda's city of Sonitapura near the ocean. The citizens noted a number of bad omens and informed Bhanda about them. He decided to
have a council of war and went to the council chamber accompanied
by his brothers.

One of them addressed the council and said that the gods were
sending an army of women to fight with them. Bhanda laughed in
scorn when he heard this, but his brothers advised him not to dismiss
the army as being unworthy of him but to send a counterforce immediately before it reached the city.

Bhanda said, "Even if all the gods came to their aid, they would still
be unable to withstand our forces." However, he called his commander-
in-chief and told him to guard all the entrances to the city. He also
sent one of his generals, Durmada, to forestall the advancing host.

> *Spiritual beauty illumining human sight,*
> *Lines with its passion and mystery Nature's*
>   *mask.*
> *And squanders eternity on the beat of Time,*
> *As when a soul drawn near the sill of birth,*

Adjoining mortal time to Timelessness,
A spark of deity lost in Nature's crypt.

—*SAVITRI* BY SRI AUROBINDO

Thus ends the seventh chapter of *Shakti,* known as "Lalitha," describing the birth of Bhandasura and the advent of Devi as Lalitha.

Aum Aim Hreem Kleem

ॐ

Aum Mahashaktyai Namaha!

8

Tripurasundari

Ya Devi sarvabhuteshu, trishna rupena samsthita,
Namasthasyai, namasthasyai, namasthasyai namo
namaha!

O Goddess who resides in all creatures in the form
of thirst,
Hail to thee, hail to thee, all hail to thee!

Seeing the *asura* hosts marching toward them, one of Lalitha's generals, Sampatkari, along with her *shaktis,* offered to meet them. When Durmada, the general of Bhanda's army, found that he was being beaten by Lalitha's general, he decided to confront her himself. He was riding on an enormous camel, while Sampatkari was on an elephant. A bitter battle was fought, and Durmada jumped onto the elephant and wrested the crown jewel from Sampatkari's tiara, much to the delight of his followers. But their mirth was short-lived, since she then smote him on the head and killed him in one stroke.

Bhanda was astonished to hear of this and commanded one of his best generals, Kuranda, to wreak vengeance on Sampatkari. Kuranda was an expert in creating illusions, but another *shakti* called Aparajita killed him in no time.

Bhanda now sent five commanders with a huge army that created an illusion in which thousands of reptiles swarmed over the goddess's militia and harassed them sorely. At last Lalitha's army hymned Lord Vishnu's vehicle, called Garuda, which was an enormous eagle that was the enemy of all snakes, and thus they overcame the illusion created by the reptiles and killed all five commanders.

Bhanda was dumbfounded and sent the seven great warriors known as the Balahaka brothers to meet the opposing army. They enveloped the *shakti* army in total darkness, but the *shakti* known as Tirasankaranika caused all seven brothers to become blind and thus killed them easily.

This news totally paralyzed Bhanda, and he realized that the opposing host was not to be trifled with. He called a secret war council and ordered his general Visunga to attack the army from the rear, for he had heard that Lalitha was stationed at the back and he felt that if she were captured, the others would be demoralized. The army left without music or any outward show and stealthily crept behind the camp, where Chakraraja, Lalitha's own chariot, was stationed. In the meantime another general approached from the front and fought a battle with the *shaktis* who were positioned there. Lalitha soon came to know of the attack from the rear; she went forth as Kameswari and put Visunga to the sword. This battle was fought in the night, and by dawn the whole *asura* host had been routed.

Lalitha's army now decided that it had to protect itself from all sides, since the *asuras* were up to all types of unrighteous acts like creeping up from the back and fighting in the night. So the whole army settled in a camp encircled by a garland of fire made by the *shakti* known as Jwalamalini. Lalitha's chariot was kept in the center, flanked by the chariots Geyachakra and Kirichakra.

Hearing about these preparations, Bhanda asked his own sons, who were thirty in number, to proceed to the front and to take Lalitha alive by hook or by crook. The expedition set out with great enthusiasm. When this news reached the *shakti* camp, Lalitha's nine-year-old daughter

Kumari, sometimes known as Bala, begged to be allowed to fight the sons of the demon chief. Lalitha demurred, but she gave in reluctantly when she saw that the child was adamant. She gave the child her own armor and weapons. Bala set forth in Chakraraja with Mantrini and Dandanatha on either side. She fought with great skill and dexterity and was untired even though the battle went on for two days. Everyone was surprised at the ease with which Kumari vanquished the enemy. Finally she defeated and killed all of them by sending the powerful *astra* (missile) known as the Narayanastra—the weapon of Lord Narayana (Vishnu).

Bhanda was heartbroken when he heard of the death of his sons, but he rallied and ordered another general to go forth immediately. When the general saw the ring of fire that protected Lalitha's camp, he threw a *yantra* into the camp, creating laziness and sloth in the minds of the *shaktis*. Mantrini and Dandanatha alone were not overcome with lassitude, and they reported the matter to Lalitha. She immediately deputed Ganesha, her elephant-headed son, to go forth and counteract the effects of this *yantra*. He did this so successfully that Lalitha granted him the boon than any ritual done to any deity should begin with the worship of Ganesha.

Next Bhanda sent his two brothers to war. Dandanatha and Mantrini fought with the two of them and slew them. Bhanda was wild with rage when he heard this and decided to go himself. All the remaining males in the city were mustered, and Bhanda marched forth with them to meet the mother of the world. A mighty battle ensued in which Lalitha countered every missile that Bhanda sent with its countercorrelative. For example, when he sent a fire missile she would counter with one carrying water, which would put out the fire, and so forth. Thus we find that in the Sahasranama she is invoked as *Bhanda-surendra nirmukta, sastrapratyastra varshini*, which means "she who countered all Bhanda's weapons with their opposites." Despite this many of her *shaktis* fell to Bhanda's missiles, and Lalitha was pained to see this.

She created a *shakti* called Yashaswini who was given weapons by all the gods. Yashaswini rode on a lion and plunged into battle with terrific war cries. Bhanda did not lose heart. He called forth all the great *asuras* of yore, starting with Hiranyaksha and Hiranyakashipu, Ravana, and Kamsa. Lalitha retaliated by calling all the *avataras* of Vishnu, from the boar to Rama, Krishna, and Kalki. Then she asked Kameswara (Shiva) for his weapon, the great arrow called Paasupata, and with this the whole army of the *asuras* was decimated. This gave rise to another appellation for the goddess in the Sahasranama: *Mahapaasupatastragni, nirdaghtasura sainaka,* meaning "she who destroyed the whole army of the demon with the great arrow known as the Paasupata." Bhanda was undaunted and fought on by himself. At last Lalitha slew him with the Mahakameswarastra, the missile of pure divine love of her husband, Kameswara. This led to yet another appellation in the Sahasranama: *Kameswarastra nirdagdha sa Bhandasura sainika,* meaning "she who slew the buffalo demon with the weapon of divine love given to her by her husband Kameswara."

Thus the object of the *avatara* of the Divine Mother as Lalitha was fulfilled, and the gods rejoiced and praised her.

Let us examine the esoteric significance of this battle. It is not just a bloodthirsty war, as one might imagine. Bhanda represents the reproductive energy of nature gone wild. He is a caricature of Kama, the god of love. In him the sacred magnetism of love is used to manipulate and destroy. It is no longer love but lust—lust for power and for self-aggrandizement. You will find that even the greatest of sages have been overcome by this Bhandasura—this demon in the form of lust for power and sex. Every stage of the battle represents a stage in spiritual purification. The battle is an allegorical representation of the march of the human soul from bestiality to humanity and thence to divinity. The *shaktis* are the various divine forces within us, which the Divine Mother gives us in order to overcome the negativity that tries to bring us down again and again. Even with the most sincere will in the world, many spiritual aspirants find that they fall prey to all types of difficulties. Most of these come from within their own mind. The external enemies are easier to overcome. For instance, one of Bhanda's tricks was to induce lassitude and laziness among the *shaktis*. Such feelings are common among *sadhakas* (those who practice spiritual disciplines). Bhanda's forces of *tamas* try to tell the aspiring *sadhaka* that it is not necessary to strive so hard. Why not go back to sleep for a few more minutes? Why should we be so disciplined? Here we find that only the two supreme *shaktis,* Dandanatha, representing breath control, and Mantrini, representing the power of the *mantra,* were strong enough to overcome this. So obviously the advice for all aspirants is to resort to *pranayama* (breath control) or to sit down and start vigorous chanting of the *mantra* to help us overcome laziness.

Next we find that Lalitha calls Ganesha to come to her aid. So too, when we feel we are failing in our spiritual determination, can we call upon Lord Ganesha to remove the obstacles in our way. He represents firm determination and good humor. If our mind is resolute and we can keep up a sense of humor, we will be able to proceed on our path.

Bhanda's attack by producing darkness over the camp is an allegory for the darkness of ignorance and despair that might assail the mind of the *sadhaka* now and again. The sincere seeker is asked to practice *pranayama* to ward off this evil. Mantrini and Dandanatha are Lalitha's most trusted generals. They are constantly alert and trying to repair and reinforce the weak points of the army. So we find that the chanting of the *mantra* and *pranayama* should be practiced diligently every day, and this will help us control our minds and overcome our weaknesses.

The two of them protect the whole campus while Jwalamalini created a ring of fire. Likewise, command of the *mantra* and the power provided by *pranayama* can indeed build around us a ring of fire that will protect us at all times. Meditating *yogis* and evolved souls at the time of death often experience this ring of fire or a shining globe, which seems to be surrounding the highest truth. Only *yogis* are supposed to be able to pass through this inner sun and proceed on their onward journeys. (The Bhagavad Gita, in fact, mentions that the departing *yogi* has to pierce the orb of the sun.)

Lalitha's daughter Bala is an allegory for all who consider the divine to be our own mother. We will be allowed to fight for the cause of righteousness and justice if we so wish. She will provide us with every aid, including her own armor and accoutrements, to protect us and help us pass all the spiritual tests enumerated in this battle. We are all children of the Divine Mother, and she loves us more than we are capable of realizing. In the chariot of our body, we ride into the battle of life protected by two *shaktis* of our Divine Mother, who will never leave our side.

In the final stage of the battle, when Lalitha herself comes to confront Bhanda, we find that she destroys each of his *astras* with its opposite or countercorrelative. He dispatches missiles of fear, illness, materialism, apathy, and neglect of sacred teachings. She counters them with the missiles of courage, health, spiritual insight, compassion, and the countless *avataras* like Krishna and Rama who put us on the right path. Finally Bhanda dispatches the missile known as Mahamoha or the supreme delusion. This is the delusion that makes us believe that sacred and secular are different—that everything exists by itself without any necessity for the divine, unsupported by God.

Lalitha blasts this view as well as Bhanda himself by the Mahakameswarastra, the missile of pure divine love that none can gainsay. Thus the most powerful force in the universe—the power of divine love—kills Bhanda, who represents selfish lust, borne from the ashes of love. Bhanda's capital city, Sonitapura, sometimes called Shunyaka, is also destroyed. *Shunya* means "zero" or "nothingness." This citadel that the power-hungry, lusty ego builds for itself is nothing but emptiness, for it does not recognize the divine truth of an all-embracing love. Bhanda's boon—that he would be able to drain half the energy of his opponent—worked in all cases except this one. Lalitha is the fullness of the infinite, and the truth is that you can never deplete the infinite even if you keep taking from it. The Veda says, *"Poornamada poornamidam, poornath poornamudachyathe, poornasya, poornamadaya, poornamevaavashishyathe.*" (That is full and this is also full. If you take away the full from the full, fullness alone will remain.)

After the battle, all the gods appeared to eulogize Lalitha as Tripurasundari, the most beautiful in all the three worlds. They begged her to restore to life Kama, the god of love, and make Rati happy and bless him with success in his second endeavor with Lord Shiva. They wanted Shiva to marry Parvati and thus get a son—Kumara, who alone would be able to vanquish the great demon Taraka. Lalitha brought Kama to her mind and immediately Rati felt her husband materialize beside her. Lalitha blessed him with power to roam about the world creating love in the hearts of all. She also commanded him to go to Shiva and promised him that this time his arrow would not fail, and so it came to pass that Shiva opened his eyes just as Kama's flower-tipped arrow pierced his heart. Just at that moment he saw Parvati and fell in love with her.

> *A nature throbbing with a heart divine*
> *Was felt in the unconscious universe;*
> *It made the breath a happy mystery,*
> *And brought a love sustaining pain with joy;*
> *A love that bore the cross of pain with joy*
> *Eudaemonised the sorrow of the world.*

—*SAVITRI* BY SRI AUROBINDO

Thus ends the eighth chapter of *Shakti,* known as "Tripurasundari," describing the battle with Bhandasura and his demise.

Aum Aim Hreem Kleem

ॐ

Aum Kamakshyai Namaha!

9

Kameswari

Ya Devi sarvabhuteshu, kshanti rupena samsthita,
Namasthasyai, namasthasyai, namasthasyai namo
  namaha!

O Goddess who resides in all creatures in the form of
  patience,
Hail to thee, hail to thee, all hail to thee!

During the time of the Brahmanda Purana, the goddess was worshipped by most people in the form of Lalitha. The principal centers of her worship were Srinagar in Kashmir and Kanchipuram in Tamilnadu.

The work of building her city of Srinagar, which exists even today in the Himalayas, was entrusted to Vishvakarma, the architect of the gods, and Mayan, his principal engineer. The city was also known as Kameswaripuri or the city of Kameswari, the queen of love, one of Lalitha's incarnations. The city was designed similarly to Mani Dwipa, the Island of Jewels, except that Srinagar is placed in the midst of nine mountains while the island was in the middle of the ocean. Srinagar was also made of multiple enclosures in the shapes of *yantras* and *mandalas* intersecting at various points, thus producing many types of mathematical figures filled with the ability to concentrate the mind. Here also was the *chintamani griha,* the sanctum sanctorum of Maha Devi made of the sacred, wish-fulfilling gem *chintamani.* The Lalitha Sahasranama names this enclosure the Mahapadmatavi, and it is the place where the goddess's sacred chariots, Chakraraja, Geyachakra, and Kirichakra, were kept. In the southeast, which is the direction of Agni, the fire god, was the big pit known as the *chidagnikunda* in which a fire blazed for all eternity, for this was the cremation pyre of all creatures. This whole town was lit by bejeweled lamps and in the center was the splendid throne of Kameswari, which had miraculous powers.

The ninth enclosure of the city was known as the Bindu Peetha. *Bindu* means "point," and this is the place from which all creation emanates. Here is the sacred cot, the four legs of which are Brahma, Vishnu, Maheswara (Shiva), and Iswara (the Supreme who has taken on form). On this cot lies Kameswara, the lord of desire, the ever-youthful consort of Kameswari. Lalitha as Tripurasundari reclines on his lap. The twenty-five *tattvas* form the steps to the cot.

Esoterically speaking, the city of Srinagar is the human body. The human body is a huge *yantra,* and the many palaces and abodes are the mysterious places through which the mind of the meditating *yogi* has to pass before reaching Bindu Peetha, where the union of the *jivatman* and the Paramatman (the supreme self or Brahman) takes place.

The different enclosures in the city represent the different *chakras* of the body. The many enclosures are the petals of the *sahasrara chakra,* the thousand-petaled lotus, which is the vortex of psychic energy established in the roof of the brain. Kameswari herself is *kundalini,* the psychic power coiled at the base of the spine that must be unwound and taken up to the thousand-petaled lotus on the crown of the head before this blissful union can take place. The Brahmanda Purana gives the esoteric *puja* (ritual) devoted to the goddess that will bring about this union and eventual liberation from mortal coils: Getting up early in the morning, the *sadhaka* should bathe, put on clean clothes, and worship the sun. Then she should enter the *puja* room. Remaining in silence for the duration of the rite, she should meditate on the city of

Srinagar within her heart *chakra* and do the *puja* as prescribed in the Agama Shastras. After this she should undertake *japa,* or repetition of the sacred *mantra* of Lalitha, thirty-six *lakhs* (hundred thousands) of times. One who does this daily can gain many extraordinary *siddhis* or supernormal powers.

The city of Kanchipuram is in the state of Tamilnadu in southern India. The author's *guru* is the Shankaracharya (the chief pontiff) of this place. Here Kameswari is known as Kamakshi, or the one with eyes filled with love. Here the navel of Sati, wife of Shiva, is supposed to have fallen (see chapters 14 and 15), and hence it is a Shakti Peetha (place where divine energy is felt) of great importance, since the navel is the place of the *manipura chakra,* a seat of enormous spiritual potential.

It was in Kanchipuram that Brahma performed *tapas* in order to propitiate the Maha Devi. At last there appeared before him Lakshmi, accompanied by Lord Vishnu. Seeing her eyes brimming with love for humanity, Brahma addressed her as Kamakshi. He begged her to permeate that holy spot with her presence in order to bless all people for eternity. She agreed, provided her brother, Vishnu, would also establish himself there. The Sri Chakra (supreme *yantra* of the goddess or Rajarajeshwari) was established in this spot, and Brahma, Vishnu, and Shiva are supposed to have worshipped it and gained glory. The priests of the Kamakshi temple perform daily worship of the Sri Chakra.

The Brahmanda Purana describes the mode of making these Sri Chakras and people buy these *chakras* and install them in their homes. The *chakras* should be worshipped only according to the advice of the *guru,* however. The Devi Suktam and the Lalitha Sahasranama are normally chanted at the end of the *puja.* Everybody, irrespective of caste or sex, can adore the goddess in this way.

The worship of Lalitha is the sweetest and most effective form of the adoration of the Divine Mother. Those who cannot do daily *puja* can still worship effectively by practicing *puja* on full-moon days.

He heard the far and touched the intangible,
He gazed into the future and the unseen.
He used the powers earth instruments cannot use,
A pastime made of the impossible.
He caught fragments of the Omniscient's thought,
He scattered formulas of omnipotence,
Thus man in his little house made of earth's dust,
Grew towards an unseen heaven of thought and
 dream,
Looking into the vast vistas of the mind,
On a small globe, dotting infinity,
At last climbing a long and narrow stair,
He stood alone on a high roof of things,
And saw the light of a spiritual sun.

—*SAVITRI* BY SRI AUROBINDO

Thus ends the ninth chapter of *Shakti*, known as "Kameswari," describing Srinagar, the abode of the goddess, Kanchipuram, and her method of worship.

Aum Aim Hreem Kleem

Aum Durgayai Namaha!

10

Durga

Ya Devi sarvabhuteshu, jati rupena samsthita,
Namasthasyai, namasthasyai, namasthasyai namo
namaha!

O Goddess who resides in all creatures in the form of birth,
Hail to thee, hail to thee, all hail to thee!

Durga is one of the most impressive and formidable goddesses in Hindu
mythology. She is a warrior queen with eighteen arms, each wielding
a particular weapon. Her primary function is to combat the demons
that threaten the stability of the cosmos. Despite this, she maintains a
benign look on her face. This reflects the fact that she attacks not in
order to kill but only when we invite her to come and deliver us from
the devilish ego that threatens our spiritual life.

There are many accounts of Durga's origin, but the most well known
is told in the Devi Mahatmyam ("text of the wondrous essence of the
goddess"), which describes her as an unconquerable, sublime warrior maid
who was birthed from the combined powers of all the gods gathered in
council. She was created to combat the buffalo demon Mahisha, who
could be killed only by a female power (see chapter 12).

Another story of Durga's origin is found in the Devi Bhagavatam:

87

Once there was a great *asura* known as Durgama. He realized that the Vedas were the main source of the strength of the *devas* (gods) and decided that the best way to weaken the gods would be to steal the Vedas. With this in mind, he started to do rigorous *tapas* to the creator Brahma. When Brahma appeared, Durgama asked for the gift of the Vedas, which Brahma promptly gave over to him.

With the disappearance of the Vedas from the world, the Brahmins forgot their chanting and *mantras*. No longer did the gods receive the fire sacrifices by which they had been nourished, and they became weaker and weaker. Unrighteousness reared its ugly head in the world. There was a severe drought; the earth refused to yield any grain and famine swept the land. Countless numbers of people, cattle, and plants died for want of food.

The Brahmins went to the Himalayas and did great penance to invoke Adi Shakti, the supreme power. They begged her to restore the Vedic *mantras* to them so that they could again perform their daily rituals.

At the end of their penance, Maheswari, the great mother of the universe, appeared before them in all her glory. Her color was dark blue, the color of eternal space. She had a hundred eyes, large and lustrous like blue lotuses, and her breasts were round and elevated. She had four hands. On the right, one hand held arrows and the other a lotus. On the left, one hand held a great bow and the other vegetables, fruits, flowers, and roots. She was the essence of beauty, luminous like a thousand suns, the ocean of mercy. When she heard the sad tale of the Brahmins and saw the pitiful condition of the earth she began to shed waters from her lovely eyes. For nine days and nights tears poured down from her eyes until all the rivers and ponds and lakes began to fill up. This incarnation of the goddess was known as Satakshi (the hundred-eyed). The gods who had been hiding in caves and mountains now started to come out and began to sing her praises. The goddess now showered the earth with plenty. Grains, vegetables, fruits, and roots were made available for all. Grass started to sprout so that the cattle could feed. From that day she came to be known as Shakambari (the giver of edible vegetation).

When the demon Durgama heard of this he was furious and set out to fight with the goddess. Seeing this, Shakambari produced from her own body countless *shaktis* who started annihilating the army of the *asura*. But Durgama vanquished the *shaktis* and eventually came before the goddess. She shot fifteen arrows at him. The first fourteen arrows killed his horses and charioteer, pierced his two eyes, and cut off his arms and flag, and finally the fifteenth arrow pierced his heart and killed him.

The world became a peaceful place once more, and the *devas* extolled the goddess. She blessed them and said, "The Vedas are parts of my own body, so cherish them well. If you lose them, great calamities will fall on you, as you have seen. Henceforth I will be known as Durga, since I have killed the demon Durgama."

Sometime around the fourth century, images of Durga slaying a buffalo began to be common throughout the subcontinent. By the sixth century Durga had become a household word and was worshipped everywhere. Lalitha is always depicted as a *shanta murti* or one with all peaceful qualities, despite the fact that she killed the demon Bhanda, but Durga is ever the warrior goddess, often seen astride her fierce vehicle, the lion.

Durga's enormous appeal seems rather strange when you consider the fact that she violates the norm of the model Hindu woman. She is not submissive, nor is she subordinate to any male deity. She does not fulfill household duties and excels mainly in battle. She doesn't lend her power to any male deities but takes from them in order to perform her own heroic exploits. On the other hand, the male deities are said to willingly surrender their potencies to her! She is not the *shakti* (power) of any male god but is pure *shakti* unattached to anything else. She herself is shown to contain various *shaktis* that she can call forth any time she wills. She is not the consort of any male. Some of the demons become enamored of her beauty, but she will have nothing to do with them and refuses to marry any of them.

Durga exists outside normal social structures and provides an invigorating view of feminine power, which lies repressed in most societies. The law books of Manu (the great lawgiver whose books are taken as the basis for the different types of behavior of various classes of people in all walks of society) declare that a woman should always be protected by a man: in childhood by her father, in youth by her husband, and in old age by her sons. In other words, a woman was considered to be incapable of looking after herself and was always to be kept under the protection of some male. It is to the credit of the ancient *rishis* that in Durga they portrayed a goddess who totally violates all the traditional views of women.

Thus Durga portrays the divinity who stands outside the so-called civilized order of established *dharma* and can be found only by one who has the courage to step out of the orderly world as we know it. The gods themselves refer to her by many dubious names. She is known as Mahamoha, the great deluder; as Mahasuri, the great demoness; as Kalaratri, the black night; as Maharatri, the great darkness; as Moharatri, the night of delusion; and as Tamasi, the delusion. As these names imply, she is full of numbing, deluding, and dark qualities. Continuously she is referred to as Maha Maya, the power that throws people into the bondage of delusion and attachment.

The juxtaposition of auspicious and terrible qualities in Durga is meant to show that she is really a portrait of the macrocosm. The universe is conceived as a living organism in the form of the goddess. In her auspicious forms she depicts the world as unceasingly fruitful, beautiful, and filled with the energy of the divine, which supports and nourishes. As the mother she dotes on her children and spoils them with all her bounties. As food she gives herself to be eaten by her children, and as sexual desire she prompts all creatures to take part in the universal dance of creation and procreation. She gives generously. She is life itself.

The Puranas describe nine different aspects for Durga, known collectively as the Navadurga. First and foremost, she is the goddess of inspiration, who gives us the impetus to start on the spiritual path. Second, she is the goddess who tells us to undertake studies from spiritual books, which will encourage us to continue on the path. Third, she is the goddess of spiritual practice, who motivates us to take up some sort of *sadhana* (spiritual discipline). Fourth, she is the goddess of inner refinement by which our mind is progressively cultured. Fifth, she is the goddess who takes us closer to the divine within us. Sixth is she who makes us completely pure. Seventh is the goddess who enables us to give up this delusion of duality. Eighth is the goddess who urges us to unite with the inner light, and ninth is the goddess who grants us liberation. The Navadurga are worshipped by all Hindus, though only the *yogis* know their esoteric significance. They represent the nine psychic forces that will lead us to our spiritual goal. At every moment on the spiritual path, one or the other is guiding us.

Durga's association with food is one of her distinctive characteristics. She is that mysterious power that transforms apparently lifeless seeds into life-giving food when they are sowed. All types of fertility are apparent in her. She possesses the power to invigorate all beings and give them a new lease on life. All plants and creatures on this planet are identified with her, for she is the manifestation of the fertile power that resides in the earth and brings into life all creatures. She manifests as infinite organisms that in turn feed more complex organisms. She is also the sexual impulse that characterizes all created beings. She is manifest wherever sexual desire appears. Kama, the god of love, is her agent.

The biggest festival connected with this goddess is Durga Puja, sometimes known as Navaratri. It is celebrated during the first nine days of the bright half of the lunar month of Aswin, in what we know as October, which coincides with the autumn harvest in northern India. On the very first day a clay pot containing Ganga (Ganges) water, sheaves from the harvest, and some banana leaves is decorated and placed on the altar. This pot is identified with the pot of the nectar of immortality that the gods churned from the Sea of Nectar. This story of the churning of the Sea of Nectar is mentioned in almost all the Puranas. It took place at a time when the gods had lost their youth and vitality and Vishnu advised them to churn this sea to get the nectar, which would return their youthful vigor.

To one side of the altar some earth is kept in which are sowed the *navadhanyas* or the nine types of grain. As each type of grain is sowed, the priest chants, "*Aum,* you are rice [or wheat or barley, etc., for each of the nine grains], you are life, you are the life of the gods, you are our life, you are our internal life, you are long life, you give life. The sun with his rays gives you the milk of life and Varuna nourishes you with water." This ritual denotes Durga's power to induce plant fertility. By the tenth day these grains sprout and are distributed as *prasada* (leftovers from offerings to the gods). In some parts of India, especially Bengal, animal sacrifices are offered during this festival. The buffalo especially is killed to indicate Durga's killing of the buffalo demon Mahisha.

But Durga is paradoxical. If she is life, she is also death, which is necessary to sustain life. If she gives life, she must also be nourished by life in the form of death. A gain in any part has to be compensated by a loss somewhere else. Just as there is no life without death, so also there is no gain without loss. Hence Durga is also shown to have many terrible manifestations. She reveals the inescapable truth of this world: that if life and nourishment are to continue, continuous slaughter and death must also continue. Food that sustains life can be procured only through death and carnage. Life and death constitute a continuous process of giving and getting, a process in which the energy of the goddess is continuously recycled.

Both beautiful and grotesque, maternal and martial, Durga can take terrifying forms that demand blood for nourishment and finally the very lives of all creatures. Her thirst for blood is established in various texts. The Mahanirvana Tantra, for example, describes her as drenched in blood, grinding up the world at the time of dissolution.

In the Devi Bhagavatam the gods ask Durga to show them her *vishwarupa* or universal form, just as Arjuna asked Krishna to show his universal form in the Bhagavad Gita. She agrees, and the gods are stunned to see her. She has thousands of heads, eyes, and feet; her entire body blazes with fierce, destructive flames and her teeth make horrible, grinding noises. Her eyes burn with flames brighter than a million suns, and the gods tremble as they see her consume the universe. They plead with her to resume her gentle aspect.

In the Devi Mahatmyam, she is said to quaff wine at intervals and roar and behave in a most atrocious manner. At the end of the episode she asks her devotees to worship her with their own flesh and blood.

All the negative qualities found in the world are found in Durga. Her greatness lies in the fact that she alone is qualified to destroy these qualities in us, because she possesses all these qualities within herself. She exemplifies the homeopathic principle of like destroying like, and for these reasons her worship has a great hold on society, even today. During the process of *yoga*, the human consciousness is lifted up from *chakra* to *chakra*, starting from the *muladhara chakra* at the base of the spine to the *sahasrara chakra* at the top of the skull. During this time it encounters inner demons ranging from immature emotions like jealousy, fear, greed, and lust up to more serious forms of derangement including paranoia and megalomania. Each weapon in Durga's hands is meant to eradicate these negative emotions. The devotee can meditate on any of Durga's weapons in order to clear these negative emotions. Her weapons in fact serve two purposes: they can combat negativity as well as instill positive traits of thought, like self-discipline, introspection, selfless service, prayer, devotion, clarity of vision, and a cheerful outlook.

Durga's fierce aspects are meant to portray those dark qualities in the human being that thirst for violence and warfare. She is the personified wrath of the whole of humanity. When she apparently loses control over herself, she personifies the mob mentality, the thirst for violence, that ever lurks in the human heart: the prod that drives the rabble to kill, ravage, rampage, pillage, and destroy, that causes even the mildest of men to slaughter and kill and undertake bloodcurdling deeds. Durga depicts this part of the dark nature of the human being when she dances on corpses and drinks human blood. In these aspects she portrays the distilled, furious, savage power and lust of the frenzied warrior. Thus she shows how such a power, when left to itself, can prove to be a terrible threat to the world.

Durga is indeed the victorious force of the divine, and it is by her grace, passion, and speed that great achievements can be made. She is the warrior maiden who never shrinks from battle. In ancient India all kings invoked Durga for victory in battle. The Mahabharata states that when King Yudhistira set out to battle with the Kauravas, he remembered the promise made by the Divine Mother in the Devi Mahatmyam and praised her with the famous *Durga Stotram* (hymn to Durga) before proceeding for battle:

> *Twilight, night, light, sleep, moonlight, loveliness, patience,*
> *compassion.*
> *When honored, you cause to perish the bondage of men,*
> *Their delusion, death of sons, loss of wealth, sickness, death,*
> *and fear.*
> *Fallen from my kingdom, I submissively take refuge in you,*
> *Just as I have bowed my head to you, O Goddess! Queen*
> *of the gods!*
> *Protect me, one of lotus-petal eyes! Truth! Be true to us,*
> *Be a refuge for me, O Durga!*
> *O refuge! O One who is fond of her devotees!*

Durga answers,

> *Victory in battle will soon be yours,*
> *Having by my grace conquered and slain the Kaurava*
> *army,*

Having made your kingdom free from troubles,
You will again enjoy the earth,
Together with your brothers, O King,
You will obtain abundant favor,
And by my grace, happiness and health will be yours.

—MAHABHARATA

Thus ends the tenth chapter of *Shakti*, known as "Durga," describing the form and function of the warrior goddess.

Aum Aim Hreem Kleem

11

Chandika

Ya Devi sarvabhuteshu, lajja rupena samsthita,
Namasthasyai, namasthasyai, namasthasyai namo
  namaha!

O Goddess who resides in all creatures in the form
  of modesty,
Hail to thee, hail to thee, all hail to thee!

The Devi Mahatmyam is a part of one of the early Puranas known as the
Markandeya Purana. It is more commonly known in northern India as
the Durga Saptashati, since it contains seven hundred verses to Durga. It
is also frequently called the "Chandi," since the goddess is often referred
to in the text as Chandika. The Devi Mahatmyam is one of the most
famous of the Shakta and Tantric literatures. Though it is part of the
Markandeya Purana, it has always had a separate life of its own. This is
because of the pristine quality and exquisite beauty of its hymns. Every
verse is a *mantra* by itself. The very first line of the book, "Listen to the
story of King Suratha, who was the eighth Manu," which gives the outward meaning, also holds the esoteric meaning, "Now I shall describe
to you the glory of the *mantra hreem*." This is the *bija* or seed *mantra*
of the Divine Mother. Similarly, every line contains some esoteric mean-

ing, which only Tantric initiates can decipher. It is truly a majestic poem that describes to us the epic march of the human soul to its destination, which is liberation from the cycle of births and deaths. Countless devotees through the ages have chanted the verses sung by the *rishis* in this book.

The manuscript describes the different battles fought by Durga with demons who were tyrannizing the world. This is in keeping with the purpose of her advent. She herself says in verse fifty-five of the eleventh chapter, "Whenever troubles arise from the fall of religion, I shall incarnate myself and destroy the enemy."

Some people complain that the Chandi is full of battles and cannot generate a feeling of devotion. This is only a superficial understanding of the book, because all its battles have esoteric meanings. It is an allegorical representation of the life of the human being, which is beset with battles of opposing interests. Life itself is a struggle against opposing forces. The fight between good and evil is an eternal one, on both a cosmic and an individual level. The story of the Devi Mahatmyam is that of the combat between the higher and the lower self in the evolved human mind.

For example, the demon Mahisha, whom Durga destroys, is symbolic of the conditioned ego, which projects its own distorted view of the universe. Everything is defined within the narrow limits of its own selfish interests. Everything has meaning only if it is connected with these interests in some way. The higher self has no other recourse than to embody all its spiritual qualities in the form of the Divine Mother of the world, who alone has the power to kill this bloated ego. She will come to our aid only if we importune her to do so. We have to admit that we are lost in the forest of *samsara* (worldly life), beguiled by our narrow vision of the world, abandoned by those whom we consider dear because they happen to have been born from our loins. If we have the courage to give up everything and beg her to save us, Durga will most definitely do so. This is the esoteric meaning of the story of this battle in the Durga Saptashati (Devi Mahatmyam).

The book is grouped into three sections, each devoted to a different goddess and describing one of the three aspects of the march of the soul to freedom. During our ascent up the ladder of evolution we come to three major stopping places where we experience a complete transformation of outlook and attitude. These three transformations are presided over by the deities Maha Kaali, Maha Lakshmi, and Maha Saraswati. We invoke Maha Kaali to destroy our negativity, then we pray to Maha Lakshmi to plant the seeds of positivity in our minds, and finally we beg Maha Saraswati to give us liberation. In the first section Adi Shakti awakens Maha Vishnu so that he may destroy the original demonic forces (see chapter 5). In the second stage Durga manifests as Maha Lakshmi and overcomes the demon Mahisha (see chapter 12). In the third stage, Durga takes on the incarnation of Maha Saraswati and destroys the demons Raktabija, Shumbha, and Nishumbha (see chapter 13). These three divine forces represent the powers of the spirit manifesting within us and urging us onward to freedom. They tell us that when we walk along the spiritual path, we do not walk alone. The forces of the Divine Mother walk beside us.

Now let us take a quick look at the different chapters before going into a detailed study. The goddess is given a number of names in this text, with the most common being simply Devi (*devi* translates as "goddess"). Each name is a *mantra* on its own. The book is charged with the power of Shakti and is capable of giving *bhakti* and *mukti*—devotion as well as liberation. It is also supposed to fulfill the desires of anyone who reads it with faith and devotion. The normal way to read it is to complete the text in seven days. It is also usually recited daily during the nine-day festival in October known as Navaratri or Durga Puja. In fact, many Devi devotees recite the Chandi every day. Every verse in this text is pregnant with the *shakti* of the Divine Mother. As mentioned at the beginning of this chapter, the first verse of the text implies that the whole book is an explanation of the seed *mantra* of the goddess—*hreem*. The book has had many commentaries, some giving mystical explanations and some giving a straightforward account of the battles, but whatever the manner in which we read it, we cannot fail to be amazed by the power of the hymns, which are charged with great spiritual potential. This book is capable of averting both individual and universal calamities. A regular daily recital of this amazing scripture can avert wars and epidemics and help us destroy our inner psychological enemies.

The name Chandika, meaning the violent and impetuous one, is applied to the goddess twenty-nine times in the Devi Mahatmyam; hence its nickname Chandi. In the poem *Chandikashtaka,* a composition of the seventeenth-century poet Bana, Chandika is described thus:

> *Spoil not thy coquetry, O brow;*
> *O lower lip, why this distress?*
> *O face, banish thy flushing;*
> *O hand, this Mahisha is not living;*
> *Why dost thou brandish a trident, with desire for combat?*
> *Caused by these words as it were, the Devi Chandi*
> *Caused the parts of her body that displayed signs of rising*
>   *anger,*
> *To resume their normal state.*
> *Her foe, which took away the life of Mahisha*
> *Foe of the gods was set down upon his head.*
> *May the foot of Devi, Chandi, destroy your sins!*

Since the Devi Mahatmyam is a Shakta text, its main aim is to postulate the ultimate reality as feminine. It also aims to prove that the reality of the goddess is both transcendent and immanent. Her transcendent character is established at the very outset of the text. But she is also immanent, operative both *as* the material world and *in* the material world. As Prakriti, she is nature, or the whole of the material world, in its multifarious forms. She is also the one who protects and the one who responds instantly to the cries of her devotees.

By characterizing the goddess as Maha Maya and Yoga Nidra, under whose influence Lord Vishnu lies in *yoga nidra* or the mystic sleep, the Devi Mahatmyam shows that it only by her withdrawal that Vishnu can act at all. The transcendental state that is normally ascribed to Lord Vishnu seems to apply equally to the goddess. She is also shown as being an interior and inward phenomenon. She is *nitya,* the eternal, and *sraddha,* the movement of the heart with faith. Over and above all she is Shakti, the universal expression of power, regardless of how she is projected in the external form of its manifestation. The devotee of Shakti sees both sides of the Divine Mother. She is both gentle and terrible. She is soft and mellow with devotees, but when dealing with evil forces she is forceful and even violent. In her gentle forms she is surpassingly beautiful, and in her fearful forms she is exceedingly terrible. Devotees have to see her in both forms. They must steel themselves against all weaknesses. They must give up all fears, hesitation, and selfishness and be prepared to overcome all obstacles. They must have the courage of the lion on which the Divine Mother is seated. They must brandish the sword of faith and fearlessness and fight against all types of negativity.

The Markandeya Purana is set in the eighth *manvantara,* known as Savarnika, or the epoch of the Manu Savarni. The first chapter starts with the story, told by the sage Markandeya, about how Devi had promised King Suratha that he would be born as Savarni, the son of Surya, the sun god, and would become the Manu of the eighth *manvantara.* The frame of the text is very simple: it deals with the deep sorrow of the *kshatriya* (warrior) Suratha and the *vaisya* (merchant) Samadhi, with their families and with life in general, and how they turn to the sage Medhas for comfort.

Suratha, a king of the illustrious Surya Vamsa (lineage of the sun), was defeated by his enemies and had to flee the country. Deprived of his wealth and retinue, he took shelter in the forest. He wandered about dejected and forlorn, and all the time his mind kept returning to the very people who had deprived him of everything: his family, his countrymen, and his ministers. Lost and helpless, he stumbled upon the hermitage of the sage Medhas. It was a beautiful *ashrama* (sanctuary) filled with trees and flowers, full of peace and tranquility. He decided to stay there. While at this place he met a *vaisya* (merchant) called Samadhi, whose story was very similar to the king's. He had lost all his wealth and had been thrown out of his house by his own relations and family. He too was forced to wander in the forest and had at last taken shelter at the feet of the sage Medhas.

The king and the merchant found that they had a lot in common. Both had lost their wealth and been cheated by their own people. Both were puzzled by the nature of the mind, which despite the cruelty they had received from their kinsmen kept returning to the very people who had spurned them. They discussed the character of the mind, which keeps lingering on the very things that have caused it sorrow. Unable to discover the reason for this, they approached the *rishi* and begged him to instruct them. The question voiced by the king and the merchant is one that poses a burning problem for the whole of mankind. The entire Devi Mahatmyam is the reply of the *rishi* to this question. The seer expatiates on the relativity of knowledge and the folly of sensual attachment.

The word *suratha* means "attention"; *samadhi* is "a state of superconsciousness" in which the mind is not aware of the external world; and *medhas* is "intelligence infused with divine love." The esoteric meaning of the simple story is that the *jivatman* that has lost its focus with the higher self (as both the king and the merchant have lost their wealth) must turn to the intelligence infused with love, which will redirect them to their essential wealth.

The sage told them:

O best of men! Human beings crave for offspring in the belief that they will reciprocate their feelings and help them when they are old. This is how they fall into the pit of delusion made by their own egos. This mysterious delusion forces them to cling to those very objects and persons who have subjected them to so much pain and suffering. All creatures have been given a certain amount of intelligence, yet they keep falling into the pits created by their own weaknesses. Their intelligence seems to be used mainly for filling their bellies and satisfying their animal wants. Moths are drawn to a blazing fire and keep hurling themselves into it, regardless of the fact that they will be consumed in the flames of their own attraction. Men fall into the fire of sensual objects. What difference is there between the two?

The blessed goddess Maha Maya, who is the cause of this cosmic delusion, forcibly seizes the mind of even the man of knowledge. All are deluded and controlled by that great power of Maha Maya. It is due to her power that this whole world functions. Because of her all are suffering. She drags down even great men of knowledge. She creates this whole universe of movables and immovables. It is due to her mysterious veiling power that the one seems to have become the many and the formless appears to have taken many forms. She is nothing but the power of Brahman, emanating from him and setting into motion the mighty cosmic drama of creation, preservation, and ultimate withdrawal into the transcendental state of pure being. It is her *lila* that binds, in order to release. She is the cause of both bondage and liberation. She is the supreme knowledge (Maha Vidya) that grants final liberation.

Naturally both the king and the merchant want to know more about this mysterious power. The sage expounds on the nature of the Divine Mother of the universe in the seven hundred verses of the Devi Mahatmyam. In the first chapter, before the *rishi* goes into the actual account of the goddess's glories, he recounts the story of Yoga Nidra (see chapter 5). From this we can see that the *asuras* thought they could defeat the divine only because of Maha Maya's mysterious powers of delusion. The implication is clear: she is the great deluder who entices human beings into believing that they are the greatest, thus perpetuating this wheel of existence (*samsara chakra*). But she is also Maha Vidya, knowledge supreme, who makes us finally realize that this ego, with its conflicting and constant demands and its total belief in the reality of this existence, is nothing but a myth.

The word *maya* comes from the Rig Veda, where it means "wile" or "magic power." This meaning connects the word with the *asuras,* who are noted for their wiliness and magic powers. From this it follows that Maha Maya is herself the supreme *asura.* In fact, Brahma, in his hymn to the goddess before Vishnu kills the demons Madhu and Kaitabha, calls her Mahasuri, the great *asura.* In other words, one of the reasons the goddess has such power over the *asuras* is because she is one of them, just as she is also one of the *devas.*

The *rishi* Medhas goes on to explain the workings of Maha Maya to his questioners: "She is *nitya* (eternal), having the universe as her form. She spreads all this out. Even though eternal, she is said to be born when she becomes manifest for the sake of accomplishing the purpose of the gods. It is through the power of this Maha Maya that people impose solidity on this ephemeral universe." From this we can understand that the goddess is both eternal and coexisting with the manifest universe at the same time. The text also tells us that at certain times she takes on a tangible form.

"Thou art *svaaha* (the word used when offering oblations into the fire), thou art *swadha* (the word used when offering oblations to the ancestors), and thou art *vasatkara* (special term in which a Sanskrit mantra is split in two). Speech is thy very soul. Thou art the nectar of the gods. Thou art imperishable and eternal, and thou art the one who abides in the threefold syllable. Thou art she, the goddess, the supreme mother—Savitri." From this we can understand that wherever the spoken word is operative, the goddess is present. She is "the highest of all things, high and low—the highest queen." She is the essence of the three deities Brahma, Vishnu, and Shiva.

The first chapter gives the goddess's orientation as transcendent to the cosmos. The second chapter shows that she is identified with the universe and is a crystallization of the glories of all the deities. The third, which involves the killing of Mahisha, describes the goddess's exuberant plunge into the mundane. It points out not only that she has an earthly career but also that she is the supreme ruler of the changing world. She is shown to be the ultimate agent of power in the universe. This is very necessary, for she is called upon to grapple with the forces of the mind as typified by Mahisha, Shumbha, and Nishumbha. Only one who wields ultimate power in the world's own terms can cope with all these disturbing elements in the mind.

The fourth chapter describes the eulogy of the gods and the promise of the goddess to help them whenever they call her. The fifth chapter gives the story of the origin of the demons Shumbha and Nishumbha, in which once again the *devas* request Durga's help; the famous hymns starting with "Ya Devi," which are sung by the gods, come in this chapter. (Almost every chapter of the book you are holding begins with a couplet from these famous hymns.)

The sixth, seventh, and eighth chapters describe the fight between the goddess and the various agents of Shumbha, including Chanda, Munda, and Raktabija. The ninth and tenth chapters describe the battle between Durga and the brothers Shumbha and Nishumbha and the demons' final annihilation. The eleventh contains the beautiful hymn Narayani Stotram, in which the gods praise her as the goddess Narayani and Devi foretells all the different incarnations she will take in the future to protect the universe. In the twelfth chapter, the goddess promises to look after and bless all those who read this book and all those who worship her with faith and devotion.

Medhas concludes his account of the goddess's extraordinary manifestations thus: "O King! The goddess comes to manifest herself in the world from time to time for establishing righteousness and for protecting her devotees. She deludes the whole world as Maha Maya, yet protects it as the Divine Mother. All this is pervaded by her alone. That great power creates this whole universe of pleasure and pain. Thus, she herself is the cause of both sorrow and joy!"

The thirteenth chapter brings the tale of the king and the merchant to its happy conclusion. They are both deeply impressed by the tales of the goddess and decide to undertake severe austerities immediately. Both penetrate the thick forest and begin doing rigorous penance on the banks of the river. After three years of intense *tapas,* in which they deny themselves even the bare necessities for life, Devi appears to them separately and asks them what they want. King Suratha asks that he might be given back his kingdom.

Devi declares, "O King! In a few days you will regain your kingdom and possessions and become a mighty monarch and rule the land happily for many years. After death you will be born as the eighth Manu, called Savarni."

When the goddess appears before Samadhi, his request is totally different. He asks for spiritual knowledge that removes sorrow and delusion forever. The Divine Mother is charmed with his request and grants it immediately. She says, "O wise one! Your desire shall be fulfilled. You will get both wisdom and liberation!"

> *O death thou lookest on an unfinished world,*
> *Assailed by thee and of its road unsure.*
> *Peopled by imperfect minds and ignorant lives,*
> *And says God's not and all is vain.*
> *How shall the child be the man?*
> *Because he is ignorant shall he never learn?*
> *In a small fragile seed a giant tree lurks,*
> *In a tiny gene a thinking being is shut.*
> *A little element in a tiny sperm,*
> *It grows and is a conqueror and a sage.*
>
> —*SAVITRI* BY SRI AUROBINDO

Thus ends the eleventh chapter of *Shakti,* known as "Chandika," which outlines the story of the Devi Mahatmyam.

Aum Aim Hreem Kleem

Aum Raudrayai Namaha!

12

Mahishasuramardini

Ya Devi sarvabhuteshu, shanti rupena samsthita,
Namasthasyai, namasthasyai, namasthasyai namo
namaha!

O Goddess who resides in all creatures in the form
of peace,
Hail to thee, hail to thee, all hail to thee!

The Devi Mahatmyam contains three myths describing the glorious
doings of Durga (sometimes called Chandika) The first myth is the
one connected with the two demons, Madhu and Kaitabha, the second
is the killing of Mahishasura, and the third the killing of Shumbha
and Nishumbha. The second, third, and fourth chapters exalt her as
Mahishasuramardini, or the killer of the buffalo demon Mahisha.
While the Madhu-Kaitabha episode stresses her cosmic and transcendental stature, this incident describes the reason for her incarnation on
Earth and her universal purpose, which is the saving of all creatures.

Once upon a time two *asuras,* known as Rambha and Karambha,
practiced great austerities in order to be granted the boon of begetting
sons. *Asuras* are noted for undertaking impossibly severe austerities in
order to force one of the gods to grant them boons meant for their own

selfish purposes. Karambha did *tapas* under the waters of a river. This infuriated Indra, the king of the gods, who knew well what all this austerity was leading up to. Indra killed Karambha before he could conclude his *tapas*. Rambha heard about this and decided to make the supreme sacrifice of immolating himself in fire in order to force one of the gods to come to him. Agni, the god of fire, did materialize before him and advised him to desist from this stupid act, since it would serve no purpose. Instead, Agni told Rambha to ask for a boon and it would be granted.

Rambha concluded that this was a sensible suggestion and asked for a son who would be able to assume different personalities at will, conquer the three worlds, and destroy all his enemies. Agni granted him this boon, and Rambha roamed the forest to find a suitable mate. His eyes fell on a beautiful she-buffalo who was in full heat. He fell for her charms and had intercourse with her. When she conceived, he took her off to the netherworld to keep her under his protection, but unfortunately another buffalo became enamored of her, and in the battle that ensued Rambha was killed. His carcass was cremated, and the disconsolate she-buffalo decided to immolate herself in the fire. When she jumped in, an astonishing thing happened: the fetus in her womb rose up from the fire and achieved enormous proportions; he became the *asura* Mahisha. Rambha also rose up from the fire in a new form and became known as Raktabija, close friend and ally of Mahisha.

Mahisha proceeded to the mountain known as Sumeru and performed severe *tapas* there for many years. Pleased with his austerities, Brahma appeared and asked him to choose a boon. The *asura* immediately asked for immortality.

Brahma replied, "O Mahisha! Birth has to be followed by death and death by birth. This is the inevitable law of nature. The highest mountains and the deepest oceans and all created things will come to an end when the time comes. So I cannot grant immortality, but you can choose some other boon."

Mahisha immediately said, "O Grandfather! Grant me the boon

that I can never be killed by any god, demon, human being, or animal of the male sex."

Brahma acceded to this request, and Mahisha exulted, for he didn't dream that any woman could stand up to his might.

Puffed up with pride after his success, Mahisha first proceeded to conquer the earth. Then he looked toward the heavens and routed the gods, forcing them to take to their heels. The dejected gods went to Brahma and asked for his help. As usual, he was unable to help them, so they went to Kailasa, the abode of Shiva.

Shiva cast a meaningful look at Brahma and said, "O worshipful one! You are the one who has given this demon these boons that have made him invincible. None of us will be able to defeat him. How can we ask our wives to go and fight with this fiend? That is not possible, so let's go and ask Vishnu to find a solution."

The gods repaired to Vaikunta, the abode of Vishnu.

Smilingly, Lord Vishnu said, "O *devas*! Since this demon cannot be killed by a male, the only remedy is to create out of our combined energies a female who will surely be able to defeat him."

Hardly had he finished speaking when a fiery red energy rose out of the face of Brahma. It was soon joined by a silvery white fire from Shiva, a dazzling blue light emanating from Vishnu, and a multicolored glow from Indra. Masses of fiery sparks soon came from the other gods and united to form a huge, mountainous mass of energy, blazing like a thousand suns. These energies eventually took on the form of a ravishingly beautiful young woman adorned with divine clothes and ornaments and having eighteen arms, each wielding a different weapon.

Her enchanting face was created from the fiery energy of Shiva; her glossy black hair came from Yama, the god of death; her three eyes emitting sparks of anger came from Agni, the god of fire; and her arched eyebrows came from Sandhya, the spirit of twilight. Her ears were fashioned from the light of Vayu, the god of wind; her nose from that of Kubera, the god of wealth; and her pearly teeth from that of Daksha, who was one of the patriarchs. Her deep red lips came from the energy of Aruna, the charioteer of the sun, and her eighteen arms from the glory of Vishnu. Her breasts came from Soma, the moon god, and her navel from Indra. Her thighs and legs came from Varuna, the god of waters, and her loins from Prithvi, the earth deity. Her form was exquisitely beautiful, and the *devas* were in rapture when they saw her.

The milky ocean in which Vishnu reclined brought forth for her an exquisite crystal necklace and some heavenly clothes, bright red in color. Vishvakarma, the architect of the gods, bedecked her with intricately designed jewels intended to adorn each and every part of her body. Varuna, lord of waters, presented her with a crown of never-fading lotuses and a *vanamala* or garland of mixed wildflowers. The mountain Himalaya offered a tawny lion as her vehicle.

Now Vishnu asked the gods to present her with their separate weapons. Vishnu created another discus with a thousand spokes and offered it to her. Shiva gave his trident and Varuna, a conch. Agni offered her a splendid blazing weapon known as Shatagni, and Vayu, a bow and unlimited arrows. Indra gave his thunderbolt and Yama gave his staff, which he uses to take away the life of all beings at the time of death. Kubera gave her a golden goblet filled with intoxicating wine. Brahma gave his own *kamandalu* or water pot, filled with Ganga (Ganges) water. Vishvakarma made a mace for her, and the sun gave his sparkling rays to surround her head like an aureole.

It's important to understand that the gods did not create this goddess out of their own imaginations. Instead they consciously constructed a body through which the unborn and deathless mother of the universe could manifest in this plane of reality. They willingly abdicated their various masculine attitudes so that the demon might be destroyed. Into the hands of the Divine Mother they delivered their various weapons, utensils, ornaments, and emblems containing their particular energies and traits. Into the all-comprehending source out of which they themselves had originally evolved, they now merged their separate natures and powers of action.

On beholding this most auspicious personification of the supreme energy of the universe, the gods rejoiced and paid homage to her. They called her Tripurasundari, "the fairest maid of all the three worlds." She was the perennial, primeval female in which all the particular and limited forces of their various personalities had powerfully amalgamated. Such an overwhelming totalization signified omnipotence. By a gesture of perfect surrender they had returned their energies to the primeval Shakti, the fountainhead of power from which they had stemmed. The result was a great renewal of the original state of universal potency. When the cosmos first unfolded into a system of different spheres and forces, life energy was parceled out into a multitude of individual manifestations. But these had now lost their force. The Divine Mother, the life energy as the primeval maternal principle, had reabsorbed them into her universal womb. She was now ready to go forth in the fullness of her being as the goddess Durga (Chandika).

Seeing her thus resplendent and adorned, filled with startling beauty, the gods extolled her: "O Devi! Thou art ever constant and ever existent. Thou art *nirguna* (without qualities), yet for the sake of thy divine play, thou dost assume different forms, *sattvic, rajasic, and tamasic,* like an actor who takes on various roles for the entertainment of the people. Pray help us rout this wicked *asura* who has driven us out of our abode and is bent on destroying the entire universe."

Durga now spoke in a melodious voice and assured the gods that she would accomplish their purpose and slay the demon.

Sitting astride the huge lion, she gave a mighty roar that reverberated through heaven and earth and made the earth and sky rock with its impact. The oceans churned and volcanoes belched lava. Heavens and hells trembled with fear. Her head grazed the sky while the ground sank beneath her feet. The *devas* were delighted to see this spine-chilling form of Devi, which was guaranteed to make the mightiest *asura* quake with fear. Along with the *rishis,* they extolled her with many hymns.

When Mahisha heard this hideous, fiendish laughter it is said that for a minute even his adamantine heart trembled with the unknown sentiment of fear. He ordered his ministers to go and find out the source of this dreadful sound. They returned with the message that the sound had emanated from the enormous figure of a woman, undoubtedly beautiful but, all the same, fearful to behold. She appeared to be quaffing wine from a golden goblet and was seated on a vicious lion. She twanged her gigantic bow with her eighteen arms and made the very air shiver with its vibrations.

When he heard that his enemy was a woman, Mahisha decided to use conciliatory methods and told his ministers to try to win her over with sweet words and bring her to him, and he would make her his consort. The ministers scurried to do his bidding and tried their best to beguile Durga with many sweet words in the hope of tempting her.

Durga smiled sweetly and said, "I am pleased with your words, but know me to be the mother of the universe. Understand that I have come here at the request of the gods with the express purpose of killing Mahisha and giving heaven back to them. I have come here alone, without an army. Tell him to restore heaven to the gods and return to the nether regions or else fight and be killed by me."

One of the ministers replied, "My master is invincible. All the gods have fought with him and failed to kill him. How can you, a delicate female, alone and helpless, ever hope to subdue him? Far better for you to surrender to him and become queen of all the three worlds."

Durga laughed at his words and said, "Your master received a boon from Brahma that he could be killed only by a woman, and that is why I have taken on a woman's form. Inherently I am neither male nor female. I am the supreme Purusha itself. Tell your master that when death beckons even a grass can turn into a thunderbolt, so why not a woman? Your master's end is approaching, and not all his warriors or his own valor can save him."

When Mahishasura heard this, he decided on battle and sent his commanders one after the other to kill Durga. To his amazement, one by one each of his best generals was killed, even though they were supported by huge numbers of infantry, cavalry, and elephants. Seated on her lion and wielding her weapons to deadly effect, Durga made short work of the *asuras*. The lion also did his bit, gobbling up those who came near him. Those who remained ran back to their master and gave a report about this unnatural turn of events.

At last Mahishasura decided to face Durga himself. But first he exchanged his buffalo form for that of an elegant human shape so as to entice her. Puffed up with pride and armed with all his accoutrements, he advanced toward her, confident that she would succumb to his charms. When she saw him, Durga blew the conch that had been given by Varuna. The sound made all the worlds quail with fear. Mahisha advanced toward her and spoke flattering words, designed to beguile her.

"O lotus-eyed one!" he said. "I will make you queen of all the three worlds if you will give in to my request and become my wife. I have already defeated the gods, and there is no one in the universe that is capable of withstanding my prowess."

Durga laughed and said, "O *daitya* (demon)! I do not desire anyone other than the supreme lord. I am his power of will—his Prakriti. Because of his proximity, I appear as the eternal consciousness, manifesting itself as this cosmos. As iron can be moved due to the power of the magnet, so I, who am inert, work consciously due to his proximity. Formless, birthless, and deathless am I, yet at times I take on forms to uphold *dharma*. If you are desirous of saving your life, make friends with the gods and go your way, and I will not harm you. But if you desire to die, then fight, for I will undoubtedly kill you!"

Rather reluctantly Mahishasura decided to fight, for he was quite enamored by her charms. He started to shoot arrows filled with virulent poison at Durga. In the meantime his warriors surrounded her and kept raining arrows from all sides, while he kept hurling missile after missile at her. She laughed as if in sport and reduced his weapons and his army to ashes in a second. Mahisha could not believe his eyes. He fell upon the lion with his club, but the lion rent his leg with his claws. The *asura* immediately took on a lion's form and clawed the lion. Durga became very angry at his assault on her pet lion and rained inexhaustible arrows at him. He now turned into a maddened elephant and hurled huge boulders at the *devi* with his trunk. But she shattered them to pieces with her arrows. The lion sprang at the head of the elephant and rent it with his claws. The *asura* immediately assumed the form of a *sarabha,* an animal more powerful than any creature known to man. Durga, however, instantly tore the *sarabha* to shreds.

Once more the *asura* resumed his original form of a mountainous buffalo, and he started to harass the goddess, piercing her with his horns, kicking her with his hooves, and lashing her with his gigantic tail. Then he fell on the lion with a mighty sword, but the lion tore his legs into pieces. Undaunted, Mahisha lashed his huge tail and scattered the clouds, which scuttled across the sky. The oceans rose up as if they had been thrashed. His horns rent the sky and his hooves plowed the entire earth.

Then Durga opened her third eye in fury and roared, "O wicked one! Your end is nigh! Go on ranting a moment more while I sip my fill of this delicious brew." She took a deep draft of wine from her golden goblet and then, tossing it aside, leapt into the air and came down on the back of the buffalo. Pinning Mahisha's throat with her foot, she drove her trident into his heart. The demon tried to escape through the buffalo's gaping mouth in the shape of a heroic warrior, but before he could drag himself out, she caught his hair and cut off his head with her discus. The severed head rolled to the ground like a colossal mountain. The headless buffalo body remained upright for a few minutes and appeared to be vibrating to the beat of the drums. Then it fell to the ground with a tremendous thud that shook the earth with its impact. Blood flowed like a river from the headless body. The lion was delighted with all the blood and lapped it up. He also chased and devoured those warriors who were fleeing for their lives. The gods and sages rejoiced. The earth and its denizens were free once again to worship the supreme, and the *yakshas* (celestial guardians of wealth) and *gandharvas* (celestial musicians) danced with joy.

The gods now extolled her with many hymns: "O Devi! You are the prime cause of the preservation and destruction of this whole universe. You are the supreme origin of the whole world. The gods are helpless to do anything without your energy. You are Gauri, Lakshmi, and Saraswati. How beautiful you are, yet how dreadful! Salutations to you, O Mother! Having vanquished this *asura,* you have brought peace to the whole world. Pray protect us from all sides."

Having blessed them, the Divine Mother repaired to her own abode, Mani Dwipa or the Island of Jewels. She was born again through the body of Parvati in order to kill the demons Shumbha and Nishumbha (see chapter 13).

The killing of Mahisha, as with all the other bloodcurdling stories told in the Devi Mahatmyam, has to be seen from an esoteric angle before we can understand the great impact it has had on the mind of the Indian subcontinent.

The bewildering series of transformations that Mahisha undergoes is an example of the mythological trait of externalization or projection often found in the Puranas. The buffalo demon, employing his illusory power, which again is a power of the goddess, projects his vital energy into new forms. His aggressiveness, his ambition, his will to win—he projects all into form after form and relinquishes one after the other in order to survive.

Similarly, the human vital energy of body and soul, when aroused, flows forth in either beneficent or destructive forms, demonic or divine, depending on the nature of the desire that prompts it to externalize. The battlefield of the world is filled with such demonic and godly characters—the Hitlers, the Mussolinis, the Ghandhis, and the Christs. In fact, the universe itself and our individual worlds are just such transformations of the absolute. Each one of us projects our individual *shakti* (vital energy) into our own little universe—our immediate environment. We color the neutral screen of the supreme consciousness with the dramas and dreams of our inner personalities and get caught in the web of our own make-believe world. The world that we perceive and react to is the product of our own *maya* or delusion. Thus we are captives of our own *maya shakti* and get caught up in its dramatic events, delights, and calamities. Whenever we are entangled and enmeshed in any vital or passionate issues, we are dealing with the projection of our own imaginations. This is the spell of *maya*, of creative, life-engendering, life-maintaining energy. It is also the spell of nescience or ignorance. Since the mind is the chief producer of our personal dramas, ancient Indian wisdom is based on mind-transcending experiences in *yoga* and meditation, and aims at a total transmutation of human nature, a new awareness of both the world and itself. It seeks to release human beings from the spellbinding projections of their own *maya shakti* and thus expose their hidden divinity.

It is an interesting fact that in all the statues depicting her slaying of the demon, Devi's face shows no signs of wrath. She is steeped in the serenity of eternal calm. Though the deed in time and space has to be accomplished, the expression on the countenance of the goddess reduces its importance to the minimum. For her, the whole course of this cosmic performance, including her own appearance, is only a part of the celestial dream. It's only another scene in the universal drama. She has assumed a form in order to play her part in the universal dream and enacts the leading role, fully aware that it is only a dream. She remains unconcerned with her own triumphant manifestation. Our Mahisha ego is constantly striving to elude this cleansing power of the divine within us. We have to have recourse to the sage Medhas, who is the loving intellect that is full of inspiration and joy, in order to show us the way to Durga.

Durga or Chandika represents the ever-victorious higher principle within us; her weapons include self-discipline, chanting of the *mantra*, selfless service, introspection, prayer, devotion, meditation, and cheerfulness. Mahisha represents the demonic ego continually seeking to elude the transformative powers of the divine force within. Mahisha is the personification of the selfish ego at its basest form, filled with pride and sensuality. His legions are spite, pettiness, greed, falsehood, and all the other negative emotions. His chief commanders are desire, anger, arrogance, attachment, greed, and self-centeredness. Fortified with these powers, he usurps the gods, who represent the divine powers of the mind. Once this mighty *asuric* ego is killed, the gods or the helpful forces within us resume their rightful roles in our lives.

> *O slayer of the demon Mahisha,*
> *The gods themselves worship you for the protection of the*
>   *universe.*
> *You are victory itself and therefore give victory in battle,*
> *Goddess, blazing with light, be kind to me!*
> *Show mercy in my hour of darkness,*
> *Grant me conquering power.*

—FROM THE *DURGA STOTRAM*
IN THE MAHABHARATA

Thus ends the twelfth chapter of *Shakti*, known as "Mahisha-suramardini," which describes the killing of the demon Mahisha.

Aum Aim Hreem Kleem

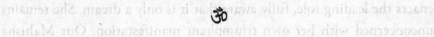

Aum Chamundayai Namaha!

13
Chamunda

Ya Devi sarvabhuteshu, sraddha rupena samsthita,
Namasthasyai, namasthasyai, namasthasyai namo
namaha!

O Goddess who resides in all creatures in the form of faith,
Hail to thee, hail to thee, all hail to thee!

The fifth through the tenth chapters of the Devi Mahatmyam are
devoted to the killing of the *asuras* Shumbha and Nishumbha and their
allies. This third section of the epic is devoted to Maha Saraswati. It
deals with the overthrow of another most powerful enemy: ignorance
of reality or *avidya*. All our human troubles arise from the fact that we
are in total ignorance of who we are, what is happening to us, and what
may happen to us. Thus *ajnana* or ordinary ignorance is the subtle
power that really binds us. The mind churns and desires only because
we do not know the nature of supreme truth. When the sun of wisdom
is covered with clouds, our minds experience a darkness in which the
cyclone of desire can sweep us off our feet and project us into a mael-
strom of hate and anger. As long as the *jivatman* is unaware of its own
effulgent nature, the tornado of desire will keep blowing.

Human nescience has its root in the three cosmic *gunas: tamas, rajas,* and *sattva.* The epic story of the destruction of Shumbha and Nishumbha represents the overcoming and transformation of cosmic nature in the form of these *gunas. Sattva* is a subtle medium of obstruction. It is like a clear pane of glass that does not obstruct your view but obstructs your approach to the reality within. Psychologically, it manifests as feelings of complacency and satisfaction with what we think we have achieved. Esoterically, these feelings are typified by Shumbha and Nishumbha. Only Maha Saraswati, the power of higher wisdom, can dispel them. Liberation is not an individual effort. It is a cosmic endeavor in which we are helped by the great celestial powers. When you step into the spiritual path, you have to leave your petty individual concepts behind and cross into the way of cosmic relationships. A spiritual seeker is not just another individual like millions of others but a special person, for he or she has connected with the universal reality. The Devi Mahatmyam involves us in this cosmic dance that overcomes the powers of *tamas, rajas,* and *sattva* and helps us attain supreme realization. In this we are helped by the great forces of Adi Shakti.

In days of yore two mighty *asuras* called Shumbha and Nishumbha decided to practice *tapas* in order to wrest some boons from the creator. They undertook severe austerities in the lake known as Pushkara until eventually Brahma revealed himself and prompted them to ask for a boon. Of course, in the nature of all demons they immediately asked for immortality, which was denied to them. Brahma told them to ask for any other boon, and after due consideration they requested, as Mahisha had done, that they should be granted invulnerability from the hands of any male creature, whether demon, god, animal, or bird. This Brahma promptly approved. (No doubt Brahma knew in his heart that he could always depend on the goddess to rescue him. The constant repetition of this pattern makes us think that Brahma must be reenacting the whole drama only in order to give us a chance to enjoy the divine *lilas.*)

The brothers returned and installed Shumbha, who was the elder, on a golden throne made for him by the sage Brighu, whom he had propitiated. They then started to amass a large army of *asuras* headed by their powerful commanders Chanda, Munda, Dhumralochana, and Raktabija. The demon Raktabija was said to be invincible because he had been granted the boon that every drop of his blood that fell on the ground would give rise to another *asura,* equal to him in valor and carrying the same weapons. Many heroes arrived and pledged their allegiance to Shumbha and Nishumbha, until their army swelled and rolled like a mighty ocean. Shumbha's army marched to the heavens and conquered the host of gods lead by Indra in no time. He then proceeded to overthrow the rulers of the quarters and established his suzerainty over the three worlds.

The dejected gods went to their *guru,* Brihaspati, and begged him to chant some *mantras* that would free them of their troubles. Brihaspati told them that good by itself could not resist evil since good is only the countercorrelative of evil. Only that which is neither good nor evil— *nirguna,* without qualities—can defeat evil.

"Don't you remember," he said, "at that time when she killed the mighty *asura* Mahisha, the Divine Mother promised to help you whenever you were afflicted by evil? Go to her therefore and praise her with hymns, and she will surely come to your aid."

The *devas* hopefully departed to the Himalayas, the abode of the goddess, and started to extol her with many beautiful hymns. They said, "Salutations to the blessed *devi*. Salutations again and again to Prakriti, the auspicious. Prostrations to the dreadful, to the eternal, to the pure and the effulgent. Prostrations to Durga, the essence, the doer of everything. All hail to her who manifests in all creatures as Vishnu Maya, as consciousness, as intellect, as sleep, as hunger, as shadow, as power, as thirst, as forbearance, as birth, as modesty, as memory, as mercy, as contentment, as mother, and as delusion, and who is known among all beings as the sustainer of all. May that *devi* bestow her blessings on us, who are forlorn and helpless."

Hardly had they finished eulogizing her when they saw the goddess Parvati coming out of her cave in order to take her bath in the river

Ganga (Ganges). She was incredibly beautiful, adorned with divine clothes and jewels. In sweet accents she asked the *devas* what they wanted. They made their request and begged her to help them.

As they spoke she smiled, and out of her bodily sheath or *kosha* another supremely beautiful form emerged, known as Kaushiki, a form of Durga. When Kaushiki came out of her body, Parvati's body changed color and became black and terrible to behold. She came to be known as Kalika or Kaali. Kaushiki told the gods to return to their own abode and promised to settle the matter with their enemies.

The beautiful Kaushiki or Durga then seated herself on the branch of a tree while Kalika sat below her and started to sing in a melodious voice. Just then, Chanda and Munda, the bodyguards of Shumbha and Nishumbha, happened to pass by. They saw the enchanting form of the goddess seated playfully on the tree. They were enthralled by her appearance and ran to inform their masters of this beautiful vision.

Asuras are noted for their vanity and lust, and immediately Shumbha asked his minister Sugriva to go and woo the beauty and ask her to become his bride.

The minister pleaded his master's case with great dexterity: "O Devi! Shumbha, the king of the *asuras,* is lord of the three worlds. He has sent me here to request you to become his bride. He is capable of giving you anything you desire."

The goddess smiled sweetly when she heard these words and told the minister, "I have no doubt that you are speaking the truth and that your master is the greatest in all the three worlds. I will gladly marry him. But there is a condition attached. I have taken a vow to marry only one who can defeat me in battle. So let either Shumbha or Nishumbha come here and defeat me, and I assure you that I will marry the one who vanquishes me."

The messenger was shocked when he heard this and begged her to reconsider her foolish vow, but the goddess merely smiled her secret smile and told him to return to his master and repeat her words.

When Shumbha heard this strange vow, he decided to send his general Dhumralochana to capture and bring her to him.

Dhumralochana tried his best to persuade Kaushiki to accompany him back to his master, but she refused to talk and merely sent Kalika to confront him. After a fierce fight Dhumralochana charged at Kalika, shouting imprecations. Kalika merely gave a mighty *ham* (seed *mantra* of *akasa*) and he was immediately burnt to ashes. His frightened soldiers ran back to Shumbha to give a report of these extraordinary happenings. Shumbha was astounded to hear this and did not know what to do. His brother Nishumbha now offered to go and conquer Kaali, but Shumbha said, "It is not necessary to send an elephant to kill a rabbit, so let us send our generals Chanda and Munda. They will be able to kill Kalika easily and bring Durga to me."

Now it was the turn of Chanda and Munda to march toward Durga and try their hand at defeating her. When they tried to lay their hands on her, she became furious. Her face became black with rage and from her furrowed brow there emerged another hideous form of Kaali. The demons were horrified when they saw her. She was gaunt and terrifying with thin, pendulous breasts and sunken, bloodshot eyes. Her tongue lolled from her bloodstained, cavernous mouth and she belched fire. She was clad in tiger skin with a necklace of human skulls, and she wielded a many-colored staff topped with a skull. Her eyes rolled revoltingly as she gave the most hideous, bloodcurdling roars. The *asura* army fell unconscious at the very sound. The earth trembled with every step she took. Taking up handfuls of *asuras* in her enormous hands, she stuffed them into her cavernous mouth and munched them with apparent relish. Chariots, elephants, and horses went the same way. She swallowed even the weapons they flung at her, crunching them like biscuits. Soon the entire army was destroyed. Undaunted, Chanda and Munda ran at her with upraised weapons. She caught hold of them as if they were puppets and brought them to Durga, who was sitting on the lion, and presented them to her as human sacrifices. Taking up her axe, Kaali cut off their heads, offering them to Durga, and drank the blood that gushed from their severed necks.

Durga said, "Since you have brought me the heads of Chanda and Munda, you will be renowned in the world by the name of Chamunda."

An eighteenth-century poem by Bhavabhuti glorifies her thus:

Hail! Hail! Chamunda! Mighty goddess hail!
I glorify thy sport, when in the dance,
That fills the court of Shiva with delight,
Thy foot descending spurs the earthly globe.
The elephant hide that robes thee, to thy steps,
Swings to and fro; the whirling talons rend
The crescent on thy brow;
And from the torn orb the trickling nectar falls,
And every skull that gems thy necklace
Laughs with horrid life!

The remaining soldiers were terrified by this gruesome spectacle and ran back to their masters to report all that had taken place on the battlefield. Shumbha now ordered his best general, Raktabija, to go with another huge army to capture Durga. The *asura* hordes encircled the goddess, her lion, and Kaali and prepared to rush at them. At this time the watching gods sent their powerful *shaktis* to help her. The energy of Brahma appeared as Brahmaani, riding on a swan, carrying a *kamandalu* (water pot). The energy of Shiva came as Maheswari, riding on a bull, holding aloft a trident, wearing the crescent moon in her hair. The force of Skanda came as Kaumari, riding on a peacock, holding a spear. The energy of Vishnu appeared as Vaishnavi, flying on the eagle Garuda, holding the discus, conch, mace, and bow. The energy of Indra came as Indrani, riding the white elephant and brandishing the thunderbolt. The *shaktis* of Vishnu came as Vaarahi the boar and Nrisimhi the lady-lion. Another fierce *shakti* came out of Durga herself, howling like a jackal; she ordered Lord Shiva to go as her ambassador to Shumbha and Nishumbha, and therefore she came to be known as Shivaduti—one who sent Shiva as an emissary.

First to arrive on the scene of battle was Brahmaani, who sprinkled the waters of her *kamandalu* over the *asura* army and drained their strength. Then came Maheswari, who flung her trident, discus, spear, and thunderbolt at them and arrested the onslaught. The boar Vaarahi came next and tossed the *asuras* hither and thither with her tusks, and then came Nrisimhi, who began to devour them.

Seeing this destruction, Raktabija came forward. From every drop of blood that was spilt from him there arose another demon, as fearsome as he. All of them started to fight Durga with renewed vigor. With one throw of her thunderbolt she severed his head, but again every drop of blood that fell on the ground turned into a clone of him. Thousands of warriors rose from his flowing blood, enough to fill the earth. The gods were filled with horror when they saw this. Then all the *shaktis* and the Sapta Matrikis (seven mothers)—Brahmaani, Maheswari, Kaumari, Vaishnavi, Vaarahi, Indrani, and Nrisimhi—fell on Raktabija, but thousands of Raktabijas rose up and filled the battlefield, to the dismay of the watching gods. The whole world seemed to be filled with *asuras,* and only the Sapta Matrikas, Durga, and Kaali were left on the battlefield to fight with these hordes.

Then Durga told Kaali, "Widen your face and spread your tongue as far as the eye can see. When I kill these *asuras* with my weapons, don't let even a drop of blood fall on the ground. Drink up every drop with your wide and long tongue, and eat up as many *asuras* as possible at the same time. Only then will we be able to stop this demon's onslaught."

With these words, Durga pierced Raktabija with her trident, and Kaali spread her tongue and drank up his blood before a drop could fall on the ground. Raktabija roared with pain and fell upon Durga with great force. She put an end to his life with her discus, which caused a great flood of blood. Kaali drank all the blood and ate all the *rakshasas* (giants of darkness and evil) who had been created by the few drops that had escaped her tongue.

The remaining *asuras* fled in terror and reported the matter to Shumbha: "O King! The goddess Durga has killed all the *asuras* and Chamunda has drunk all their blood and ate the rest. We advise you not to keep on with this battle if you fear for your life. She is not an ordinary woman. She is Maha Maya. There is no doubt about this. She has manifested herself only to help the gods and is bent on destroying our whole race."

Shumbha was furious when he heard this and told them scornfully, "You are all cowards to be chased by a woman. You may go down to the netherworld if you wish, but I will go and destroy her myself."

Then Nishumbha said, "Brother! Fear not! I will go first and kill this woman. There is no need for you to bestir yourself."

Seeing the approaching army, Durga laughed and spoke in her soft, sweet voice to Kaali: "O Kaali! See how foolish they are. Hope springs ever in the human breast. Even after witnessing the death of so many of their generals they still think they can defeat me."

Nishumbha fell upon Maha Maya and fought with her various manifestations, including Kaali and the Sapta Matrikas (Vaishnavi, Maheswari, Brahmaani, Kaumari, Indrani, Vaarahi, and Nrisimhi). Shumbha followed, close on the heels of his brother, and supported him from the rear. When Nishumbha wounded her lion, Durga (Chandika) became angry and stuck him down. He rose up immediately and came forward to fight with Durga. He flew at her in his chariot, holding aloft many weapons. Seeing him approach, she blew her conch, and the sound made the blood freeze in his bones. However, he rallied himself and fell upon the lion with his club and then made as if to lunge at Durga. She immediately struck off his head with her axe, but to the horror of the *devas,* the headless demon danced around, lashing at everyone with his club. Durga then cut off his hands and feet, and at last the lifeless trunk fell to the ground with a mighty thud.

The soldiers ran back and told Shumbha about the death of his brother and advised him not to proceed.

Shumbha said, "Fools! Do you expect me to run away and save my skin when I have been the cause of the death of my brother and my ministers? This woman is a woman only in name. She has the strength of a hundred heroic warriors. Since death is certain for every creature, let me die on the battlefield rather than rot in the netherworld!"

So saying, Shumbha got into his chariot and advanced toward Durga. When he set eyes on her, he was smitten by her charms and tried to woo her with conciliatory words: "O thou of delicate limbs, why do you want to fight with me? A woman's eyebrows are her bow and her looks are her arrows. Her gestures and postures are her weapons. Give up these fierce ministers of yours, this ugly Kalika and Chamunda, and come with me. I shall serve you as you deserve to be served."

Durga laughed at his words and said, "O stupid one! If you think I'm too beautiful to fight with you, then fight with this ugly Kalika or fierce Chamunda. I will stand and watch."

Then turning to Chamunda she said, "O Chamunda, your nature is violent and this person likes to fight with ferocious people, so please go and humor him."

Hearing this command, Chamunda pounced on Shumbha with her axe and cut off his left hand, which was adorned with jewels and weapons. Then Shumbha said, "O wicked Durga, you are fighting with the help of so many others while I am all alone."

Durga replied, "Look at me. I am alone. There is none other than I. I alone exist in this whole universe. You are imagining that you see people other than me."

As soon as she said these words all her other *avataras,* from Kaali to the Sapta Matrikas, reentered her body, and Durga remained alone, holding aloft her trident. But Shumbha was too immersed in his own ego to understand the message. He continued to think that he could conquer the divine. He failed to understand the inner meaning of the show she had just put forth: that he was also a part of her and could merge himself in her if he so wished.

Shumbha now waged a terrific battle with the goddess. He hurled his most powerful weapons at her, and the gods watched with bated breath as she smashed his chariot and made him fall to the ground. He fell on her with his most powerful *astra* (missile), but she sliced it with her arrows. Now he hit her on the breast with his club. She retaliated and beat his chest with her mace, and he fell down senseless. She waited until he regained consciousness. Then he soared into the sky and rained arrows on her. She immediately flew after him and brought him down to the ground. The infuriated Shumbha charged at her as if to throttle her with his bare hands. Thus the fight went on and on. The Devi Mahatmyam says that Durga allowed Shumbha to wrestle with her for a long time.

At last Durga decided to put an end to Shumbha's life and tore his chest in two with her trident. As he fell, the whole earth trembled and oceans churned. The celestials rejoiced and danced. The trees began to bloom and the rivers to flow swiftly. Fires in all hearths burned vibrantly, and the wind blew softly while the sun shone brightly. The earth had been rid of her burdens.

The gods rejoiced and came to hymn Durga (Chandika) with the famous *Narayani sthuti* (praise).

O Narayani! Destroyer of woes! Be pleased, O Mother of the universe. Supreme controller! Protect us all! You are the support of the universe.

You are Vishnu Maya, cause of both bondage and liberation. All knowledge is thy form. All women are thyself, O Mother!

O Narayani! Thou art time, space, and causation. All this is filled by thee alone.

Thou art intelligence, O Narayani!

O blessed refuge of the distressed, O Narayani! Salutations to thee!

O destroyer of all troubles of the devoted, who take refuge in thee, O Narayani! Salutations to thee!

O Devi, whenever evil prevails, you manifest yourself.

You are that power of the eternal that manifests as the power of creation, sustenance, and destruction. O queen of all, you protect all. Having all for your very soul, you support all.

O Mother of all the worlds! Destroyer of woes! Support of the universe! Please continue to protect the world. O Brahmaani, carrying the *kamandalu,* riding on the swan; O Maheswari, with the trident sitting on a bull; O Kaumari, with the spear sitting on the peacock; O Vaishnavi, carrying the conch, discus, mace, and bow, seated on Garuda, salutations to you!

O Devi of the dreadful form of Vaarahi and Nrisimhi, O Narayani, salutations to you!

O Lakshmi! O Kaali! O Saraswati! Pray protect us.

O Narayani! Salutations to you again and again!

Wherever there is unrighteousness, there will you manifest. Those who take refuge in you have no cause for fear.

O adorable one! Pray protect us who rest under your feet!

O Mother, be gracious! Just as you rescued us from the demons today, please promise to save us whenever we call out to you in all the times to come.

The goddess was pleased with the hymn of the gods and told them of her future incarnations:

In the Vaivasvata *manvantara,* in the twenty-eighth Dwapara Yuga, I will be born in the house of Nandagopa in Yasoda's womb and will destroy Shumbha and Nishumbha once again in the Vindhya mountains, where I will take up my abode and be known as Vindhya Vaasini.

Again I will be invoked by *rishis* at the time of a universal famine, and I will be born in order to relieve the distress of the people. At that time I will be known as Satakshi and Shakambari.

Whenever there is oppression by evil forces I shall descend into the three worlds and save you, if you call to me with hearts full of faith. Whoever contemplates my saving grace with full concentration and loving devotion will be relieved of disease and misfortune. They need fear neither weapons, fire, nor floods. I will never abandon that abode where prayers are offered to me continually. Listening to the tales of my deeds, one becomes fearless and is unaffected by evil dreams and the influence of malefic planets.

Whenever there is trouble anywhere I shall manifest myself and bring peace on Earth. The mere reading of my stories will destroy the troubles of my devotees.

Thus saying, she blessed the gods and disappeared from their sight.

Shumbha typifies that part of our nature that keeps resisting the truth that we are all fundamentally the same and all emanate from the supreme. We are confirmed individualists and will not give up our separate egos even if we are promised the kingdom of God. We find it difficult to accept the fact that we cannot force the divine to obey our will. When she doesn't bend to our will, we feel the same frustration and anger as Shumbha. We are allowed full freedom to entertain this idea and combat with her for a long time—until the moment comes when she decides that we should be made aware of our true nature.

Shumbha's general Raktabija is an allegory for our unhealthy thoughts, which multiply if left to feed on the negativity that surrounds us. They have to be caught before they take root in our subconscious and multiply beyond our control. Kaali has to be invoked to do this. If left alone, these thoughts will harden into our personality, and then we will never be able to eradicate them. As Swami Shivananda says, "Constant vigilance is the price of spiritual liberty."

The Devi Mahatmyam is the story of an inner battle. Victory comes to us only when we find the strength to surrender our negative emotions to Durga's purifying influence. The different types of conflicts that are described here actually happen daily within our hearts and in the external world. We are constantly waging a war between our negative and positive emotions. It is a battle that has to be fought by every generation. The answers have to be given by the Divine Mother herself. Unless we surrender to her, we can never end the conflict. If, like Chanda and Munda, we try to defy the goddess and usurp her special powers for our own benefit, she become enraged and out of her beautiful form will emanate the terrible figure of Kaali, the power of time, who will devour us with her fierce fangs.

> *When worshipped by your devotees,*
> *You remove their ignorance and bondage,*
> *Their fear, disease, and threat of death.*
> *You protect their children and their goods.*
> *I, who have lost everything, appeal to you for help.*
> *Protect me, O lotus-eyed savior.*
> *I am fighting for truth,*
> *Protect me with all the power of truth.*
> *O Durga, shelter me in your wide lap.*
> *You who are ever loving and merciful to devotees,*
> *Help me!*

—FROM THE *DURGA STOTRAM*
IN THE MAHABHARATA

Thus ends the thirteenth chapter of *Shakti*, known as "Chamunda," which describes the killing of the demons Shumbha and Nishumbha.

Aum Aim Hreem Kleem

Aum Sathyyai Namaha!

14
Sati

Ya Devi sarvabhuteshu, kanti rupena samsthita,
Namasthasyai, namasthasyai, namasthasyai namo
namaha!

O Goddess who resides in all creatures in the form of beauty,
Hail to thee, hail to thee, all hail to thee!

As we have seen, Maha Devi takes on various incarnations in order to
fulfill the demands of her devotees and for the protection of the world.
One of the most famous of these is her incarnation as Sati, daughter of
Daksha.

Brahma is the creator in the Hindu trinity. He is self-born and
he created many other beings out of his mind, including thousands
of sons. Most of the great sages were created in this fashion. Brahma
wanted them to take up the task of creation but they refused. At last
he produced Daksha who was another of his mind-born sons. He was a
prajapati, or patriarch. Because Brahma was tired of creating endlessly
from his mind, he gave the responsibility of creating through cohabita-
tion to his son Daksha (one who is skillful). Daksha was an arrogant
man with a long face and deep furrows on either side of a hooked nose.
He was the champion of orthodoxy and conservatism. His lips curled

with disdain at anything that did not meet with his ideas of propriety. He was addicted to rites and ritualism and was the greatest supporter of the Vedic tenets.

Up until this point creation had taken place only through the mind of Brahma, and it was not proving very successful in populating the world. So Daksha's father, Brahma, asked him to marry and create people through the normal way of union between male and female.

Daksha took two wives, named Asikni and Virini. From his first wife he got two thousand sons, whom he commanded to marry and thus multiply the human species. Unfortunately, the sage Narada advised them instead to become ascetics and contemplate the supreme truth, thus deflecting the boys from their marital plans. Daksha was furious and cursed Narada. He decided that daughters might prove to be more pliable, and so he begat sixty daughters on his second wife. When they came of age he married them to suitable husbands among the *rishis* and demigods. Much to his relief, their progeny slowly started to fill the world.

But for the one daughter on whom his mind always dwelt with great fondness, he had been unable to think of a suitable groom. He remembered her birth. Brahma had asked him to do *tapas* to Maha Devi and beg her to be born as his child. He had undertaken intense austerities and eventually had a vision of the goddess. She appeared as a haze of darkness in which appeared two pinpoints of light. One point turned out to be a brilliant blue lotus and the other a flashing sword. And then as he peered into the gloaming, he saw her: Durga seated on a lion and looking at him with great tenderness. He got up and threw himself down before the growling lion and begged the goddess to become his daughter. She graciously agreed.

Daksha returned home and, along with his wife Virini, worshipped the goddess and begged her to keep her promise. The supreme mother of the universe now took birth in the house of Daksha. As she was the personification of supreme truth, she was named Sati (the embodiment of truth).

Brahma had instructed Sati while she was still young that the only fitting mate for her was Mahadeva: Shiva, the lord of lords. Her mother noticed that she was quite unlike her sisters. They would laugh and gossip and invent stories of the ones they would marry, but Sati kept to herself. She was often found wandering alone in the forest singing to herself and painting pictures of the lord of Kailasa. The face she drew was frightening, and quite incomprehensible to her mother and sisters. When she reached adolescence, Sati approached her mother and informed her that she was going to undertake a year-long vow in order to propitiate Shiva. She underwent rigorous tortures of her body until one full year had passed. At the end of the year she concluded her worship of the three-eyed lord and sat and concentrated on him. This news was reported to Daksha, who was quite dismayed. He was the patriarch of organized religion, following strict rules and conducting continuous fire sacrifices (*yajna*) to the gods, who in turn were supposed to support and upkeep the sanctity of the social order. Shiva stood for the very opposite of all this.

Daksha ranted and raved, "I will never agree to my beloved daughter marrying this crazy man, this woman stealer! He is the enemy of all rules and rites, he smears himself with the ashes of the dead, and he consorts with the lowest of the low, grows his hair long, and bedecks himself with bones. He stands for the opposite of everything that I stand for. Why did I compose so many rites and rituals and why did I beget the mother of the universe if she is to be snatched away from me by that madman? I will never agree to this marriage! You may tell her that!"

But though her mother and sisters tried their best to dissuade her and warned her of the dire consequences of her father's wrath, Sati was adamant and refused to be deterred from her firm resolve. She determined not to stir from the place she had chosen for her austerities until the lord of her heart appeared in person to take her. As the months passed, she grew thin and emaciated, yet her body shone with an extraordinary luster. Even the sages came to see her, for she had reached an exalted state. They determined to make her wish come true, and along with the gods they went to Lord Vishnu and begged him to intercede with Shiva on her behalf. All of them now proceeded to Kailasa and praised Shiva and begged him to accept Sati as his wife.

Shiva said, "O sages! Only a person of imperfect knowledge will desire marriage. It is a great bondage. I am a *yogi*, ever delighting in the bliss of the self. I'm always engaged in *tapas* and total detachment from the world. What interest would I have in marriage? Moreover, I'm the friend of ghosts and goblins. I visit the burning *ghats* and crematoriums. My body is covered with the ashes from the cremation ground. Serpents and reptiles are my ornaments. Which woman would want to marry me?"

The gods begged him to reconsider his decision, so Shiva smiled and said, "If you can find a woman who will meet my requirements, I shall certainly marry her. When I am *yogi*, she will have to be a *yogini*. When I desire her, she will have to be a wife. When I go into *samadhi* (a superconscious state), she should not approach me, for she will be burnt to ashes in the fire of my austerity. If she refuses to do what I say, I shall abandon her. Now see if you can find such a woman."

Brahma was delighted at these words and said, "Indeed, O Lord, such a woman has already been born in the household of Prajapati Daksha. She is known as Sati and is a fitting mate for you. At present she is performing rigorous penance in order to secure you as her husband. She is an incarnation of Maha Devi, who takes on many forms in order to bless the world."

Shiva was intrigued by this description and agreed to meet Sati. On the eighth day of the bright half of the month of Aswin (September/October), Sati observed her final fast, which concluded her one-year worship of Lord Shiva. She sat in the dense forest engrossed in meditation on his form. Suddenly she felt her whole body tremble. Her mind became agitated and refused to concentrate. Wondering what had happened to distract her, she opened her eyes and saw her beloved standing before her, just as she had imagined him. He appeared before her in his incomparable form with five faces, three eyes, and a crescent moon adorning his locks. He was holding a trident and drum, and his neck was entwined with serpents. He was covered with ashes and clad in a tiger skin. Such was his brilliance that Sati could hardly look at him.

Although he knew her desire, Shiva asked her to choose a boon, for he wanted to hear her wish from her own mouth. But she was very shy and would not speak. Again he urged her to openly express her desire. At last she whispered, "O Lord! Why do you play with me? You know my desire. Let me have the bridegroom of my choice."

Hardly had she finished when he replied, "You shall indeed be my wife, O Dakshayini (daughter of Daksha)! I shall take you away to my mountain abode immediately, before anyone sees us. Your father would surely obstruct us if he could."

Sati begged him to approach her father and marry her with all proper rites. Shiva shook his head in foreboding, but since she insisted he gave in to her wishes. He grasped her tender hand in his strong one and hastened to Daksha.

Daksha, the impeccable priest of orthodoxy, looked at Shiva in utter contempt. He was a wild beggar clothed in the stench of pyres. Daksha broke out in a fierce expletive when he saw that Shiva held Sati tightly in one strong arm while he stroked his garland of bones with the other. Sati herself looked different. She was no longer his beautiful daughter. The long year of penance had turned her skin dark. She was clad in dirty and torn clothes, but her eyes were bright and radiated happiness. She was looking adoringly at her divine lover and seemed oblivious of her father's wrath.

"You scoundrel!" Daksha exclaimed. "What have you done? Are you trying to snatch my beloved daughter from me?" Looking at Sati he said, "I will never let you marry this wretch."

"O Father!" said Sati. "I have made my choice. This is the man I wish to marry, and none other."

"In that case you can marry him without my consent and without my blessings. You will be shunned forever, condemned to wander like an outcast with this madman!" Daksha exploded.

Sati's eyes pleaded with her father for understanding, but he refused to meet them with his own. This child who had been so dear to him was now cast out of his heart and house. Sati clung harder to Shiva's arm. Without a word he lifted her into his arms and placed her on his vehicle, the bull Nandi, who had been waiting for his master's command. The couple set off without any pomp or show. There was no music or trumpets, no priests, and no rituals. They had no home or shelter. From the palace of Prajapati Daksha, in which she had enjoyed every comfort, Sati was taken to a bleak and barren mountain where there were only beasts and reptiles to welcome her. She cared not for the lack of comforts. All she wanted was to roam about wildly in the wake of her unpredictable husband, across the desolate Himalayan ranges and peaks inhabited by wild animals, followed by a horde of goblins. At first Shiva tested her resolve and hardly glanced at her, but she ignored this callous treatment and continued to follow him. At last one day he chased his followers away and gathered her into an embrace that lasted for twenty-five years, without his ever emptying his seed into her.

The embrace of Sati and Shiva represents the union of Purusha and Prakriti as one. Sati's role was to make Shiva function in the mundane world. He was *bhava* (pure being), and she *bhavani* (becoming). Unless she bestirred herself and broke out of his embrace, all creativity would be at a standstill. The portrait of Shiva always alternates between the extremes of asceticism and eroticism. Shiva's stored-up potency that accumulates during asceticism has to be coaxed into being released into the world to invigorate creation. Sati's and later Parvati's role was to lure Shiva from this ascetic isolation to creative participation in the world.

At last Sati uncurled herself from that endless embrace and started to question Shiva on the meaning of the self: "Ever since I was a little girl I have practiced *tapas*, not for liberation but to get you as my husband. Now that I have my desire, I long for liberation too. I have been told that you are liberation itself. All my devotion has been to you, but now I want knowledge."

Shiva said, "O Sati, in the age that is to come, the Iron Age of Kali, devotion is the easiest method of getting release. So you should continue with your devotion to me and I shall set you free."

"My lord, I know what devotion is, but I would like also to learn about *jnana* (wisdom)."

"You don't need it, O Sati, for you and I are one. That is knowledge."

"But who are you?" asked Sati.

"I am That," said Shiva.

"What is That?" she insisted.

At last Shiva, the supreme soul, gave in to the wishes of the Divine Mother and gave her, who is omniscient, all wisdom in order to benefit the world. He said:

O Sati, I shall give you that knowledge that shall free all souls in bondage. O beautiful one! Know that supreme knowledge consists of experiencing the great truth, "I am Brahman." In the enlightened intellect, nothing else is remembered. This sort of consciousness is very rare in this world. But O beloved! Remember that I myself am the supreme Brahman, as is Vishnu. As for you, my love, you are nothing but the supreme Shakti (Parashakti). You are not separate from the Brahman. Devotion to you or to me or to Vishnu will give liberation from these mortal coils and is easier to practice. One who is steeped in devotion enjoys perpetual bliss. Devotion has the power to attract me as nothing else can. Why do you think I was attracted to you? I go even to the houses of outcasts if they are devotees. In the decadent age of Kali, wisdom and detachment have been misused and neglected. People who can grasp them are rare. Devotion or *bhakti* can give the same benefits and is more appealing.

Listening to this discourse, Sati was satisfied. She questioned Shiva on a thousand other things also. These wonderful dialogues between Sati and Shiva form the basis of much of the sacred lore found in Hindu philosophy. Thus Shiva and Sati, who are both intrinsically nothing but the supreme Brahman, who are all-knowing and eternal, carried on their dialogue in the Himalayas in order to help human beings rise out of the ocean of *samsara* (the wheel of human existence).

When Shiva was immersed in *samadhi*, Sati would sometimes wander off by herself. At these times she would feel a weight of grief pressing on her breast, for she knew that her father Daksha hated Shiva. She remembered the great *yajna* that the *rishis* had once conducted at Prayaga (the confluence of the three sacred rivers of the Indian subcontinent: the Ganga, Yamuna, and Saraswati). She had gone there with her lord, and all those assembled had gotten up from their seats to pay homage to Mahadeva. When Daksha arrived with his entourage, everyone except Shiva rose from their seats to honor him. Daksha's face became dark with rage when he noticed this lack of humility on the part of his son-in-law. He broke out into a host of invectives against Shiva.

"How is it that when the rest of the world honors me, this fellow alone refuses to pay me homage? His monkey eyes are not fit to meet the doelike eyes of my lovely daughter. By giving her to him, I have given the fragrant flowers of the Veda into the hands of an unclean outcast! In the future he shall not be given a place in any of the *yajnas* conducted by anyone!"

Sati would have jumped up immediately to vindicate her husband, but Shiva restrained her with a touch.

"My dearest," he said, "this is not the time and place for you to denounce your father. Don't you know that I myself am the sacrifice, the sacrificial rite, and the very self of the sacrifice? Who is this Daksha? Who are you? Who are all these people? In reality I am all. Knowing this, you should not grieve. Daksha has done this out of pride, for which he will be forced to pay a heavy price. But you are my wife and should be free from anger!"

So Sati had held her tongue, but often as she wandered alone on the mountain slopes she felt a great sadness. She felt sure that some dire incident was approaching. She knew that her husband did not reciprocate Daksha's hatred, for he had no aversion to anything in the world, but still the nameless sorrow gnawed at her.

One day as she was wandering on the mountainside she noticed many of her sisters traveling in their aerial vehicles up in the sky, accompanied by their husbands. Many other celestial beings were going the same way. She called to them to find out where they were proceeding.

They said, "Don't you know that our father is conducting a grand *yajna* to which everyone has been invited? It is going to be the greatest show the world has ever known. I'm sure you will be invited, and we will meet you there."

Sati ran to Shiva and asked him whether they had received an invitation. Shiva replied, "I thought you knew that your father hates me. He is conducting this *yajna* (fire sacrifice) with the express purpose of humiliating me and will certainly not invite us."

Sati looked crestfallen and said, "Of course you cannot go to a place where you have not been invited, but I am his daughter. Children can go to their father's house without invitation. Moreover, I long to see my mother and sisters and talk to people other than Nandi and the goblins, so will you permit me to go?"

"I cannot stop you from going where you please," said Shiva, "but remember that no good will come of it. In fact, you may face dire consequences if you go. You will be dishonored and forced to listen to your father's insults!"

But Sati was adamant. She had made up her mind and nothing could deter her. With great sadness Shiva watched her depart. He sent Nandi as her vehicle and all his *ganas* (Shiva's attendants, who are a motley crew of goblins and spirits) to protect her if necessary. She wore pomegranate flowers in her hair. Her pet parrot sat on the bull beside her. The white umbrella of royalty was held above her head, and pennants and banners waved merrily beside her. Trumpets and conches blared forth as she set out. Shiva watched her sadly, for he knew that he would never see her in this form again.

Sati came from the realms of established religion, the order of *dharma*. She married into the order of asceticism, thus combining the two conflicting worlds. Her role was to act as the mediator between these two opposing poles, both of which are basic to the Hindu tradition. Her final sacrifice of herself forced Shiva to look favorably on the sacrificial cult that is meant to maintain and nourish creation and from which he had so far kept aloof.

> *How has He through the thickets of the world,*
> *Pursued me like a lion in the night,*
> *And come upon me suddenly in the way,*
> *And seized me with His glorious golden leap.*
> *Unsatisfied He yearned for me through time,*
> *Sometimes with wrath and sometimes with*
>   *sweet peace,*
> *Desiring me since first the world began.*
> *He rose like a wild wave out of the floods,*
> *And dragged me helpless into seas of bliss.*

—*SAVITRI* BY SRI AUROBINDO

Thus ends the fourteenth chapter of *Shakti*, known as "Sati," which describes the advent of the goddess as Sati, daughter of the patriarch Daksha.

Aum Aim Hreem Kleem

Aum Shivaayai Namaha!

15

Dakshayini

Ya Devi sarvabhuteshu, smriti rupena samsthita,
Namasthasyai, namasthasyai, namasthasyai namo
namaha!

O Goddess who resides in all creatures in the form of
memory,
Hail to thee, hail to thee, all hail to thee!

When she arrived at her ancestral home, Sati hardly recognized it, for
it was spectacularly decorated and abounded with wondrous sights.
She descended from the bull Nandi and went inside alone. The *ganas*
waited outside in trepidation. They knew that something momentous
was about to happen. As Sati entered the sacrificial hall, those gathered
there froze and none dared to look at her face, for fear of Daksha. Only
her mother and sisters flocked to welcome her, but she waved them
aside. Her father alone was totally unaware of her entrance, for he was
immersed in his rituals. She instantly noted that offerings had been
made for all the gods except Shiva. His place was deliberately empty
and bare. With measured steps she walked toward the center of the
yajnashala (hall of the *yajna*), where her father was seated beside the
blazing fire, offering ghee and various other herbs into the pit, mutter-

ing incantations all the while. Everyone watched with bated breath as Sati approached.

Sati's complexion, which was normally quite dark, became even darker. Her long, black tresses, which had been knotted up, shook loose and swung like a black cloak around her. Her lotus eyes were red with anger and blazed like hot coals, and as she looked at her father, sparks of red light flew out. Daksha turned and saw her and visibly paled beneath her scorching gaze. It was the first time that Daksha had broken off his mutterings in the middle of a ritual.

Sati looked at him with scorn and said,

O Father! Your end is near. You are trying to perform a sacrifice without inviting the one who is the very soul of all sacrifices. Shiva is the essence of fullness, and you have excluded him from your *yajna*. You think the world revolves around your rites. The flowers of your ritual are but rain that falls from the feet of Shiva. You have insulted him—the great lord, Mahadeva, without whose blessings no sacrifice can be complete. My lord warned me of what I would find here and I disregarded him. How can I return to him? I can no longer bear to have my beloved call me Dakshayini (daughter of Daksha). This body that was born from your seed is hateful to me. I can no longer inhabit it. Your daughter shall be the supreme human sacrifice for your great *yajna*. Here and now I shall abandon this body that sprang from your loins.

So saying, Sati turned toward the north and fixed her mind on her lord. She covered herself with her upper garment and went into a *yogic* trance.* She raised her *kundalini* from the *muladhara chakra* at the bottom of her spine up to the *sahasrara chakra* on the crown of her head. Her spirit disappeared through the orifice at the crown of her head,

---

*In India it is normal for people to cover their heads with their upper garments or shawls when they sit for meditation. This is to keep the vibrations that arise through meditation within themselves.

leaving the empty, calcified shell of her body standing like a translucent statue. Everyone gazed in terror at what remained of Sati's body.

The *ganas* flew back to Shiva and reported to him the wretched story. Shiva jumped up from the rock on which he had been sitting, plucked off one of his braids, and dashed it against the rock. From it sprang the gigantic figure known as Virabhadra. He had the same features, embellishments, and dress as Rudra, the destroyer. He had hundreds of feet and arms, brandishing a multitude of weapons. He was decked with snakes, tiger skins, and flower garlands. Shiva commanded him to proceed to Daksha's palace and destroy the entire hall of sacrifice. Virabhadra set out, followed by Kaali and a host of goblins and spirits.

Far away in Daksha's *yajnashala* there was total silence and gloom. Into this silence crept a noise, which grew and grew like the awesome approach of a tornado. It approached inexorably from the north. Virabhadra's arrival was heralded by a dust storm that filled every nook and crevice in the hall. Then out of the shadows came his mountainous figure with flailing arms and weapons, indiscriminately destroying every single thing in the hall. Those who could flee ran for their lives; others had their limbs torn from them and still others were brutally trampled upon. The once beautiful *yajnashala* had become a battlefield soaked with blood and scattered with limbs. The *ganas* desecrated the entire place, urinating in the hollows in which fires glowed and splattering blood on the offerings. Virabhadra, looking around for the master of the sacrifice, at last spied Daksha huddled in terror near the altar. One of Virabhadra's hands gripped him by the neck and hauled him off to the pit where the animal sacrifice was normally done. Virabhadra cut off Daksha's head and threw it contemptuously into the fire as the final offering: the head of the master of the sacrifice.

Having done their worst, Virabhadra and the host returned to their lord. In the meantime Brahma and Vishnu had gone to Kailasa and begged Shiva to withdraw Virabhadra and allow Daksha to complete the sacrifice for the well-being of the world. Shiva agreed, but since Daksha's body now had no head, he told them to fix the head of a goat on him.

Though he had forgiven Daksha, Shiva was filled with agony at the death of his beloved Sati. Picking up her lifeless corpse, he wandered over the world, holding her aloft. His *ganas* followed him silently, tears rolling down their cheeks, not knowing how to console their grief-stricken lord. He wandered on, repeating the steps of the *thandava,* the dance that precedes creation and destruction. The whole of creation was filled with grief, and the gods begged Vishnu to do something before the whole world drowned in Shiva's sorrow. Vishnu took his discus and cut off pieces of Sati's body, limb by limb. At last, when the whole body had been cut apart, Shiva realized that there was nothing more in his arms. He retired to his mountain fastness and went into deep *samadhi* and refused to meet anyone.

Those places where Sati's limbs had fallen came to be known as Shakti Peethas, where the power of Maha Devi is most keenly felt. One hundred and eight in number, they are found all over India and even today attract devotees from all over the country. Shiva is always present in the Shakti Peethas, so these places are considered doubly holy. Sati's *yoni* (vulva) fell in the place called Kamarupa or Kamakhya in the state of Assam. It is said that Shiva assumed the form of the *lingam* (penis) and plunged himself into her, and there the two remain conjoined eternally. There is a saying in Sanskrit that the penis will always ejaculate automatically when placed in a vagina. But this is not true of Shiva. He has completely obliterated lust from his consciousness. His *lingam* always resides in Sati's *yoni,* and yet he never loses his semen. The same story is repeated with Parvati, when she and Shiva embrace each other for eons with no apparent display of lust. This is why Shiva is known as the perfect *yogi.* Esoterically, the *yoni* stands for all womankind and the *lingam* for all mankind, and this story is meant to show that men and women will continue to attract each other eternally.

Sati's eyes are said to have fallen in the holy spot of Varanasi, and here she is known as Vishalakshi (the wide-eyed one). Her navel is said to have fallen in Kanchi, a famous Shakti Peetha, and here she is known as Kamakshi (the one with love-filled eyes). She is known as Kumari in

Haridwar, as Rukmani in Dwaraka, and as Radha in Vrindavana. She is Sita in Chitrakuta and Vindhya Vaasini in the Vindhya mountains. These places are said to be her favorite abodes. In the form of truth she is present in the hearts of all creatures all the time.

Even in death Sati succeeded in her attempt to bring Shiva from ascetic isolation to creative participation: he dwells forever in the form of the *lingam* embedded in her *yoni*. She performed the same feat when her body was cut to pieces and fell to the earth. By following her, Shiva was literally forced to return to the type of life that he had hitherto shunned. Previously he had dwelt in the mountains and was totally immersed in *tapas,* indifferent to creation. But Sati succeeded in involving the great ascetic god in the world of creation by capturing him in her *yoni* and forcing him to accept a creative role. Thus, even though Shiva keeps performing his asceticism in his mountain retreat, he continues to be accessible to the world in the form of the *lingam.* This theme is fully developed in the story of Parvati.

> *A spirit within looks into the Eternal's eyes.*
> *It hears the words to which our hearts were deaf,*
> *It sees through the blaze in which our eyes grew blind.*
> *It drinks from the naked breasts of Truth,*
> *It learns the secrets of eternity.*

—*SAVITRI* BY SRI AUROBINDO

Thus ends the fifteenth chapter of *Shakti,* known as "Dakshayini," which describes the sacrifice of Daksha.

Aum Aim Hreem Kleem

ॐ

Aum Yoginyai Namaha!

16

Parvati

> *Ya Devi sarvabhuteshu, vritthi rupena samsthita,*
> *Namasthasyai, namasthasyai, namasthasyai namo*
> *namaha!*
>
> O Goddess who resides in all creatures in the form of
> activity,
> Hail to thee, hail to thee, all hail to thee!

One of Sati's sisters was called Swadha, and she had been given in marriage to the *pitris* or the *manes*. (The *manes* are ancestors who occupy a world of their own. It is normal in India to offer oblations to them at certain specific periods. The oblation is offered with the word *swadha*.) She had three daughters, called Mena, Dhanya, and Kalavati. Once, in their youth, the sisters had gone to Vaikunta to receive the blessings of Lord Vishnu. They had failed to show respect to the four boy sages known as Sanat Kumaras, who happened to be visiting Vishnu at the same time. As punishment for their disrespect, the sages had cursed them with the fate of being born on Earth as mortals. The sisters felt very sad and begged the sages to retract their words. The Sanat Kumaras told them that the curse of a sage was always for the good of the world; it always fulfilled the inscrutable purpose of the lord. They comforted Mena by telling her that she would become the wife of Himavan, the king of the Himalayas, and that Maha Devi herself would be born as her daughter and would be known as Parvati. Dhanya would become the wife of the great sage-king of Videha known as Janaka, and Lakshmi would be born as her daughter and would be called Sita; this Sita would become the wife of Vishnu in his incarnation as Rama, prince of the land of Kosala. The third sister, Kalavati, would be born into a cowherd family and would be married to their chieftain, Vrishabhanu. The goddess Parashakti would be born as her daughter Radha and would become the beloved of Krishna.

The sisters were very happy when they heard this, and they thanked the sages for their curse that would prove a blessing not only to them but also to the whole of humanity.

After the death of Sati, Shiva had become a permanent recluse. He wandered to those holy sites where the different parts of Sati's body had fallen, immersed in meditation on that supreme Parashakti who had embodied herself in human form as Sati and spent some years with him. How could he forget? Because of his intense *tapas* the rivers dried up and the earth lost its prosperity. The hearts of all beings lost the power to love. All creatures became immersed in an ocean of sorrow from which there seemed to be no reprieve. Disease and famine stalked the world.

The only one who prospered was a demon called Taraka, whose story we first encountered in chapter 7. As described there, he had received from Brahma the boon that he could not be killed by anyone but the son of Shiva. Since he knew Shiva to be a confirmed ascetic, he felt secure in committing atrocities on gods and humans alike. He had all the three worlds under his control and declared himself to be Indra, king of gods. Indra himself ran in despair to Brahma, even though he knew Brahma to be the cause of all their troubles since he insisted on giving boons indiscriminately to fiends like Taraka. Where could they find a woman who was capable of luring a *yogi* like Shiva into marriage? They trouped off to Vishnu and begged him to help them in their impossible task. Vishnu told them that their only hope lay in enticing Lord Shiva to marry and get a son, since only such a person could kill Taraka.

Parashakti, the Divine Mother, was the only fitting bride for Shiva, so they prayed to her and begged her to incarnate herself as the daughter of Himavan. At the end of their great *tapas* the goddess appeared. "O *devas!*" she said. "I know your desire and my *shakti* will incarnate as Parvati, in the house of Himavan. She will become the wife of Shiva and will beget a son who will destroy the demon known as Taraka."

The gods were very happy to hear this and departed. Himavan, however, stayed back and begged the goddess to give him true knowledge. The advice she gave him is known as the Devi Gita, as described in chapter 1.

Along the northern boundaries of India stand the magnificent mountains known as the Himalayas (abode of snow). They are some of the highest peaks in the world. This was the place loved by Lord Shiva. It is known as the land of the gods, for sages from time immemorial have performed austerities there and the place is saturated with spirituality. The intense *tapas* practiced in these regions have soaked into the very rocks so that the heat of austerity shimmers in the air. Himavan was the king of these mountains. His wife was called Mena. This was the fortunate couple meant to be the parents of Parvati (she who dwells in the mountains), the incarnation of the Divine Mother. Though her parents had many heroic sons, their fond gaze always followed the antics of their beloved daughter.

Once the sage Narada visited the palace of Himavan and foretold the future prospects of the child: "The palms of your daughter, O Himavan, are filled with auspicious signs. She will heighten the glory of her parents and delight her husband, but her husband will be a naked *yogi*. He will have neither mother nor father and will be indifferent to honor and dishonor. His manners and mode of dressing will appear inauspicious."

Mena and Himavan were greatly distressed to hear this, but Parvati smiled her secret smile, for she knew that the description tallied with the portrait of Shiva, which she had imprinted in her heart from birth.

Seeing the distress of the parents, Narada comforted them: "O Lord of the mountains, don't be unhappy. Lord Shiva will be her bridegroom. In him there is neither good nor bad, neither auspiciousness nor inauspiciousness. He is *nirguna* (beyond qualities). Let her propitiate him with austerities and he will definitely agree to wed her. Love such as is found between them will not be found anywhere in the world. She will become part of him and he will take the name Ardhanareeswara, meaning half male and half female."

Himavan had doubts. "O celestial sage, I have heard it said that after the death of the daughter of Daksha, Shiva has sworn never to marry again and is always in *samadhi*. How will he agree to marry Parvati?"

Narada, the omniscient sage, replied smilingly, "Have no fear, O Himavan! This daughter of yours was formerly the daughter of Daksha called Sati. There is no doubt that she will become the wife of Shiva. Now she resides on your lap, but her permanent place will be the lap of Shiva!"

The main theme in the story of Parvati is similar to that of the story of Sati. Shiva represents the ideal of asceticism and Parvati the ideal of the householder. These two typify the eternal tension in Hindu philosophy. One path insists that the world is *maya* and should be shunned, and the other asserts that the world is real and leading an ideal householder's life can also lead to the goal of liberation from mortal coils. Parvati's mission was to lure Shiva into a world of marriage, sex, and children—to lead him away from asceticism, *yoga,* and solitude. Shiva had no family, no lineage, and no interest in progeny. He lived beyond the pale of established society, outside the recognized law of *dharma*. Parvati came from a noble family and longed for marriage, children, and a home. Shiva is the destructive fire that burns up the juices of life, and Parvati the flowing sap that promotes life.

The famous fourteenth-century saint of Tamilnadu, Manik-kavachakar, calls Shiva the madman and Parvati the goddess who tames this unpredictable *yogi* and makes him behave in a civilized manner.

Parvati's mother, Mena, was not too happy about Narada's predictions and did not want her lovely daughter to marry a madman, but she was persuaded by her husband to allow Parvati to go to the mountains to perform austerities in order to attract the ascetic.

Just at this time it is said that Shiva himself came to the territory of Himavan in order to do penance. Himavan hastened to welcome him and asked him how he could serve him. Shiva replied that the only service he could do for him was to leave him alone. Himavan took some fruits and offerings and went to wait upon Shiva, accompanied by Parvati. He begged Shiva to accept the services of his daughter, who was anxious to provide him with all his needs.

Shiva took one look at Parvati, who was in the first flush of youth, beautiful beyond words, and quickly averted his eyes. Very sternly he told Himavan, "A woman is a phase of illusion. What use would I have for a young woman as beautiful as your daughter? Please don't send her here in the future."

Himavan was struck dumb and didn't know what to say, but Parvati was undeterred in her determination to woo him and spoke boldly. "O Lord!" she said. "Have you considered that all activity comes under the sway of Prakriti? Even *tapas* can be done only with the consent of Prakriti."

Shiva replied, "I am destroying the *gunas* of Prakriti with my penance. In reality I am *nirguna* (without attributes)."

Parvati spoke up again, emboldened to make a bid for her love: "Don't you know that I myself am Prakriti as you, O Lord, are Purusha? Without me, you will be attributeless no doubt, but you will also be actionless and incomprehensible."

Shiva laughed and said, "O Parvati! I see that you are a champion of the Samkhya system of philosophy but seem to know little of Vedanta. Know me to be the supreme Brahman, beyond *maya* and beyond Prakriti, comprehensible only through spiritual insight."*

Quick as a thought Parvati countered, "If, as you say, you cannot be affected by Prakriti, why should you fear me? Why can't I serve you? Surely I cannot pose a threat to one like you?"

Shiva was delighted with her quick wit and determination and agreed to let her serve him.

Parvati was elated by her success. Every day she went to Shiva with all the prescribed materials for *puja* (ritual), washed his feet with holy water, and made all offerings to him. She sang and danced for him and cleaned the ground around him with her own hands. Many years elapsed like this, with the lord in deep *samadhi*, totally oblivious to what happened around him. Parvati continued to serve him day after day, unperturbed by his indifference.

But the gods were getting worried. Taraka's harassment went on unabated and Shiva showed no signs of responding to Parvati's lures. Indra decided to employ Kama, the god of love, to help them in their mission.

"I can overthrow both gods and demons with a single arrow from my bow," boasted Kama, "so why not Lord Shiva?"

Kama's five arrows were flowers and his bow looked as if it were made out of a row of bees, for spring followed him wherever he went and the inebriated bees were drunk with the nectar of the flowers. As described in chapter 7, he proceeded to the territory of Himavan accompanied by his soul mate, Rati, to the place where Shiva was doing *tapas*. Kama and Rati, desire and pleasure, always went together. They were followed by spring with her full retinue of perfumed breezes and running brooks. Spring danced like a breath of fresh air into the wintry surroundings where Lord Shiva sat in motionless contemplation. Everything she touched or glanced at turned into beauty. Ice flowed into gurgling brooks and bare boughs became loaded with fragrant flowers and buds. Spring even crept into the

---

*The Samkhya system of philosophy postulates two realities—Purusha and Prakriti— whereas Vedanta postulates only one reality—the Brahman. Prakriti is only a derivative from the undifferentiated unity of the Brahman and has no existence of its own.

hermitages of the *rishis,* who began to feel an indescribable longing for all that they had forsaken.

Kama crouched behind a thicket and watched, fascinated, as Parvati came forward to perform her daily worship of the lord. As she placed flowers at his feet, Spring sent a little breeze that lifted her shawl and exposed her enticing breasts, covered only with a scanty bit of cloth. Just then, as luck would have it, Shiva opened his eyes and saw Parvati in the full beauty of her budding youth. Her complexion was that of a blue lotus; her maturing breasts ended in a slender waist that could be spanned by his two palms. Her black, curly locks tumbled about her shoulders as she bent forward. Kama, who was waiting for just such an opportune moment, shot one of his flower arrows straight at Shiva's chest with unerring accuracy. Usually if Shiva happened to open his eyes, he would close them again without any change in his demeanor. But at that moment, thanks to Kama's intervention, he could not tear his gaze away from Parvati's delectable form. He gazed deep into her eyes and thought to himself, "She is indeed a storehouse of perfection. If I get so much pleasure just from looking at her, how much would I get by embracing her?"

Thinking thus, he was just stretching out his hands to touch her when Kama shot a second arrow. At the twang of the bowstring, Shiva turned his head and saw Kama standing proudly with Rati beside him. The full blast of Shiva's wrath swept over Kama like a fiery flame. Mentally he invoked the help of Indra and the other gods who were lurking in the bushes to see the show. Before they could come to his aid, Shiva opened his third eye. A great flame of fire shot up into the sky like a fiery meteor. It dropped to the earth and covered the ground, engulfing the trembling Kama and reducing him into a heap of ashes that eddied around with the dust. Rati scrambled on the ground trying desperately to save what she could of her lover's remains.

Rati's loud sobs shook Parvati out of her petrified state. She ran home sobbing to the arms of her mother, followed by her terrified maids, who described the whole ghastly scene to her parents.

The gods were frightened out of their wits and did not know how to comfort the sorrow-stricken Rati. They begged Shiva to restore Kama to life.

"What have you done?" cried Rati in agony. "By killing Kama, you have condemned all creatures to live a life devoid of desire. Life will come to a standstill and collapse if desire is destroyed. The bull will forsake the cow and the horse the mare, the bees the flowers, and man his wife. Desire is not just the cause of suffering but the basis of all joy. What is life without love? It is mere existence, like a flower without perfume. Life has its price, which is suffering, but it also has its reward, which is joy, and it cannot exist without Kama."

Shiva's anger was always short-lived, and he could not bear the sight of Rati's suffering. He said, "I destroyed Kama's body but not his spirit. He will live on as Ananga, the bodiless one, and will be reborn as Pradyumna, the son of Krishna, and you, O Rati, will be joined with him once again as his wife."

So saying, Shiva lapsed into silence, closed his eyes, and went into deep *samadhi*.

(Chapter 7 continues the story of Kama, describing the creation of the demon Bhanda from Kama's ashes and the incarnation of the goddess Lalitha to defeat him.)

> *And now his burning breath assailed the soil,*
> *The tiger heats prowled through the fainting earth.*
> *All was licked up as if by a lolling tongue,*
> *The Spring winds failed; the sky was set like bronze.*
>
> —*SAVITRI* BY SRI AUROBINDO

Thus ends the sixteenth chapter of *Shakti*, known as "Parvati," which describes the birth of Parvati and the death of Kama.

Aum Aim Hreem Kleem

ॐ

Aum Mahamayayai Namaha!

17

Aparna

Ya Devi sarvabhuteshu, daya rupena samsthita,
Namasthasyai, namasthasyai, namasthasyai namo
namaha!

O Goddess who resides in all creatures in the form of
compassion,
Hail to thee, hail to thee, all hail to thee!

Parvati returned home in a highly agitated frame of mind. "What is
the use of physical beauty if it can't get me the one thing I most desire?
Shiva is a true *yogi*. Physical charms have no fascination for him. What
he admires most is asceticism, so that is what I should practice if I want
to marry him."

She decided to go to the forest and practice intense austerities. At
that time the sage Narada came to the palace and spoke privately to
Parvati. He gave her the famous five-syllabled *mantra* of Shiva and told
her that if she concentrated totally on that, she would surely win him
over.

Parvati went to her parents to get their consent. Himavan was agree-
able, but her mother could not bear to see her go. "Why don't you meditate
in the house?" she asked. "All the facilities are here, and I'll see to it that

you are left alone. *U-ma.*" *U-ma* means "don't go"; thus Uma came to be another of Parvati's names.

But Parvati was adamant. Discarding her fineries and ornaments, she clad herself in the bark of a tree tied at the waist with a girdle of grass. She told her maids not to accompany her and went straight to the place where she had last seen Shiva after Kama had been burnt down. It was bare and empty; the leaves had withered, and the season was no longer spring. Parvati could have wept for her lord, but she controlled herself and took her seat in the same place where Shiva had sat. She made a *lingam* out of mud in front of her and started her penance. Still and steady as a rock, she kept her mind fixed on the beloved form of her lord and kept repeating the *mantra* Narada had given her.

In the summer Parvati sat in the midst of five fires, in the monsoons she sat in the rain and did not seek shelter, and in winter she sat in the snow, inured to the icy winds that howled around her. For the first year she subsisted on fruits alone, and in the next year on leaves, thus becoming known by the name Aparna (one who subsists on leaves). Her mind was a canvas on which was painted the picture of Shiva alone. She had neither father nor mother, indeed no other life except this one. She felt as if she had been meditating all her life. Her parents came to try to persuade her to return to them, but she didn't even notice them. The heat created by her *tapas* was so great that the ground under Indra's feet began to burn. He ran to Brahma to find out the reason for this phenomenon. Brahma was equally perplexed, and they went together to Lord Vishnu, who told them the reason for the sudden rise of heat in the world. It was the power of Parvati's *tapas,* and she had sworn not to stop her austerities until Shiva became her husband. So they went to Shiva and eulogized him and begged him to save them from the threat of Taraka and the heat that was being produced by Parvati's penance. They told him that only he could save them from both dangers.

The great *yogi* looked at them with a glimmer of a smile in his eyes. He said, "I thought you'd be happy that Kama is out of the way and you can do your meditations without being troubled by his arrows. If I marry Parvati, Kama will have to be revived and you will be unable to perform penance!"

Vishnu now spoke: "Your beloved wife Sati has been reborn as Parvati, the daughter of the mountains, and she is performing intense *tapas* to procure you as her husband. Only a son born of your loins is capable of killing the demon Taraka. So for the good of the world, please accept her as your wife."

Shiva mused to himself, "A wife is ruinous to the life of a *yogi*. Even the Vedas say that, but then I have always been a rule to myself. Nothing can fetter me, not even a wife. Moreover, I'm always anxious to please my devotees. How can I resist her plea when she's undergoing such tortures for my sake? She has proved that she can be a *tapasvini* (female who practices austerities), fit to be the wife of a *tapasvin* (male who practices austerities) like me."

He told the seven sages* to go to the place where Parvati was performing austerities and test her resolve. Seeing her emaciated form shining with brilliance, they bowed to her and begged her to give up her *tapas*. Shiva was a confirmed *yogi*, they said, and had declared that he would never marry.

"In that case I shall die unwed," said Parvati, with no change in her composure. "As you know, I am the daughter of the mountain and therefore immovable. Don't waste your time on me. It's better for you to go back to your contemplations. The sun may rise in the west, fire may refuse to heat, but my words will never be false. I shall continue my penance until he comes to me or I shall give up my body in this very place."

---

*The seven *rishis*, or sages, are the mind-born sons of Brahma and they are the custodians of the spiritual heritage of the Sanatana Dharma. All Brahmins down to the present day claim to have been born from their lineage. They have created an unbroken line lasting for thousands of years. To this day, a Brahmin will claim that he belongs to the Atri *gotra* or the Bhrigu *gotra*, etc. *Gotra* means "lineage." Atri and Bhrigu are two of the sages. Different names are given to the seven sages in different *manvantaras*. But in all lists you find Atri, Angiras, Vasishta, Bhrigu, and Kashyapa. Pulastya, Pulaha, Kratu, Marichi, and Agastya are added in certain lists.

The sages were delighted with her determination and reported the matter to Shiva. Now Shiva himself decided to test her. He appeared before her in the guise of a very old sage in ascetic's garb and told her to desist from her *tapas,* since Shiva would never marry her. Parvati merely smiled and said, "In which case I shall immolate myself in the fire that I have kept ready."

Without speaking another word she lit the pyre and jumped into it, but the fire became cool and could not burn her. The old man stopped her from making another fire and listed all of Shiva's bad qualities to her.

Parvati was furious and cried out, "Why have you come here to poison my mind with your vile accusations against my lord? Whatever Shiva is or is not, I love him and will have none other as my husband."

She turned away in disgust and was on the point of running away when Shiva assumed his real form and caught her by the hand.

"Why are you running away from me?" he teased. "You have won me by your extreme austerities, and I am your ardent slave. Come with me to my abode in the Himalayas."

But Parvati could not be persuaded so easily. "My lord," she said, "I eloped with you once in my incarnation as Daksha's daughter, and you know what happened. This time I want a proper marriage with all due rites and with the full consent of my parents. So you will have to go to them and ask for my hand if you want to marry me."

"My sweet Parvati," said Shiva, "this entire world in one of illusion. I stand above all prophecies and planets. But if it's your wish to perform the marriage rites by propitiating all the planets, so be it. I can refuse you nothing. I shall approach your father and ask for your hand in the proper manner."

Parvati returned home jubilantly and was welcomed back with great love. But as one might expect, Shiva could not conform to rules. He went to Himavan's court in the guise of a mendicant dancer and delighted the court with his skill. Mena offered him money and jewels, which he refused.

"What is it you want then?" she asked.

"I want your daughter," he replied.

Mena was furious and ordered that he should be chased out of the court. Parvati alone had been shown his true form, and she begged him mentally to take on a more conventional appearance. So the next time he came, Shiva took the guise of a noble Brahmin, a devotee of Vishnu with crystal beads in his hand and a *saligrama* (a stone with the image of Vishnu on it) around his neck. The Brahmin strongly advised Himavan against giving his daughter to Shiva. He then left the way he had come, muttering on his beads. Parvati was desperate and prayed to him to stop playing these tricks.

So Shiva commanded the seven sages once again to go to Himavan and request the hand of his daughter. Overjoyed to do his bidding, they went to Himavan and said, "Shiva is the father of the universe, and Parvati its the mother. It behooves you to give your daughter to him alone. By this gift your life will be fulfilled."

Himavan was very happy to hear this, but Mena was stubborn in her refusal to give her tender daughter to a madman, as Shiva appeared to be. The gods then sent Arundhati, the wife of the sage Vasishta, who was noted for her wisdom and chastity, to persuade Mena to agree to the union of her daughter with Shiva. Arundhati told her, "Parvati is the great cosmic intellect, the mother of the universe. You will gain honor and glory only if you give her in marriage to Shiva."

Hearing this, Mena was pacified and agreed to the betrothal. Preparations were immediately started for the consummation of the joyful event.

Himavan was determined that this should be the grandest occasion ever held in the world. Everyone who was anyone was invited—the gods, the sages, the rivers, the mountains, and the *gandharvas* (celestial musicians), *apsaras* (celestial dancers), and all other celestial beings. Different mansions were made for the gods, with the best one reserved for the bridegroom. On the auspicious day, all the gods went to Kailasa to accompany Shiva. They begged him to dress as befitting a bridegroom. He smiled his secret smile and complied with their request.

The crescent moon took the place of a crown, his third eye became a beautiful jewel adorning his forehead, and the serpents twined around his ears turned into earrings and the ones around his neck into necklaces and garlands. The ashes that were smeared on his body turned into sandal paste and the elephant hide into a silk garment. The *ganas* from all over the world flew in to accompany the bridegroom's party. Nothing could dissuade them from coming.

Thus the members of the wedding party set out amidst the blare of trumpets, beating of drums, and blowing of conches. When they reached the outskirts of the mountain city, Himavan came out with a large retinue to meet them. He was enchanted to see the divine form of Shiva totally contrary to what he had been expecting. The lord had taken on the form of Sundaramurti, the handsome one. He was seated on the white bull of crystal purity and beauty, the very symbol of *dharma*.

As can be imagined, Mena was in a fever of impatience to see the man for whom her daughter had been prepared to forsake everything she held dear and spend so much time doing intense austerities. She went to the balcony and looked down on the bridegroom's party, which was just arriving. Shiva knew of her qualms and decided to play one of his usual pranks. Mena was delighted to see the splendid procession. First came the *gandharvas,* the celestial musicians noted for their sartorial elegance. Heavenly nymphs waving banners of brilliant hues accompanied them. Mena thought that one of them might be Shiva but was told that they were merely his attendants. How striking he must be, she thought, if his attendants were so handsome. Then came the gods Agni, Yama, and Indra, all looking equally fantastic. When Vishnu arrived on the scene, Mena nearly fainted. She had never seen such a handsome personality before and was sure that this was Shiva, but again she was disappointed. Next came Shiva himself, accompanied by the *ganas.*

"Here is your daughter's bridegroom," someone whispered in her ears. Mena stared aghast at the motley crew of *ganas* that now appeared. The spirits, ghosts, and goblins came first. Some of them were in the form of violent gusts of wind, making hissing sounds; some had crooked faces and deformed bodies; some were lame and some blind; some hobbled on one leg and others carried staffs and tridents and had distorted faces.

Were these creatures Shiva's escorts? Mena could hardly believe it.

"There is Shiva! There is the bridegroom," the wedding guests shouted.

On seeing him, Mena trembled and nearly fainted. He had five faces and three eyes. His hair was matted and had the crescent moon on it. His body was smeared in the ashes of annihilated desire, and he had ten hands, each brandishing a gory weapon. His upper garment was an elephant's hide, and lower a tiger's skin. He had a wild look in his eyes and appeared to have been drinking. In fact, the whole party seemed to be intoxicated, its members rolling about in a drunken orgy and singing obscene songs. They flung skulls and bones up into the air instead of flowers.

Mena gazed at this horrifying scene for a few seconds and then mercifully fainted. As soon as she recovered she wept and cried and swore that she would certainly not give her charming daughter to such an unkempt and uncivilized creature whose sole attendants seemed to be a motley crew of fiends.

"What shall I do?" she moaned. "My life is utterly doomed and so is my daughter's. Where are those sages who have cheated us? I shall pluck out their beards with my own hands." Turning to her daughter, she cried, "Is this the fruit of your penance? Surely your intellect must be deranged. Setting aside cooked rice, are you bent on eating the husk?* O! What have I done to deserve such a fate?" So saying, the poor lady beat her breasts and wept uncontrollably, bewailing her lot.

Narada and the other sages came to reason with her, but Mena would not listen. Her husband came and told her that this was all the

---

*When she uses this idiom, Mena asks Parvati why she prefers to marry a strange person like Shiva when she could have married any of the other handsome gods.

sport of Shiva, who wanted to test her. She shut her ears. Brahma came and told her that Shiva had many forms and this was all his divine *lila*. She was unconvinced.

Parvati asked her, "O Mother! Why has this delusion overtaken you? Please give me to Lord Shiva. I have wooed him mentally, verbally, and physically for many years. I shall wed none other." Mena cried bitterly when she heard this.

At last Lord Vishnu approached her and spoke to her in sweet accents. "O Mena!" he said. "You are the beloved daughter of the *manes,* and you should be able to appreciate the greatness of Maheswara (Shiva). He is devoid of all attributes yet possesses all attributes. He is hideous as well as handsome. It is only because of your daughter's great penance that he has agreed to marry her. Consider yourself to be fortunate that he has blessed you. O wife of Himavan! Stop your tears and accept him as your son-in-law and all will be well."

Hearing these soothing words, Mena relented and said, "I will agree to this wedding only if he assumes a pleasing aspect. Otherwise, whatever any of you might say, I will not consent to this marriage."

Vishnu reported the matter to Shiva, and Parvati prayed to her lord to stop playing tricks. Shiva laughingly agreed, and when the appropriate time came for the bridegroom to enter the marriage hall, Shiva strode in. Much to Mena's surprise, his form was wondrous to behold.

He was fair and handsome and his face shone with a divine radiance. He was the personification of masculine splendor. His dark silky hair flowed to his broad shoulders. His long, lithe limbs were clad in silk, and he wore a garland of fragrant jasmine flowers. His lustrous dark eyes turned toward Mena and penetrated to the very depths of her soul. There was a glimmer of a smile on his face as he noticed Mena's discomfiture. Mena went forward with her husband and worshipped him, offering sandal paste and whole rice grains mixed with turmeric. The wives of the sages waved ghee lamps and camphor flames in front of him and escorted him to the ceremonial stage reserved for the bridal pair.

Now the wives of the sages brought Parvati forward. Her beauty entranced all those present. Her complexion was as dark and radiant as a blue lotus. Her thick black hair was plaited and covered with flowers and jewels. Necklaces covered her breast, and bangles and bracelets her arms. Her lips, which had been colored with red lac, opened slightly to reveal her pearly teeth. Her pink feet tinkled with the sound of anklets as she walked. She carried an exquisite mirror set with gems in one hand and a lotus in the other. The intoxicating perfume of sandal paste, musk, and saffron emanated from her body. On seeing this fascinating form of the mother of the universe, all the gods stood up and bowed. She looked up for a second and met Shiva's appreciative eyes and gave a small, secret smile.

Taking his daughter's hand, Himavan repeated the age-old *mantras* of the Rig Veda and then gave her hand to Lord Shiva.

Shiva grasped the lotuslike palms of Parvati and repeated the appropriate *mantras*. He then placed the auspicious red mark on Parvati's forehead. Grasping her trembling hand in his strong one, he led her thrice around the sacred fire and thus plighted their troth. Thus was the wild one tamed and made to conform to the rules of normal society.

Thinking this to be an appropriate time, Rati, the wife of Kama, came forward and begged to have her husband restored to his bodily form. Shiva smilingly agreed, and much to Rati's delight, Kama appeared before them, looking as handsome as ever.

As was the custom, Shiva stayed for four days in the mighty mansion made for the bridal couple. He, who was used to sleeping on rocks and stones and in cremation grounds, was cajoled by Parvati to lie on silken coverlets covered with flowers. At last the festivities came to an end and Shiva returned to Kailasa, accompanied by Parvati and followed by the host of *ganas*.

> *But now the destined spot and hour were close,*
> *Unknowing she had neared her nameless goal.*

For though a dress of blind and devious chance
Is laid upon the work of all-wise fate,
Our acts interpret an omniscient force,
That dwells in the compelling stuff of things,
And nothing happens in the cosmic play,
But at its time and in its foreseen place.

—*SAVITRI* BY SRI AUROBINDO

Thus ends the seventeenth chapter of *Shakti,* known as "Aparna," which describes the wedding of Shiva and Parvati.

Aum Aim Hreem Kleem

Aum Bhuvaneswaryai Namaha!

18
Gauri

Ya Devi sarvabhuteshu, matre rupena samsthita,
Namasthasyai, namasthasyai, namasthasyai namo
namaha!

O Goddess who resides in all creatures in the form of the
  mother,
Hail to thee, hail to thee, all hail to thee!

Though she had moved from the comfortable palace of her parents to
the chilly caves of the Himalayas, Parvati was in a state of bliss. She
had chosen her path; she was fully conscious of the type of person
she had married and had no regrets. Henceforth these caves would be
her boudoirs, and these snowy slopes her gardens. She had goblins in
lieu of maids, and her only friend was Nandi, the bull. The brilliant
peak of Kailasa was the place chosen by Shiva for his wife's delec-
tation. Close by was the scintillating lake Manasarovar (lake of the
mind), where celestial damsels sported with their lovers. In these icy
waters Parvati had to bathe. The austere beauty of her new residence
enthralled her. She was fully aware that she had conquered the heart
of this great *yogi* only due to her asceticism, and she had come prepared to pay the price.

163

Parvati sported with Shiva on the frosty mountain peaks and verdant slopes of the Himalayas and bathed in the icy waters of Lake Manasarovar amidst lotuses and royal swans. She was as gentle and graceful as he was wild and forceful. When he performed the dance known as *thandava*, filled with vigor and violence, she would do the steps of the *laasya*, full of grace and soft, slow movements. This was the perfect combination. If Shiva's principal function was destruction, hers was preservation and reconstruction, thus offsetting his violence. She had a calming, civilizing influence on Shiva. Under the soothing effect of her charming presence, he changed his wild, rude, and often mad behavior.

Parvati is known to be kind and considerate to all devotees, and she herself is Shiva's greatest follower. Many Shiva devotees are said to approach Parvati first in order to have access to Shiva. The great fourteenth-century Shiva *bhakta* Manikkavachakar emulated Parvati and prayed to her to give him steadfast devotion to Shiva.

The recurring theme in Hindu philosophy is that the way of the ascetic is superior to the way of the householder. These opposing principles are brought to a successful reconciliation by Parvati. Shiva is the god of excesses, both ascetic and sexual, while Parvati is the modifier. She represents the householder's ideal of married sex that is opposed to both asceticism and eroticism. Shiva yields to her persuasions and reconciles himself to a mutual interdependence of husband and wife, which is the basis of a harmonious, married life. This interdependence is shown in many images that combine the two deities into an integrated whole: as Shiva-Shakti, as Shiva portrayed as Ardhanareeswara (half male and half female), and as the *lingam* and the *yoni*.

Many comparisons are given in the Puranas to show this interdependence. Shiva is the sky and Parvati the earth; Shiva is the ocean and Parvati the shore; Shiva is the sun and Parvati the light. Parvati is all qualities, and Shiva the enjoyer of all qualities. Parvati is the embodiment of all souls, and Shiva the supreme soul itself. Parvati is all forms, and Shiva the thinker of the forms. Parvati is speech and Shiva meaning.

The Ardhanareeswara figure emphasizes that the two deities are absolutely necessary to each other and only in union can they satisfy each other and fulfill the cosmic purpose. Transcending sexual particularities, this image demonstrates that the divine is both male and female, both father and mother, aloof and active, fearful and gentle.

The representation of the *lingam* and *yoni* also points to an aspect of this interdependence. As a great *yogi*, Shiva accumulates great sexual potency that must be released in creation so that it will not be utilized for destruction. Both Sati and Parvati enabled the great *yogi* to use his accumulated potency for the good of the world. The *lingam* and the *yoni* symbolize the creative interaction between the world of the ascetic, in which sexual abstinence is compulsory, and the life of the householder, in which sex is absolutely necessary. Shiva and Parvati portray the ideal of wedded bliss. They have a deep understanding and harmony between them. In this aspect Parvati is the perfect wife who makes herself subservient to her lord and master, unlike Durga and Lalitha. Parvati and Shiva show us that opposites can unite in perfect harmony. They represent the two poles: Shiva is the figure for *moksha* or liberation and Parvati for *dharma* or righteous living in the world. Neither of them give up asceticism entirely, thus teaching the lesson that asceticism actually enhances the intensity of sexual life and keeps the householder from being obsessed with eroticism alone. Thus *dharma* and *moksha* complement and complete each other in the divine pair.

Many years passed while the great *yogi* appeared to have been tamed by Parvati's exquisite beauty and charm. She stimulated him to share with her all the accumulated wisdom he had gained from his great *tapas*. Because of her, the whole world gained this wisdom, which is contained in the *shastras* (scriptures) and Tantra (systems of worshipping the divine as Shakti) of Hindu philosophy. There was no end to Parvati's thirst for knowledge and no end to Shiva's wisdom. She was the perfect student and he was Dakshinamurti, the perfect teacher.

One day Shiva teased Parvati about her dark color. In a fit of temper she went to the forest and started *tapas* in order to change her color. Seeing her intense austerities, Brahma came to her and asked her to take another form and rid the world of the two demons Shumbha and Nishumbha, who had been reincarnated and were terrorizing the world.

Acceding to this request, the goddess Parvati shed her dark skin and became fair in color. In this form she came to be known as Gauri, the radiant one, the shining one, the fair one. Her dark outer skin took the form of Kaali, the virgin goddess, with the luster of a black rain cloud. Kaali held the conch and discus of Vishnu as well as the trident of Shiva, for she had the strength of both. Gauri told her to go with Brahma to slay the demons. She went to the Vindhya mountains, where the demons were residing, and vanquished them. As Maha Devi had foretold in her incarnation as Durga (see chapter 13), Kaali stayed on there as the goddess known as Vindhya Vaasini.

Gauri returned to Kailasa and delighted her lord in her new role as the goddess with the color of molten gold. She longed to have a child and prayed to Shiva to grant her this boon. Shiva drew her to him and the couple locked together in an embrace that lasted for eons. Excess was always Shiva's norm. He never followed the *via media* and did nothing according to accepted modes of conduct. With him life was an ever-lasting turbulence or a total renunciation. Neither of these states is suitable for a peaceful life on the earth. If Shiva practiced *tapas* and ignored the world, then life lost its fragrance and drooped and died. If he indulged in a game of pleasure with Parvati, it went on for centuries until the constant friction threatened to burn the whole world. The world was capable of absorbing only a tiny fraction of his energy. Thus the gods had decided long ago that whatever Shiva was doing, he would always have to be interrupted so that the equilibrium of the world would be restored. They were still sorely troubled by the menace of Taraka, and though they had arranged the marriage of Shiva and Parvati for the express purpose of producing a child, there was no sign of such a happy event. They decided to visit Kailasa and remind him of the reason for his marriage. They went to Vishnu and asked him to accompany them.

"Shiva might well wait another eon before producing a child," Vishnu said musingly.

The gods went to Kailasa and found the entrance to the cave guarded by the *ganas*, who had been warned to keep everyone out. After waiting for a long time they became impatient and started eulogizing Shiva and begging him to come out and grant their plea for a child who would save the world. Shiva had been on the point of giving in to Parvati's request to have a child when the gods came with their incessant demands. He loosened his hold on Parvati and went out.

The seed that he had been withholding for ages now discharged into the air, flew like a fiery meteor, and fell to the earth. The earth could not contain it and begged Agni, the god of fire, to help her. Agni took up the seed, but even he could not bear the heat, and he spat it out into the Ganga (Ganges). As the fiery seed was taken down the river it became stuck in some reeds. The six stars that make up the constellation known as the Krittikas (the Pleiades) were drawn to the flame. The seed divided itself into six parts, and each of the six Krittikas nourished one part in her womb. At last out of their collective wombs the child who was to be the savior of the world was born. The reeds rustled and six pairs of hands lifted the child above the surface of the water and caressed it. The six Krittikas gave suck to him and the divine infant's six mouths sucked their milk. Hence he got the name Shanmukha, the six-faced one. Since he was born among the reeds, he was also known as Sharavanabhava (born among the reeds known as *shara*). Since the Krittikas nurtured him, he was called Kartikeya. His actual name was Skanda, the war god, born to destroy the evil created by the demon Taraka.

The gods had been keenly watching the progress of the seed. They now came down and took the child from his six mothers, much to their dismay, and wafted him off to Kailasa. When Parvati saw the child, milk oozed from her breasts, for she knew him to be her own. She said, "You are the product of my *tapas* and my bliss. Even though you were not born from my womb, you exist because Shiva touched me." She took him on her lap and caressed him. Skanda then went to Shiva's lap and played with the snakes around his neck. The fond parents gave him the childhood name of Kumara, which simply means "son."

The selfish gods hardly gave the fond parents a chance to cuddle their child. They clamored that he should be crowned immediately and sent forth to accomplish the deed for which he had been born. Water from all the holy rivers of the land were consecrated and poured over his head to the chanting of Vedic hymns. Brahma gave him the knowledge of the Vedas and the sacred *mantras*. All the gods blessed him and gave him all types of weapons and insignia. The spear was his weapon, the peacock his vehicle, and the rooster the emblem on his flag. Shiva told the gods to take Skanda as their general and fight with Taraka. A terrific duel was fought between Taraka and Skanda, which ended with Skanda defeating the demon by driving the spear into his chest.

Parvati longed to have another son who would be her very own and listen only to her, who wouldn't be appropriated by the gods for their own selfish purposes. When she asked Shiva, he was evasive. "I am not a creator, so how can I create a child?" he asked teasingly. "You know what happened the last time I tried!" Parvati didn't say a word. They were lying side by side, and her body as well as Shiva's was drenched with perspiration.

"I am the mother of the world. I can create a child for myself," she said. She anointed her body with sandalwood oil and turmeric powder and mixed it with her sweat and that of Shiva's. She rubbed her palms hard all over her body and made soft dough out of it. She shaped the dough into the figure of a beautiful little boy and breathed life into him. The child was big and handsome, filled with strength and valor. She named him Vinayaka. She gave him clothes and ornaments and told him that he should be her bodyguard alone. She gave him a staff with which to ward off intruders.

The very next day, when she went for a bath, Parvati stationed Vinayaka outside and told him to keep away anyone who tried to enter. It so happened that the first person to come was Shiva himself. He ordered to boy to make way for him. At first Vinayaka refused politely. When Shiva tried to enter forcibly, the child dared to hit him with his staff. Shiva was amazed by the boy's audacity and sent his *ganas* to capture him, but the boy defeated the *ganas,* who returned to Shiva dejected. At this Shiva became quite angry and severed the head of the boy with his trident.

Parvati was furious when she heard this and determined to create many *shaktis* to defeat the *ganas*. Shiva placated her with great difficulty and promised to restore her son to her. He told the *ganas* to cut off the head of the first creature they saw that was sleeping with its head turned to the north. As it happened, they saw an elephant first and cut off its head and brought it to Shiva, who affixed it to the boy's neck. Parvati was delighted to see her boy come back to life, even though he now had the head of an elephant. She insisted that he should become the leader of the *ganas,* and that's how he received the names Ganesha (lord of the *ganas*) and Ganapati (master of the *ganas*). She also insisted that he should be worshipped first before any *puja* or ritual commenced. Parvati adored Ganesha and always kept him by her side. He would lie beside her with his trunk curled up and scribble on leaves with his stylus. Thanks to his mother's blessings, he is one of the most adored gods in the Hindu pantheon.

> He longed to draw her presence and power,
> Into his heart and mind and breathing frame,
> He yearned to call forever down,

Her healing touch of love and truth and joy,
Into the darkness of the suffering world,
His soul was freed and given to her alone.

—*SAVITRI* BY SRI AUROBINDO

Thus ends the eighteenth chapter of *Shakti*, known as "Gauri," which describes the birth of Skanda and Ganesha.

Aum Aim Hreem Kleem

Aum Gangayai Namaha!

19

Ganga

Adharabhuta jagatastwameka,
Mahiswarupena yata sthitasi,
Apam swarupasthitaya twayaitat,
Apyayate, krithsnam alankhyaveerye.

You have become the sole support of the world,
For you abide in the form of the earth.
By you, who exist in the form of water,
All this [universe] is filled up,
O one of inviolable valor!

Indian mythology is mixed with fact and what the modern world calls fiction. But to the Indian, the Puranas are more real than the so-called realistic fiction of the modern world. The Puranic stories were based mostly on observance of terrestrial bodies and planets and the lives of great saints and kings. Laypeople came to know much of geography and science from these stories. Some of the stories have since been proved to be based on an acute observation of scientific data that has been discovered by modern science only with the turn of the twentieth century.

Many stories are connected with the birth of the river Ganga, better known as the Ganges. One of them is connected with the great sage

171

Agastya. At one time some Brahmin ascetics were being constantly harassed by a group of demons. The Brahmins would chase the demons as far as the ocean, but the next day they would return, having had their strength renewed by being submerged in the sea. At last in desperation the Brahmins appealed to Agastya, who was renowned for his proverbial ability to digest anything. He solved their problem by the simple expedient of swallowing the entire ocean. Vishnu and the other gods were able to kill the demons that had lurked in the depths of the now dry ocean, and the sages could then carry on their fire sacrifices without impediment.

When they approached Agastya and asked him to disgorge the water that he had swallowed, he smiled and told them sweetly that he had already digested it all. So even though he had solved their particular predicament, it led to a host of other problems. Rivers ran dry and the land was barren due to lack of water. The celestials were filled with distress. At last Brahma comforted them by promising to bring down the waters of the heavenly Ganga and thus fill the ocean. This task was fulfilled by the saintly king Bhagiratha, who undertook the challenge to give liberation to his ancestors.

At one time the celestial Ganga was what we know as the Milky Way. It was a stream of souls, of subtle essences. It ran from one end of the sky to the other and then flowed to the earth. Earth and sky were the two banks of this great river of stars. Where was the point at which the river passed from the celestial to the terrestrial bank? The disparity of force between earth and heaven is so great that it would have been dangerous to go directly from one to the other. The river had to break her fall on those mountains called the Himalayas that lift the earth to the heavens. Thus the Milky Way became the Ganga and Shiva caught her as she fell. If left to herself, her waters would have flooded the earth and washed it away into space. The impact as she charged down shattered the mass of water so that it came down to earth in many small streams. Life on earth became possible only because Ganga flowed unceasingly over Shiva's head, like the water that is kept in a pot suspended above the stone *lingam*. Theirs was a perennial love, renewed at every instant by a stream that knew no end. In fact, Shiva's seed, which even Agni, the god of fire, could not contain, was kept and cooled in Ganga's womb. Here the seed took on the embryonic form that was later nourished by the Krittikas (see chapter 18). Thus Ganga was not only Shiva's consort but also the mother of the war god Kartikeya (Skanda).

The Puranas vividly describe these three stages in the evolution of the Ganga. First she was a river of stars—Akasa Ganga or the Milky Way—that fell as snow on Mount Meru on the high plateau of Pamir and on the ridges and ranges that surround it. Here she was a river of snow. As the snow melted she became a river of water, divided into the four main rivers of Asia: the Huang in China, the Oxus or Amu Dar'ya that flows from Pamir Lake to the Aral Sea; the Ob in Siberia; and the Alaknanda in India, one of the headstreams of the Ganga (Ganges) river. It is said that Ganga will forsake this planet ten thousand years after Kali Yuga has passed. When she leaves, all other holy rivers will also leave.

There are many other accounts of Ganga's origin in the Puranas. The Brahma Vaivarta Purana says that at one time Lakshmi, Saraswati, and Ganga were all consorts of Lord Vishnu. But due to some misunderstanding, they cursed each other and had to take birth on earth in various forms. Saraswati suspected that Vishnu loved Ganga more than her and spoke harshly to Ganga. Lakshmi, who tried to calm her, received the brunt of Saraswati's wrath; Saraswati cursed her to take birth on earth in the form of a river and a plant. Lakshmi did not display any anger, but Ganga was furious with Saraswati and cursed her in turn to a similar fate of becoming a river on earth. In retaliation, Saraswati promptly swore that Ganga would get the same fate and would be forced to come to the earth in the form of a river. Very soon all three repented their bad behavior and begged Vishnu to release them from each other's curses. Lord Vishnu pacified the three goddesses and told them that all this had happened only to accomplish the divine plan. He said, "Calamities are really a cause of happiness to human beings. Without sorrow no one can understand the true nature of joy."

Vishnu commanded Ganga to go down to the earth to help King Bhagiratha and eventually to help fill up the ocean that had been drunk by the sage Agastya. Part of her would take refuge in the locks of Lord Shiva, and thus she would become his consort. Vishnu further blessed her, "You will be able to release thousands of souls from their sins and give them liberation."

Ganga asked, "O Lord! But what will happen to me? Will I not be tainted with the sins of so many wicked people who are constantly shedding their impurities in me?"

The lord answered, "Fear not, O dear one! Even if one pure soul washes his feet in you, all your impurities will be washed away. Such is the glory of my devotees. You shall be the cause for the redemption of thousands of souls."

Vishnu commanded Saraswati also to accept the curse and go to the land of Bharata Varsha (India) in the form of a river. Later she would go to the abode of Lord Brahma and become his consort. Only Lakshmi was allowed to remain with Vishnu in her complete portion, for her nature was peaceful. But the curse of even a pure soul could not be gainsaid, and in the course of time she also would have to go to the earth and become the river Gantaki. Furthermore, she would become the sacred *tulasi* plant, which would be loved by Vishnu.

The Brahma Vaivarta Purana describes how the Ganga came out of Brahma's *kamandalu* (water pot). After the wedding of Shiva and Parvati, in which all the gods took part, Lord Shiva is said to have extracted the sacred essences of the earth and created a water pot. He poured all hallowed waters into this pot and consecrated it with *mantras*. Since this pot was made out of the essence of earth and water, it became the cause of creation, maintenance, and destruction.

Lord Shiva handed this pot to Brahma and said, "All *dharma* is established here. Sacrifice, enjoyment, and salvation are all to be found in this. All the sins of one who bathes or drinks or performs offerings with this sacred water will perish. O Brahma, take this *kamandalu* that I have consecrated with divine *mantras* and continue with your work of creation."

Another story of Ganga's descent is connected with the *avatara* of Lord Vishnu as Vamana or the dwarf. Vishnu had taken on this particular incarnation in order to subdue the demon king Mahabali. The demon had promised to give Vishnu, in his role as Vamana, three steps of land. But when the time came for the demon to offer the gift, Vamana took on his universal form and measured the whole earth with his first step. His second stride stretched up to the heavens, where his foot pierced a hole in the shell of Brahma's world. Brahma was amazed to see this phenomenon, but he immediately took the opportunity to wash the sacred foot of Vishnu with the water from his *kamandalu*. The water that fell from the pot was the heavenly Ganga that fell on Mount Meru, as described above. Hence Ganga is also known as Vishnupadi, or the one who has come from the feet of Vishnu.

The most popular account of Ganga's descent to the earth is given in the epic poem the Ramayana. It tells the story of Sagara, a king of the solar dynasty (Surya Vamsa). He had two wives; the elder wife had one son, called Asamanjas; the second wife had sixty thousand sons. Sagara held a grand horse sacrifice known as the Aswamedha Yajna. In this sacrifice the consecrated horse was left to wander all over the earth. The king's sons had to follow and defeat anyone who tried to stop the horse. Indra, the king of the gods, became jealous of Sagara's sacrifice. He stole the horse and took him to the nether regions, tethering him next to the great sage Kapila, who was immersed in meditation. The heroic sons of Sagara, who had followed the horse, suspected the sage to be the thief and spoke harshly to him. When he didn't open his eyes, they thought he was pretending and gave him a good kick. The sage opened his eyes and looked at them. Immediately they were burnt to cinders by the concentrated power of his austere gaze.

The king was desperate at the disappearance of his sons. Nobody knew where they had gone, and the king sent his grandson, Amsuman, to find out the fate of his uncles. He discovered their whereabouts and was told that the only way to reprieve them from the heinous sin of having kicked such a great soul and disturbed his *tapas* was to bring the heavenly Ganga down to the spot where their ashes lay and allow her waters to wash over them. Amsuman started his austerities but died before he could complete them. His son Dileepa performed more austerities, but he also passed away before he could complete them.

At last Amsuman's grandson, Bhagiratha, who was a great devotee of Shiva, gave up his kingdom in order to concentrate entirely on achieving the purpose that had obsessed his family for four generations. He stood with hands upraised and performed terrific austerities in the place known as Gokarna. After Bhagiratha had performed a thousand years of *tapas*, Brahma appeared and promised to release the waters of the Ganga from his *kamandalu*. He pointed out to Bhagiratha that the earth would be unable to sustain her fall; only Lord Shiva would be able to do so. Bhagiratha was nonplussed. He knew Shiva to be the arch ascetic, sitting in splendid isolation on the solitary peak of the Himalayas, steeped in meditation, unconcerned with the petty worries of the world. It would be a Herculean task to induce him to cooperate in this endeavor. But Bhagiratha was determined. He performed another thousand years of austerities in the Himalayas at the place known as Gangotri. At last Lord Shiva appeared to him and agreed to accommodate Ganga in his matted locks.

This story glorifies the greatness of those who acquire ascetic willpower. By enduring self-inflicted suffering, the *yogi* accumulates a vast amount of psychic and physical energy. The universal life force becomes so concentrated in him that it melts the resistance of the cosmic powers and forces them to give in to his demands. This is true even of demons; they too can force these powers to bend to their will by the accumulated strength of their ascetic fire. The heat generated by *tapas* is like a laser beam that can cut through every type of resistance. Bhagiratha, by the enormous power of his *tapas*, coupled with his determination to bring salvation to his ancestors, was able to drag the heavenly Ganga down to the mundane world. In fact, his name has come to be a synonym for any task that needs superhuman effort.

It is said that Ganga was rather proud of her celestial status. She looked down upon the snowy peaks of the Himalayas from the Milky Way. She saw the bluish, tangled mass of Lord Shiva's head where she was told to break her fall before touching down on earth. She was scornful of anyone's ability to hold her.

"I'll sweep him away like a straw," she thought.

Even gods like Agni (god of fire), Soma (god of the moon), and Surya (god of the sun) were nothing to her. Was she now to be frightened of that motionless figure on the peak of Kailasa who thought he was powerful enough to break her fall? She laughed scornfully and plunged down with a mighty crash onto his head. She would sweep him off and carry him on her way over the beautiful earth. But no sooner had she touched Shiva's hair than she was lost. She was enmeshed in a labyrinth of darkness through which there was no exit. Shiva's locks were a forest of thick trees through which she turned and twisted in vain to find an outlet, but she found herself to be totally enfolded in his tresses. Through it all she was aware of a strange mocking laughter that echoed in her ears.

Ganga felt desperate. "I'll never see the light of day again if I go on like this," she thought. She had been cut up into tiny streams and made to squirm and wriggle through the maze of Shiva's hair. She felt cheated and humiliated. She had been a spoiled princess in the heavens, but now she felt her force was nothing compared to the mighty power emanating from this strange ascetic.

In the meantime, poor Bhagiratha was frantic. He performed more *tapas* and begged Lord Shiva to allow Ganga to come down to the earth and thus purify his ancestors. At last his efforts bore results. Having curbed Ganga's pride, Lord Shiva relented and released from his locks a trickle that formed the mighty lake known as Bindusaras (lake of drops). It is from here that Ganga flows down the Himalayan terrain as the mighty river that we see today. Mounted on a splendid chariot the royal sage Bhagiratha went ahead to lead her to the place where his ancestors lay. Unfortunately, as Ganga meekly followed the chariot, she happened to cross the sacrificial arena of the great sage Jahnu, who calmly drank up all her waters, since she was disturbing his penance. Bhagiratha now had to appease the irate *rishi,* who eventually released Ganga through his ear. She thus received the name Jahnavi, or daughter of Jahnu.

Ganga then resumed her course behind Bhagiratha's chariot. They were followed by a host of celestials, heavenly nymphs, demons, giants, sages, and snakes. As Ganga hurried onward in the footsteps of the royal sage, the whole multitude of created beings bathed in her sacred waters and washed away their sins. Very soon Bhagiratha and the goddess arrived at the dry bed of the ocean. From there they made their descent to the netherworld where his ancestors had perished. Bhagiratha's long penance was now approaching a successful conclusion. Ganga's purifying waters flowed over the ashes of his ancestors and redeemed them. Thus after superhuman efforts Bhagiratha succeeded in delivering his ancestors and taking them up to heaven. Nor was this the only benefit. Ever since the sage Agastya had swallowed the waters of the ocean, it had remained dry. But now with the coming of the Ganga this defect in nature was remedied and the ocean was replenished to the furthest shore. Ganga now had the name Bhagirathi (daughter of Bhagiratha) because Bhagiratha was the one who had brought her down to Earth.

We have already heard the story Parvati, Shiva's consort. But the story of his wives cannot be complete without the story of Ganga. Parvati and Kaali were countercorrelates and stemmed from the same source, but Ganga was a different personality altogether. She was a part of Shiva. Nothing could separate them. Shiva was never alone, even when he was doing *tapas,* for Ganga was always tucked away in his locks. From his long black hair she dripped constantly. Parvati was always a bit jealous of Ganga. Though she never actually saw them speak to each other, she knew that Ganga was a constant witness to all Shiva's doings. Sometimes, immersed in Shiva's cosmic embrace, Parvati would be totally lost to all mundane thoughts. However, her consciousness would come back when she was disturbed by the steady drip falling from his locks, flowing over her face and trickling to the ground. She would twist her face away from his chest and look up to meet Ganga's steady, unwavering gaze, looking at her with compassion and never with jealousy. Even though all she did was flow, Parvati was always suspicious of her.

"When Shiva has me wrapped in his embrace, he is still continuing an affair with Ganga," Parvati thought. "How can I ever immerse myself in him if I'm constantly meeting her eyes telling me of a pleasure greater than my own?"

Ganga's body remained always twisted around her lover's head in a constant caress. Parvati could not bear it. When questioned about her, Shiva told Parvati that he had allowed Ganga to break her fall over his head so that the world would not be swept away. She is turn served the world by cooling Shiva's head so that his *tapas* would not scorch the earth. With this Parvati had to be content.

Just as the sons of Sagara were redeemed from their sins and given an entry to heaven by having Ganga's waters flow over their ashes, so all pious Hindus believe that having their ashes or bones thrown into the Ganga is a sure guarantee of a safe passage to heaven. Thus she is known as the ladder to heaven: *swarga-sopana-sharani*. The Skanda Purana says that the forefathers are always singing this song: "May someone take birth in our family who will bathe in the Ganga and redeem all of us."

The Ganga is a bridge between the worlds of the living and the dead. Any of the rites of *tarpana* (libations to the *manes* and the sun god) are supposed to be more effective when done with Ganga water. Using Ganga water nourishes the ancestors, since she also acts as a means by which the rest of the offerings will reach them. Every devout Hindu household will always keep a pot of Ganga water. People come all the way from the south of India to have a dip in the holy waters of the Ganga and carry a pot of water back to their homes. This water keeps forever without any decay. At the time of death a few drops are placed on the tongue of the dying person in order to assure him or her of a safe passage to heaven.

The word *thirtha* means "crossing," and Ganga is known as a *punya thirtha* (holy river), for she is the one who aids the human soul in its crossing from the land of the living to the land of the dead. "Ganga herself is all the *thirthas,* Ganga is a grove of penance. Ganga alone is the holy place of supernatural powers. No one need doubt this," says the Skanda Purana.

Ganga water is said to be totally pure, and it is a fact that it can be kept for years without becoming putrid. The East India Company discovered this strange phenomenon in the seventeenth century; on voyages between London and Calcutta, ships found that Thames water became quite undrinkable by the time they reached Calcutta, but on the return journey the water they took from the mouth of the Ganga, though apparently polluted, remained drinkable until they reached England and even came back to Calcutta.

From Vedic times all water has been regarded in Hinduism as a tangible manifestation of the divine essence. Just as copper is the best conductor of electricity, so water is known to be the best conductor of divine energy. An important part of every ritual in India is to worship a pot of water representing the power of the divinity and sometimes even serving as a sacred object in lieu of an image. For the duration of a ritual, this pot containing water is considered to be the seat of the deity. Normally ordinary water is consecrated and made sublime by the chanting of *mantras* and by the addition of sacred herbs. But in the case of Ganga water, no such sanctification is necessary. It is already pure. As the Agni Purana says, "One becomes purified of all sins just by seeing, touching, or drinking Ganga water."

"One who touches the Ganga attains an eternal spiritual form," says the Narada Purana. Indeed, Ganga water has the magical effect of purifying the devotee who touches it, sublimating the base metal of the devotee's earthly nature. The Ganga flows from the highest eternal realm and carries the celestial essence of all three primary deities: Brahma, Vishnu, and Shiva. He who bathes in these waters becomes an embodiment of that celestial essence. This divine essence is not something remote from our life but the very core of our existence and the source of every moment of our life. The Ganga, which flows directly from that mystical realm, takes the devotee back along its blessed course to the place of our beginning and forward to our final goal, which is the ocean of existence.

After leaving the earthly regions, the Ganga is said to become a river of punishment, known as the Patala Ganga, which traverses the seven lower planetary systems and is dedicated to the ultimate purification of all lost souls. Then she becomes the river Vaitarini, which encircles the city of Yama, the lord of death. Here she has a fearsome aspect. She is thick and slimy with blood and grime, and her waters crawl with strange and gruesome creatures. All mortals have to cross this river on their way to the abode of the god of death. Persons who have done good deeds in their lifetime and given gifts and charity can easily cross it. Sinners have to wade through the putrid blood and sediment, at the mercy of crocodiles and fish that pierce them with swordlike snouts. A person who has given the gift of a cow at the time of death, known as *vaitarini,* is rowed across by the boatman without difficulty.

The human form of the Ganga is visible only to the mystic eye. The Agni Purana says that she is white in color and adorned with ornaments. Like Maha Devi, she has three eyes and four arms. She holds a jeweled pot in one hand and a white lotus in the other. Her other two hands show the *mudras* (mystic signs) of fearlessness and blessing. Her vehicle is a *makara* (crocodile) that is white like jasmine. The crocodile is associated with both earth and water and has the power to both redeem and destroy. *Yogis* have perceived the figure of a crocodile in the *swadhishtana chakra* at the base of the spine. This *chakra* has water as its element, and it is a storehouse of our *vasanas* (innate tendencies). We carry these tendencies with us from life to life, and they impel us to various actions that bind us more tightly to the materialistic life. The goddess Ganga, however, has totally subdued this crocodile of the mind's *vasanas* and stands on top of it, as if it were a domesticated animal.

The Ganga Mahatmyam (meaning "glorification of Ganga"), which is part of the Skanda Purana, offers this speech from Shiva to Vishnu:

Ganga is my own transcendental body in the form of water. Her substance is all auspiciousness. She is the transcendental source of creation and the foundation of countless universes. I carry this mother of the world, who is not different from the supreme truth, in order to protect the universe.

In Krita Yuga holy places are found everywhere. In Treta Yuga the only holy place is Pushkara. In Dwapara Yuga the only holy place is Kurukshetra, and in Kali Yuga the only holy place is the Ganga.

In Krita Yuga the cause of liberation is meditation. In Treta it is austerities, in Dwapara it is sacrifices, and in Kali the only cause of liberation is the Ganga.

O Hari (Vishnu)! One can take up residence on the banks of the Ganga only through the accumulated merit of many auspicious actions done in previous lives.

One may be competent, learned, virtuous, and charitable, but if he has never bathed in the Ganga, his life is wasted.

On the banks of Srimati Jahnavi (Ganga) all places are auspicious, all times are auspicious, and every person is a fit receiver of charity.

In the Bhagavad Gita, Lord Krishna tells Arjuna, "Among sacred and flowing things, O Arjuna, know me to be the holy Ganga!"

Adi Shankaracharya wrote the famous eight *slokas* (verses) on the Ganga known as the Gangashtakam. The fourth verse gives the entire story of the Ganga: "At first you were the water used for rituals in the *kamandalu* of Brahma, the grandfather of the universe. Then you became the all-purifying water that washed the feet of Vishnu. Then again you became the jewel adorning the matted locks of Lord Shiva, and then you became the daughter of the *rishi* Jahnu. May you, O goddess Bhagirathi, who destroys all inauspiciousness, protect me."

Let us conclude the glorious account of the divine Mother Ganga with the prayer of Kunti, the mother of the Pandavas (the sons of Pandu, representing the virtues of the evolved person), to Lord Krishna, which is found in the Bhagavad Purana: "O slayer of Madhu, just as the

Ganga flows constantly to the sea without hindrance, so let my mind be relentlessly drawn to you without being diverted to anything else."

> *The mountain trembles, the stones*
> *In vast screes clattering pour;*
> *The water, swelling and foaming,*
> *In anger and tumult roar;*
> *In their mighty exultation*
> *They would rend the mountain asunder;*
> *Mad with the morning's rays,*
> *Through earth they would crash and thunder.*
>
> *And I—I will pour of compassion a river;*
> *The prisons of stone I will break, will deliver;*
> *I will flood the earth, and, with rapture mad,*
> *Pour music glad.*
> *With dishevelled tresses, and gathering flowers,*
> *With rainbow wings widespread, through the hours*
> *I shall run and scatter my laughter bright*
> *In the dear sunlight.*
> *I shall run from peak to peak, and from hill*
> *To hill my leaping waters spill,*
> *Loudly shall laugh and with claps keep time,*
> *To my own steps' chime.*

—RABINDRANATH TAGORE IN "THE
AWAKENING OF THE WATERFALL"

Thus ends the nineteenth chapter of *Shakti*, known as "Ganga," which describes the story of the goddess Ganga.

Aum Aim Hreem Kleem

20
Kaali

Ya Devi sarvabhuteshu, branti rupena samsthita,
Namasthasyai, namasthasyai, namasthasyai namo
   namaha!

O Goddess who resides in all creatures in the form of
   confusion,
Hail to thee, hail to thee, all hail to thee!

Kaala is the Sanskrit word for time, and the goddess Kaali is divine consciousness in the form of time—relentless, all-consuming, and indomitable. She is also the beloved of Shiva. Parvati is Shiva's wife, but Kaali is his soul mate. While Parvati's role is to subdue and soften Shiva's violent nature, Kaali's role is the very reverse. She incites him to wild, dangerous, and destructive behavior that threatens the stability of the universe. She loves carnage, destruction, and violence. Friend of ghouls and ghosts, she performs the same functions as Shiva but in a more violent fashion. Even Shiva cannot tame her spirit. Her wrath is immediate and dire, especially against treachery and falsehood. She is ruthless to the haters of the divine. She cannot bear indifference and negligence in the performance of divine works. Force and strength are her characteristics. Her divinity springs out in the splendor of tempestuous action. There is an overwhelming intensity in Kaali, a divine violence hastening to shatter every limit and obstacle. Her sword is swift and straight.

Kaali imagery can be bizarre. She is portrayed in a number of different fashions, but in all of them her appearance is intimidating and intended to put off all those who are not ready to accept life as it is. She is sometimes known as Bhayankari, or the one who terrifies. Sometimes she is naked and pitch-black in color, with long, disheveled hair that flows like night behind her. She wears a girdle of severed arms and a necklace of freshly cut heads. Her earrings are children's corpses and snakes are her bracelets. She has a cavernous mouth dripping with blood, a lolling red tongue, and long, sharp fangs. She has clawlike hands with hooked nails. Her favorite haunts are battlefields, where she gets drunk on the hot blood of her victims, and cremation grounds, where she sits on corpses, surrounded by jackals, goblins, and ghosts.

This is the visage Kaali shows to the uninitiated. But this is only one of her facades. Her visible mask is that of nature bringing forth all beings from her womb, feeding them at her breast, then devouring and assimilating them back into herself. This is her public mask as known to science: a material cosmos that seems to be a superficially purposeless chaos of opposing qualities, of creation and destruction, cause and effect, light and darkness, good and evil. Here she appears as a randomly willful despot, elusive and aloof.

But the face she shows to her devotees, who value her for her own sake and not for the evanescent charms of her creation, is altogether different. To those fortunate ones, untamable nature becomes a doting mother whose sole concern is their ultimate well-being. The transformation from one extreme to the other is well brought out by an analogy of the great twentieth-century saint Swami Rama Thirtha: As long as we pursue the things of the world for their own sake, they will remain frustratingly elusive, like a shadow that flits ahead always just out of reach. At this stage the world seems alien and unfriendly. However, the moment we wake up from this elusive creation and turn around to face the creator, the shadow of creation follows dutifully behind us, as the tail of a dog. Nature supports those who sincerely turn toward God.

As the embodiment of universal destruction, Kaali is not an easy goddess to love, but if one loves her without reservation, as a child loves a mother even though she may be ugly, then she will come in any of the forms in which one wants her to come. To a Krishna *bhakta* she will come as Radha, to a Shiva *bhakta* she will come as Parvati, and to one who loves her as a child, she will become the Divine Mother, placing the devotee on her lap and teaching him or her everything. Many of the greatest Hindu saints discovered this esoteric secret and were ardent worshippers of Kaali. They realized that the secret of life lay in accepting both sides of the coin of life: the destructive and the constructive. There are two sides to the Divine Mother. One is the feminine side, representing the maternal, life-nourishing, and life-bearing principle. The other is her destructive side, which takes back and swallows the creatures she gives birth to. For Kaali is, as we've said, time, the all-producing, all-consuming principle in the flow of which everything that comes into existence has to vanish after the expiry of its brief spell of allotted life.

Adi Shankaracharya, the founder of the Advaita philosophy of nondualism, was an ardent worshipper of the goddess. He says in one of his poems:

> *Who art thou, O fairest one? Auspicious one!*
> *You whose hands hold both delight and pain?*
> *Both the shade of death and the elixir of immortality,*
> *Are thy grace, O Mother!*

The world cannot be fragmented into clean and unclean, creative and destructive, male and female, as the human mind attempts to do. The world is a unified totality of the terrible and the sublime, welded together. Through the Kaali imagery we are made to realize that to experience opposites is to be fully human. One is meaningless without the other. Such fearless affirmations from a gruesome divine power like Kaali become a comforting directive. It encourages women, who experience the so-called unclean bodily functions like menstruation and pregnancy, to feel worthy of themselves as females. In fact, the Kaali imagery has the potential to become a symbol of completion and release for all women all over the world.

Most pictorial representations of Kaali show her in the wholly negative aspect. She is often depicted as an emaciated, gruesome hag with bony fingers, protruding teeth, and prominent canines. She has an unquenchable hunger for flesh and blood. She is cold-blooded, self-centered, ungenerous, and selfish. The hunger for life that impels the infant to suck hard at the very lifeblood of its mother through her teats is shown in its most loathsome transformation. The goddess feeds upon the entrails of her victims. Her victims are all those born from her own womb. She haunts the cremation grounds, for she loves to feed on intestines that are still steaming with the last breath of expiring life. Like Nataraja (Shiva as the cosmic dancer), she has a halo of flames. These flames are the tongues of the universal conflagration that reduces everything to ash at the termination of an age or *kalpa*. But these flames are also to be found all the time; they lick incessantly at the bread of life. Life feeds on death. For every newborn creature that comes into the world, another returns to the earth from which it came. Every time we eat, it is at the cost of the death of something else.

Some Tantric texts describe Kaali as standing on a boat that floats on a sea. The sea is made up of the lifeblood of the children belonging to all species that she brings forth, sustains for a brief period, and then takes back. She stands and quaffs the warm blood from a cranial bowl. Just as her love is unending, her thirst is unquenchable.

When we conceive of totality we should never forget its ambivalent character. Both the creative and the destructive principles are one and the same. Both emanate from the same divine cosmic energy that becomes manifest in the process of the unfolding of the history of the universe. The supreme goddess Maha Devi represents both aspects of life. To accept one and ignore the other is a form of childish indulgence that Hindu philosophy does not cater to. As Tripurasundari, Maha Devi is the embodiment of the feminine principle—the personification of man's desire. But in order to show her full significance, her other side has to be revealed. She has to be shown as Kaali, old, black, and ugly, the embodiment of man's disgust, holding the symbols of destruction and death.

The eight gruesome heads strung in a garland around Kaali's neck represent the eight *pashas* (ropes of ignorance) or emotions that cloud the mind and incite it to keep performing endless actions that tighten the knots that tie us to the wheel of life and death. These eight *pashas* are lust, anger, greed, delusion, envy, shame, fear, and disgust. In a state of ignorance we possess many or all of these grinning heads. Kaali chops off these heads one by one to free us from these ropes.

Kaali's lolling tongue is meant to lick up the hundreds of *asuras* that multiply in us. These are our desires. The moment one is fulfilled, another hundred appear, like in the story of the *asura* Raktabija (see chapter 13). As soon as a drop of Raktabija's blood fell to the ground, it multiplied into many more demons. Similar is the case with our desires. If we allow them to take root, a hundred other desires crop up. We should pray to Kaali to spread her tongue and lick them up before they reach the ground.

Some of Kaali's pictures show her as having huge breasts. Breasts are the symbol of motherhood and maternal love. The baby sucks from its mother's breasts all that it needs for life and growth. Kaali also has a huge belly, for she consumes and digests all the beings in the universe. In order to cover her nakedness she wears a skirt of freshly severed human arms, dripping with blood. The Sanskrit word for "arm" is *kara*, which is closely related to the word *karma*, which means "action." So these arms represent the *karmas* (or actions) of innumerable births. If you look closely you find that both left and right arms are found in Kaali's skirt, which shows that the *karmas* include both positive and negative ones. She wears them as a covering for her navel and pubis, for most *karmas* are performed for the sake of food and sex.

Kaali's anklets are little cobras. Snakes are a symbol of our ancestors. These snakes remind us to pray for our ancestors, without whom we would never be here.

The goddess also has four hands. One holds the cranial bowl that yields an abundance of food and the other the lotus that is the symbol of eternal life. Sometimes Kaali is seen carrying a noose instead of the lotus. This is meant to convey the message that she will free us from the noose of death and confer immortality. A third hand holds the pair of scissors with which Kaali cuts the knots that bind us to embodied existence. In the fourth hand she carries a sword, which symbolizes physical extinction and spiritual determination. With this sword she cuts through our error and ignorance—the veil of individual consciousness and our doubts, false ideas, and impressions.

The famous Kaali statue at the temple of Dakshineswara that the great saint Sri Ramakrishna worshipped shows a slight variation on Kaali's four hands. Her upper left hand holds a sword. On the esoteric level this sword stands for the destructive principle of the world process. For one who sees no deeper than this, the weapon is naturally frightening. The worldly man senses, quite rightly, that the sword is directed at him; in fact it is hanging over his head. He knows not when it might fall. His spiritual evolution is still in the primitive stage, and he tries desperately to appease Kaali's wrath by offering live animals and money. He does not realize that her sword is directed at decapitating his animal instincts. In fact, this is the esoteric truth behind all animal sacrifice: we are supposed to sacrifice our animal instincts at her feet and not goats and buffaloes. The devotee, on the other hand, does not fear the sword for he knows that it is poised to sever the deadly enemies of spirituality—lust, greed, pride, and the rest of the demonic brood. Indeed, the severed head that Kaali holds in her lower left hand is a token of her inevitable success in defeating these demons that are products of our ego.

If her left arms show negative aspects, Kaali's right arms portray positive ones. Her upper right hand is raised hand, with the palm facing upward, to show the *abhaya mudra,* signifying that divine protection will be given to all sincere aspirants on the path of spirituality. The lower right hand, with the palm turned downward, offers boons and assures the devotee that whatever he lacks for spiritual evolution will be granted unasked, a gift of grace.

In the Mahanirvana Tantra, Kaali is the most common epithet used for the primordial Shakti. In this scripture Shiva, who is known as Mahakaala or the lord of time, praises Kaali thus:

> At the dissolution of things, it is Kaala (Time) who will devour all, and by reason of this I am called Mahakaala. Since you are the one who eats Mahakaala himself, you are known as the supreme, primordial Maha Kaali or destroyer.
>
> Since you are the devourer of Kaala, you are Kaali, the original form of all things, and therefore you are known as Adya (the primordial goddess). After dissolving all things, you remain alone, formless, ineffable, and inconceivable.

Kaali is destruction incarnate, the destruction that is brought about by constant generation and life-bearing. She also destroys the veil that Maha Maya has enshrouded us in. She comes like the black night that brings in its wake the dawn. Without her there would be no death and therefore no life. Terrible is the face she shows to the haters of the divine and ruthless is her mood toward them. Intolerant of hypocrisy, she deals roughly with all those who are false, treacherous, indifferent, and negligent. Her hands are outstretched both to strike and to succor, for she is the eternal mother. Her love is as intense as her wrath and her compassion as deep. Only the great, the strong, and the noble worship her. They accept her blows and know that she will melt whatever is negative in their natures and mold it into strength and perfection. She can achieve for us in one day what might take years for us to achieve by ordinary means. Nothing can satisfy her short of the supreme, the highest heights and the noblest aims.

One of Kaali's great devotees, Ram Prasad, wrote this about her:

> *O Mother Kaali, you dwell in cremation grounds,*
> *So I have made my heart a burning pit where you*
>   *can dance.*
> *One desire burns in the conflagration of my life,*
> *To watch your blazing dance!*
> *Lord Shiva lies beneath your feet*
> *Gaping up at your dance,*
> *While I sit waiting on my funeral pyre,*
> *Looking for you with closed eyes!*

The well-known pictorial representation of Kaali dancing on the prone and corpselike figure of Shiva has a deep, esoteric meaning: that that Shiva without Shakti is nothing but *shava*. The supreme by itself is inert or zero. It is Shakti that pulsates with life. She is the infinity of forms. It is only at her touch that Shiva can come alive and become the enjoyer of all forms. The master of time (Mahakaala) becomes time itself at the touch of Maha Maya, but until then he might as well be considered a corpse. This is what Parvati told Shiva when he refused to look at her; she claimed that without her, who was his Prakriti, he, Purusha, would be unable to move! So also the human body becomes a corpse when Shakti or the power of Prakriti leaves it at the time of death.

The mythological story behind this pictorial representation is quite interesting. It is said that at one time Kaali began to dance on a battlefield and eventually lost all control, since she had become drunk on the blood of her victims. Nobody could manage her or put a stop to her mad rampage. At last, to bring her to her senses, Shiva lay down on the battlefield, emulating a corpse. When she started to dance on her beloved husband she came to her senses and stopped the bloody carnage.

Kaali's most famous appearance is to be found in the Devi Mahatmyam, in which she is the personification of Durga's wrath (see chapter 13). When the demons Chanda and Munda tried to catch hold of Durga, the goddess turned black with rage and out of her furrowed brows came the hideous figure of Kaali. The Devi Mahatmyam describes her thus:

> *Carrying a many-colored staff, topped with a skull,*
> *   wearing a garland of human skulls;*
> *With a garment of tiger skin, exceedingly frightening with*
> *   her dried-out skin,*
> *With widely gaping mouth, terrifying with her lolling*
> *   tongue;*
> *With sunken, reddened eyes and a mouth that filled the*
> *   directions with roars!*

In another episode Kaali is the personification of Parvati's wrath. When the gods asked Parvati to destroy the two demons Shumbha and Nishumbha, Kaali came out of Parvati's body and went to the Vindhya mountains, where she defeated the *asuras* and remained there as the goddess of the mountain (see chapter 18). The temple of Vindhya Vaasini at Vindhyachala is dedicated to her.

Whenever Shiva went out to destroy demons, Kaali would accompany him. She was adorned with skulls and her eyes were closed with the intoxication of drinking blood. Shiva praised her as being the daughter of the Himalayas, which shows her identification with Parvati. When Shiva sent Virabhadra to destroy Daksha's hall of sacrifice (see chapter 15), Kaali was part of his terrifying entourage.

In the Mahabharata, Kaali is mentioned in the context of the killing of the Pandava children by Ashwatthama. The latter was a devotee of Shiva and had invoked him. Shiva sent Kaali to help him. The Mahabharata gives a vivid description of her:

Kaali of bloody mouth and eyes, smeared with blood and
*   garlands,*
With reddened garments, alone, crested noose in hand,
The night of death (Kalaratri) laughing derisively and
*   standing firm did the Pandavas see.*
Binding men, horses, and elephants with terrible snares
*   did she sally forth,*
Carrying various spirits who were bound with snares, their
*   hair disheveled.*

She appears again in the wonderful work *Kumarasambhava,* by the great poet Kalidasa, who describes himself as the slave of Kaali. He writes that he had been ignorant until he started to worship the goddess, who rescued him and made him the greatest poet of the land.

To be a devotee of Kaali is not an easy affair. She makes us suffer and disappoints us in terms of worldly desires and pleasures. She gives her devotee a vision of himself that is not confined to the normal physical and material limitations. As one of her devotees said, "One who loves Kaali can easily forget worldly pleasures." Nothing can satisfy her except the noblest aims. Therefore the victorious force of the divine is always with her, and it is only by her grace that great achievements can be accomplished here and now.

Kaali's devotee need not bother to ask for worldly joys because she will not give it. It is because of this that Kaali's devotees can find a reality that goes beyond worldly comfort and security. Her figure is one that is capable of destroying the comforting, mythical assumptions that one has of the world. One who thinks of the universe as an orderly, beautiful whole in which God as the protecting father sits in his heaven and tenderly looks after the needs of his children will never be able to understand the significance of Kaali.

It is only in this century that the scientists have discovered that their notion of the universe as an orderly whole, in which atoms and molecules behave in a set and understandable pattern, is a myth of their own wishful thinking. The energy field from which the whole universe rises is far from being orderly. It is a seething mass of turbulent forces made up of energy particles that seem to have no observable method of behavior. Though to the scientistific mind this may have been a shocking revelation, the Indian mind had realized it long ago. The figure of Kaali forces us to step out of the everyday world of logic into a world of unpredictability, dramatic reversals, opposites, and contrasts.

Ram Prasad writes about her:

> *You shine in deepest darkness, O Mother!*
> *So yogis worship you in dark caves.*
> *They find in your unlimited darkness,*
> *Unlimited peace,*
> *Who are you, Mother,*
> *Clothed in nothingness,*
> *Glowing in the deepest recesses of my mind?*
> *Your frenzied laughter terrifies,*
> *While your love like lightning from a black cloud,*
> *Shocks the worlds with light.*

Kaali is India's gift to the world: the eternal, horrifyingly beautiful, caressing, and murdering symbol of the totality of the world-creating and world-destroying process.

> *The gods who watch the earth with sleepless eyes,*
> *Have given to man the burden of his mind.*
> *They gave him hungers, which no food can fill*
> *His body the tether with which he's tied.*
> *They cast for fodder, grief, hope and joy,*
> *His pasture ground they fenced with ignorance.*
> *Into his fragile, undefended breast,*
> *They breathed a courage that is met by death,*

They have traced a journey that foresees no goal.
Aimless man toils in an uncertain world,
Lulled by constant pauses of his pain
Death prowls, baying through the woods of life.

—*SAVITRI* BY SRI AUROBINDO

Thus ends the twentieth chapter of *Shakti,* known as "Kaali," which describes Maha Devi in her form as Kaali.

Aum Aim Hreem Kleem

Aum Lakshmyai Namaha!

21

Lakshmi

Ya Devi sarvabhuteshu, lakshmi rupena samsthita,
Namasthasyai, namasthasyai, namasthasyai namo
namaha!

O Goddess who resides in all creatures in the form of
auspiciousness,
Hail to thee, hail to thee, all hail to thee!

There are four aspects of the Divine Mother by which she guides and
deals with the world. Two of these, Maha Devi and Maha Kaali, we
have already discussed. Her third mask, Maha Lakshmi, is one of
sweetness and harmony and beauty. She has a compelling attraction
and flair for affluence of all types. She opens to our vision the miracle
of eternal beauty, divine harmony, and the irresistible charm of God's
creation. Lakshmi is the most attractive aspect of the Divine Mother,
and that is why she is one of the most popular of the Hindu goddesses.
Maha Devi can appear too calm and distant for the earthly nature to
approach, and Maha Kaali is too formidable and swift for our weak-
ness to bear, but Maha Lakshmi throws over us the intoxicating bliss
of the sweetness of the divine. We feel profoundly happy when she is
close to us. Existence becomes rapture. Grace, charm, and tenderness

flow from her like an inexhaustible fountain, and the one on whom she smiles is plunged into bliss. Her delicate touch refines the body, life, and soul of the human being.

Monastic systems of Hindu philosophy like Advaita Vedanta and Patanjali's Yoga are responsible for giving the general impression that Hindus look down upon wealth and give it a secondary importance in their social structure. But the contrary is true. Lakshmi or Sri, as she was initially known, has been revered from Rig Vedic times to the present day. Only by appreciating the true nature of Lakshmi can one hope to attain *moksha* or liberation, which is the goal of all Hindu philosophy. Initially both names, Sri and Lakshmi, meant anything that was auspicious and brought good luck or bestowed riches. Just as the word *aum* is associated with the spiritual side of life, the word *sri* is associated with the material side. It has been the sacred symbol of cosmic auspiciousness and abundance since Vedic times. So it was but natural that the two words eventually became connected and Lakshmi, the goddess of beauty and prosperity, came to be known as Sri Lakshmi.

The *Sri Suktam* found in the Rig Veda is the most ancient invocation to this goddess:

> *Invoke for me, O Agni,*
> *Lakshmi who shines like gold,*
> *Is brilliant like the sun,*
> *Who is wonderfully fragrant,*
> *Who wields the rod of suzerainty,*
> *Who is the form of supreme rulership,*
> *Who is radiant with ornaments,*
> *And is the goddess of wealth.*

In the Lakshmi Tantra, the goddess herself says,

> *I am inherent in existence,*
> *I am the inciter, the potential that takes shape.*

I manifest myself; I occupy myself with activity,
And finally I dissolve myself.
I pervade all creation with vitality, will, and
    consciousness.
Like ghee that keeps a lamp burning,
I lubricate the senses of living beings with the
    sap of my consciousness.

Wisdom and force are not the only manifestations of the Divine Mother. Above them is the miracle of eternal beauty, the secret of eternal harmony. Lakshmi is the one who transforms dreams to reality. To realize her is to appreciate and rejoice in the wonders of life. It is due to her kindness that life on earth is made bearable. Due to the inherent transience and mortality of all things, our journey through life is filled with sorrow. Destruction haunts the footsteps of the *jiva* from birth to death. It is due to the radiant and joyful aspect of Sri Lakshmi that life becomes endurable.

Lakshmi is often called fickle or *chanchala*. It is not easy to meet the demands of this captivating divinity. She goes only where there is harmony and beauty of mind, thoughts, and feelings. She is drawn to harmony and loveliness of surroundings also. She consents to abide only with those who are responsive to the rhythms of the infinite, who respond to the call of her lord, and who strive to keep everything clean and neat both internally and externally, ever ready to welcome the advent of the divine. Her delicate steps will not tread where there is meanness or ugliness or among those who are coarse and brutal. Where there is no love and beauty, she will not deign to come. This enchanting goddess will not linger in the house and heart of one who is filled with greed, jealousy, and hatred. Neither ascetic bareness nor harshness are appealing to her, nor the repression of the soul's natural desire for love and beauty. It is through love and beauty that she yokes the human to the divine. Life is turned into a work of art and existence into a poem of delight by her touch. Even the simplest things are made fragrant by her breath.

Though we think of Lakshmi as the consort of Vishnu, originally she was supposed to belong to the demons. Demons, however, have the reputation of plundering and hoarding wealth, thus hindering its flow. This is why Lakshmi deserted them. She is said to have then gone to Indra, the king of the gods, but when he overindulged in wine, wealth, and women at the cost of his duty, she was disgusted and left him. Lakshmi has also been linked with many other gods of the Vedic pantheon like Varuna, Soma, Agni, and Kubera. It was only in Puranic times that she was truly domesticated and became the consort of Lord Vishnu. In Vishnu she finally found the perfection she was looking for, as Vishnu is the embodiment of *dharma*. Though married to the goddess of affluence, he is totally uninterested in the acquisition or hoarding of wealth. The true nature of wealth was known to the ancient *rishis*. Their formula for keeping riches was to allow it to flow, unobstructed, in the desired channels, never to obstruct its flow, never to hoard, and never to plunder. This deep understanding of the nature of money is found in all the stories of Lakshmi. She appears fickle only because she will not stay with one who hoards and plunders wealth. But what her devotees should realize is that Lakshmi has a decided partiality for those who worship her husband Vishnu and will always go to them unsolicited.

Lakshmi has four hands. One hand shows the *abhaya mudra* (sign of grace and fearlessness), and another has the palm pointing downward to show that she showers her devotees with wealth. Another hand holds the *akshaya patra*, the vessel of plenty that flows gold and grain and is never exhausted. Her fourth hand holds a lotus.

The lotus is the most popular flower in Hindu mythology, and Lakshmi is strongly connected to it. In many representations she is shown sitting on a red lotus, and many of her appellations are associated with the lotus. She is, for example, sometimes called Kamala and Padma, both of which mean "lotus," and Padmavati, which means "lotus born." The lotus takes its birth and strength from muddy waters. It symbolizes the growth of existence that is distilled from the life-giving property of water and mud. The lotus growing from the navel of Vishnu, for example, marks the beginning of another cycle of cosmic life. The lotus gives a picture of a growing, expanding world, imbued with vigorous, fertile power. This is the power that is revealed in Lakshmi. She is the essence of creation and gives it flavor and splendor. Organic life is impelled by her mysterious power to flower into the rich tapestry of the world as we know it.

Lakshmi is extremely beautiful because she is the goddess of fertility. Beauty is a life-propagating necessity and a true component of fertility. If flowers were not beautiful, pollination would not take place. Red is the color of potential energy, so Lakshmi always wears red. Gold never rusts or becomes polluted, so she is adorned with gold ornaments.

Some pictures of Lakshmi show her flanked by two elephants that shower water on her through their upraised trunks. Elephants represent life-giving rains as well as royal authority. They imbue her with those qualities, which she possesses to the highest degree.

Lakshmi gives us the best of physical life so she has eight forms, known as Ashta Lakshmis, that portray the eight things in material life that are most prized by human beings. These are Bhagya Lakshmi, or the one who gives good fortune; Dhana Lakshmi, or the bestower of wealth; Dhanya Lakshmi, or the provider of food; Gaja Lakshmi, or the one who gives power; Santana Lakshmi, or the granter of offspring; Vara Lakshmi, the granter of boons; Vidya Lakshmi, or the bestower of knowledge; and Virya Lakshmi, or the one who confers strength. These figures are very popular in southern India.

Lakshmi also has a supreme form, known as Maha Lakshmi or Adi Lakshmi, in which she is a totally independent deity of Maha Shakti. In the Pancharatra and Tantric schools she is given this independent status. While Lakshmi is the consort of Vishnu, Maha Lakshmi is the embodiment of the divine Shakti. Her nature is very much like that of the virgin goddess Durga.

One of the Tantric schools considers her to be the root of all creation. In this story, Narayana (Vishnu), the cosmic soul, was lying on the cosmic waters. The idea of objectifying his divine bliss in the form of creation appeared in his mind and his Shakti lying dormant within him burst forth, manifesting herself as Maha Lakshmi. She placed the seed of his divine desire in the palm of her hand and unleashed the dynamic forces of creation, which emerged in the myriad forms of the universe that we know.

Another story describes Vishnu sleeping on the coils of the serpent of time known as Adi Shesha or Ananta (endless time). Brahma, the creator, emerged from the lotus sprouting from Vishnu's navel and Shiva burst forth from Brahma's forehead. Ananta was conceived as floating on the cosmic waters. But what was the container of these waters? The sages declared that the waters were contained in the womb of the primeval Divine Mother, Adi Lakshmi or Adi Shakti. *Adi* means "first," implying that she existed before everything else.

The Puranas have hundreds of interesting stories that describe creation. The Brahmanda Purana states that Adi Lakshmi laid three eggs. Durga and Vishnu emerged from the first, Lakshmi and Brahma from the second, and Saraswati and Shiva from the third. She paired off Saraswati with Brahma, Lakshmi with Vishnu, and Durga with Shiva and sent them forth for the purposes of creation, maintenance, and dissolution.

Another story states that Lakshmi, Durga, and Saraswati were the personification of the three *gunas* that emerged from Adi Lakshmi. *Rajas* or activity was the essence of Lakshmi, *tamas* or negativity was that of Durga, and *sattva* or harmony was that of Saraswati.

Another interesting story about Lakshmi tells us how she got the name Bhargavi. Brahma created the seven sages at the dawn of time and taught them the Vedas. He charged these sages with seeing to the well-being of the world. Six of them used the *mantras* they had learned from Brahma to invoke Saraswati, the goddess of wisdom, through whose grace alone humanity could gain enlightenment. However, they soon realized that wisdom does not appease the hunger of the body and mind.

The seventh sage, Brighu, learned from Varuna, god of the waters, that ultimately all things are composed of food. There are only two categories of living things: those that eat and those that are eaten. He realized the extreme value of food. He used this knowledge to invoke Lakshmi, the goddess of bounty and wealth, through whose grace human beings could get food as well as anything else they wanted. Some of the impoverished sages went to Brighu and asked him to help them attain riches. He taught them the science of astrology, palmistry, and how to make use of the bounties of the earth in the correct way, by which they could acquire wealth. The collection of his works is known as Brighu Samhita. Since he was the one who taught them the science of material prosperity, the sages concluded that Lakshmi was his daughter, and thus they added another name to her collection and called her Bhargavi.

Later on Lakshmi was invoked by the demons and went to stay with them, and thus the *asuras* became very powerful. But when they resorted to hoarding and cheating and licentious living, she deserted them and went to Indra, king of the gods.

At this time Durvasa, the sage who was known for his irascible nature, took a celestial garland to Indra's court. Indra was totally inebriated and carousing with the heavenly damsels. He took the garland the sage offered and carelessly threw it over his elephant's head. The garland fell off and was trampled by the elephant. Durvasa was infuriated by this behavior and cursed Indra, saying that all the gods would lose their health, wealth, and youth and become decrepit. No sooner did the sage utter this curse than the gods lost their virility and Lakshmi disappeared into the Ocean of Milk (another name for the Sea of Nectar). Instantly the world lost its appeal. Everything became dull and listless. The earth refused to yield and the cows to give milk. The gods ran to their savior, Vishnu, who advised them to get the help of the demons and churn the milky ocean and thus get back both Lakshmi and *amrita* (the nectar of immortality), which they could take to regain their lost youth.

It was an enterprise that needed cosmic preparations. The churn was the huge mountain called Mandara (representing space) and the rope was the serpent Ananta (representing time). The positive and negative forces of life—the gods and demons—combined to churn the ocean of causality. Vishnu had to help them many times, whenever misfortune overshadowed this gargantuan enterprise. When the mountain started to slip down into the ocean, he took on the form of a gigantic tortoise and held it up. When both parties started to tire, he took a form with thousands of arms and stood in the middle and helped both sides to churn vigorously.

Many wondrous things came out of the cosmic waters. At last, pleased with the determination displayed by both parties, Lakshmi emerged from the ocean in all her glory, seated on a glowing red lotus. She was clad in a splendid red and gold sari and resplendent with jewels from crown to toe. Both parties stopped their exertions just to gaze at her. Along with her came the wish-fulfilling tree called *kalpavriksha,* the wish-fulfilling cow called Kamadhenu, and the desire-fulfilling gem known as *chintamani.* Thus Lakshmi brought with her everything that would give pleasure to humanity.

The gods, demons, and sages all wanted to please the goddess and begged her to accept them, but after inspecting them, she found some fault with each of them and refused their advances. Looking around, she saw one being who was totally disinterested in what was going on. He was sitting alone, dangling his foot in the milky ocean and gazing out over the waters. This was Vishnu. Taking her *vanamala* (garland of wildflowers) in her hands, she glided slowly toward him and placed the wedding garland around his neck. Hence it is said that Lakshmi blesses those who don't run after her. She goes unsolicited and places her garland of plenty on those who worship her husband. Vishnu accepted her and gave her a place on his chest next to his heart. He also declared that she was his Shakti and thus her name should be said before his own. So he came to be known as Lakshmi-Narayana.

As Vishnu's consort, Lakshmi lost her reputation for fickleness. She became the model Hindu wife, loyal and submissive to her husband. She is usually shown sitting at the feet of her lord and massaging his feet. The picture of Lakshmi at Vishnu's feet gives the message that one should not allow worldly power and riches to go to one's head. Wealth has the subtle ability to corrupt, and so one should always be careful in handling it. We have seen that Lakshmi's early history connected her with teeming vitality and prolific fertility. In her role as the wife of Vishnu, however, she is more involved in helping her husband keep the order of *dharma* in the world. Whenever Vishnu incarnates himself to uphold *dharma*, she incarnates along with him as his helpmate and consort.

The Vishnu Purana says, "As Hari (Vishnu) descends in the world in various shapes, so does his consort Sri (Lakshmi). When Hari was born as a dwarf, the son of Aditi, she appeared in the form of a lotus. When he was Raghava (Rama), she became Sita, when he was Krishna, she became Rukmani. In his other descents also she is his associate. When he takes a celestial form, she appears divine, if a mortal, she becomes a mortal too, transforming her own person to suit the character her husband enacts."

In her role as a model wife Lakshmi upholds the social order. Thus it is said that she is always present in a house that is clean and beautifully kept and lives with those who observe the correct social observances like telling the truth and who are generous and kind. In the Mahabharata she says, "I dwell in truth, gifts, vows, austerities, strength, and virtue."

All Vaishnava schools of philosophy insist that Lakshmi should always accompany Vishnu and be invoked along with him. In fact, the devotee prays to her to intercede with her lord on the devotee's behalf. She is the embodiment of divine compassion and she ensures easy approach to Vishnu.

Lakshmi is worshipped in every house, temple, and shop around the length and breadth of India, but one festival closely connected with her is Navaratri, or the nine-days' worship of the Divine Mother in all her forms. During the first three nights of the festival the goddess is worshipped as Durga or Kaali; in the next three nights she is worshipped as as Lakshmi and in the final three nights as Saraswati. The actual method of worshipping her has already been described in chapter 10. It is said that the festival symbolizes the act of Maha Devi standing on a point of a needle and doing terrific *tapas* for nine nights, transforming herself from the fierce, *tamasic* Kaali to the ravishing, *rajasic* Lakshmi and finally to the serene, *sattvic* Saraswati. Esoterically speaking, these nine days are to be divided by spiritual aspirants in the following fashion: During the first three days we concentrate on Kaali and beg her to remove all our negative tendencies of hate, fear, anger, and jealousy. For the next three days we worship Lakshmi and beg her to replace these negative qualities with the positive qualities of cheer, joy, and love. In such a purified heart, Saraswati, the goddess of spiritual success, may deign to come and give liberation, and we pray for that over the final three days. When we want to plant a garden we must first root out the weeds, and for this we need the help of Kaali. When the ground has been prepared we can invite Lakshmi to come and plant the flowers. Only then will Saraswati appear to give us the fruit of Supreme Knowledge.

Diwali or Dipavali, the festival of lights, is another celebration closely connected with Lakshmi. The actual festival falls on the new moon of late autumn, in October or November. But the two days preceding and two days following are also celebrated. On the thirteenth day of the waning moon, all types of shining vessels—gold, silver, copper, or steel, according to one's capcity—are brought to the house. These vessels are the tangible manifestations of the goddess. The next day is known as Naraka Chaturdasi, which is the day on which Lord Krishna defeated the demon Naraka and rescued the ten thousand damsels who had been incarcerated in Naraka's dungeon.

Diwali falls on the day of the new moon, which is the darkest night of the lunar cycle. At this time every house is lit with hundreds of little lamps to welcome the goddess. It was on this day that she is supposed to have risen from the milky ocean. On this night the sun enters the constellation of Libra, the scales. Hence all businessmen balance their accounts on this day and invite Lakshmi to come and take up her abode in their shops and houses. On the next day it is usual to distribute new clothes and food to everyone, especially the poor.

The basis of Hindu religious life is to discover our true nature. Before we do this, however, we have to experience life as it is—to know both its bounties and its pain. For this we need to worship Lakshmi, for she is the divine provider, the source of all nourishment. Adi Shankaracharya, the exponent of Advaita Vedanta, which asserts the ephemeral nature of life, wrote a famous hymn to Lakshmi known as the *Kanakadhara Stotram,* which means, "The hymn that will make gold flow." This shows that even he, ascetic though he was, realized the necessity of the blessings of Lakshmi in temporal life.

> *May the eyes that are spellbound by the beauty of Vishnu,*
> *Fall on me and bestow upon me prosperity and happiness.*
> . . . .
> *Salutations to the lotus-faced goddess who emerged from*
>   *the ocean of milk, along with the moon and the elixir*
>   *of immortality and became Narayana's bride.*
> *May the breeze of her compassion bring the clouds of*
>   *prosperity*
> *And pour rain on the barren life of this poor bird*
> *And wash away its accumulated demerits.*
> . . . .
> *With my impoverished heart I surrender myself to your*
>   *compassion*
> *That you may watch over me, bless me and forgive me.*

> —FROM THE *KANAKADHARA STOTRAM*
>   BY ADI SHANKARACHARYA

Thus ends the twenty-first chapter of *Shakti,* known as "Lakshmi," which describes Lakshmi, the goddess of auspiciousness.

Aum Aim Hreem Kleem

Aum Saraswatyai Namaha!

22

Saraswati

Chithirupena ya krthsnam ethat vyapya sthitha jagat,
Namasthasyai, namasthasyai, namasthasyai namo namaha!

She who abides in this whole world,
Having pervaded it in the form of mind,
Hail to thee, hail to thee, all hail to thee!

The universe is the creation of Maha Prakriti, and the Devi Bhagavatam identifies different parts of the world with different parts of the body of the goddess. The earth is her loins, the oceans her bowels, the mountains her bones, the rivers her veins, and the trees the hair on her body. The sun and moon are her eyes and the netherworlds are her hips, legs, and feet. She wears the stars as ornaments in her hair.

Sometimes called Punyabhoomi (which means, "the blessed land"), India has a sacred geography. The whole of the Indian subcontinent is a repository of divine power. Every region in India is dotted with sacred and holy places. The sacredness of the land, rather than its political setup, has been the force that has made India a unified nation. The whole of the subcontinent was rendered sacred by the different parts of the body of Sati that were scattered by Shiva through the length and breadth of the land. The Puranas depict the whole of India as a goddess. She is known as Bharata Mata, or Mother India. All Indians consider themselves to be children of Mother India. In many places, such as Haridwar and Varanasi, there are temples dedicated to Mother India. The land itself is an inspiring and nourishing presence to all those who are born in it. The Indian national anthem, written by Sri Ravindranath Tagore, portrays this feeling beautifully:

> *Thou art the ruler of the minds of all people,*
> *Dispenser of India's destiny.*
> *Thy name arouses the hearts of Punjab, Sind,*
> * Gujarat, and Maratha,*
> *Of Dravida, Orissa, and Bengal.*
> *It echoes in the hills of the Vindhyas and the*
> * Himalayas,*
> *Mingles with the music of Yamuna and Ganga,*
> *And is chanted by the waves of the Indian Sea.*
> *They pray for thy blessings and sing thy praise,*
> *The safety of all people reposes in thy hands,*
> *Thou dispenser of India's destiny,*
> *Victory, victory, victory to thee!*

Each act of worship to any village goddess is considered to be an act of worship to the divinity of India as a whole. Every river in the Indian subcontinent is considered a *thirtha* or sacred water. This reverence goes back all the way to the Rig Veda, where it is said that all Indian rivers have their origin in the heavens. The earthly river is only a continuation of the waters that flow from Heaven to Earth.

In the Vedas Saraswati was worshipped as a river. Her name actually means "watery." The early Indians considered this river to be most sacred. At that time it held a position similar to what the Ganga (Ganges) holds today as the prototype of all the rivers of India, in that all the waters of the land share its magic power of salvation, though to a lesser degree.

The Rig Veda proclaims that the river Saraswati is a goddess who blesses her devotees with health, long life, and poetic inspiration. The earthly river is only a partial manifestation of the heavenly deity. This river is said to have flowed through the region of Rajasthan six thousand years ago. It was a huge river, with waves so big that they could break down mountains. Its source lay in the celestial ocean and thus it was inexhaustible. But two thousand years ago it vanished and the region turned into a desert. It is believed that it became a subterranean river that flowed underground to join the two other great sacred rivers of India—the Ganga and Yamuna—in the holy place of Prayaga. This confluence is known as Thirtharaja (king of all *thirthas*). It is said that anyone who stays on the banks of the Saraswati reciting the Saraswati *mantra* will become a poet.

Anticipating her later nature as the goddess of learning, the hymns of the Rig Veda describe Saraswati as the one who inspires all songs and all gracious thought. In fact, she is similar to the Vedic goddess of speech, Vac. The ability to turn unintelligible sounds that come from the mouth into forms that can be understood by others is a unique ability of human beings, and Hindus have great respect for it. Sound is the primordial stuff of creation. The Vedas declare that ritual speech is a most powerful tool for invoking the powers of nature and making them obey the will of man. It is the power of the goddess Vac that inspired the *rishis* and enabled them to hymn the divine. She is the mysterious presence that enables us to hear, see, grasp, and express in words the nature of the world, both inner and outer. Thus Vac is an essential part of our spiritual experiences. The Vedas describe her as a glowing being, benign and bounteous, who confers on everyone the riches of language. It is due to her grace that we can communicate with each other.

As the embodiment of speech, Saraswati is present whenever and wherever a word is spoken. She is also the goddess of the intellect, which makes coherent speech possible. She is not only the power of knowledge but also the power of memory. She is behind the infinity of forms found in the universe and is responsible for the infinity of ideas created by the human mind. Thus she is the mother of all sciences—Sarvavidya Swarupini, or the embodiment of all wisdom. She is also the mother of all arts. She inspires poets, musicians, writers, and dancers. Whenever we see great culture, great art, or extraordinary intelligence, we can know that Saraswati has manifested herself. She is the divinity that has enabled the human race to become superior to all other creatures and the grace that enables them to stride across the world as demigods. Artistic creations and the power of knowledge, including philosophy, demonstrate the extraordinary ability of the human being to mold and refine the natural world into something noble and divine. Thus Saraswati is the energy of cosmic creativity that is reflected in us.

Maha Saraswati is the Divine Mother's power of intelligence, perfection, and order. Maha Devi lays down the large lines of the world order. Maha Kaali drives everything before her with her energy and impetus, Maha Lakshmi points out the beauty of their rhythms and harmony, and Maha Saraswati provides the intelligence that details their organization and execution. As described in chapter 21, she is the third of the goddesses who are worshipped during Navaratri, the nine-day festival of worship of the Divine Mother. The first three days are devoted to Maha Kaali, who roots out our negative qualities, the next three days to Maha Lakshmi, who plants in us all beauty and virtue, and the final three days to Maha Saraswati, who finally gives us liberation.

Saraswati's symbols and character contrast dramatically with those of Lakshmi. Saraswati is clad in pure white and Lakshmi in red. Saraswati's only ornament is a necklace of pearls or crystals, while Lakshmi bedecks herself with fabulous jewels. Saraswati holds books, pens, and the lute in her hands, while Lakshmi holds lotuses and the pitcher of plenty. Saraswati is associated with the wind, free and unbound, and thus she rides a swan. Lakshmi is associated with earth and water, bound and flowing, and thus she sits on a lotus. Lakshmi's name is coupled with that of many male divinities, but Saraswati is associated with only

Brahma, a god who is never worshipped. Lakshmi's color is that of turmeric and gold, while Saraswati is as fair as the full moon.

Brahma is the creator in the trinity. As Brahma Shakti, Saraswati is that power that enables human beings to create. Out of the nameless and formless, she makes this world of forms and names that we can experience. She is the goddess of inspiration, eloquence, and learning. In fact, many schools and colleges in India have statues of Saraswati to provide inspiration to students, and initiation into all learning begins with an invocation to Saraswati. Before a child is sent to school, he or she has to go through the ritual called *vidyarambham,* or the commencement of learning, and for this the supreme deity to be worshipped is Saraswati, the giver of all knowledge.

As we have seen, Saraswati was originally the wife of Lord Vishnu, but due to the curse of Ganga she was born on Earth as a river. She is sometimes called Bharati, since she came to the land known as Bharata Varsha. She is also known as Vani, or sound, since she is the presiding deity of speech. Later she became Brahma's wife. However, she quickly overshadowed her spouse. Hardly anyone in India worships Brahma, but the whole country worships Saraswati. She is rarely shown seated next to him, even when they are seen together. Their relationship seems more intellectual than conjugal. She is his dynamic counterpart. She holds the three Vedas that are chanted regularly by Brahmins in her hands (the Rig Veda, Yajur Veda, and Sama Veda), and thus she is said to be their creator.

Brahma's creations are all mental. It is Saraswati who manifests these ideas, which are in the form of divine vibrations, as concrete forms. It is she who stirs the still lake of the undisturbed energy of the absolute into the living stream of life. The first manifestation of the Brahman is Sabda Brahman or sound. This is called *spanda,* the mysterious vibration of sound that we hear as *aum.* Saraswati is the living form of this sound, so she is known as Nada Brahman (*nada* translates as "sound of creation"). In the Saraswati Rahasya Upanishad, the goddess herself says:

It was through me that the creator gained liberating
knowledge,
I am pure being, consciousness, bliss, eternal freedom,
Unsullied, unlimited, unending.
My perfect consciousness shines in the world like a
beautiful face in a soiled mirror.
Seeing that reflection I call myself you—the individual
jiva,
Pretending to be finite.

Maha Saraswati is the Divine Mother's power for accomplishing all types of works and her spirit of perfection and order. There is none to beat her in the executive faculty. She is the drive behind the impetus of all nature. She demands exactitude and certainty. That is why science, crafts, and techniques come under her province. Those who are blessed by her have subtlety and patience, the certainty of the intuitive mind, and the discerning eye of the perfect worker. Her will is scrupulous and indefatigable, though it might be slow. She is conscious of every detail and insists on flawless performance. Nothing is too small or trivial for her attention. Both in the individual and in the universe, she molds every part until it fits perfectly into the role meant for it. If we submit to her will, she will choose for us the right time, the right place, and the right conditions to produce the perfect piece of work. She dislikes carelessness, negligence, and indolence. Nothing short of perfection will satisfy her. She is ready to face an eternity of toil if necessary to produce fullness in her creation. If we are single-minded and determined to succeed, her hand will sustain our every effort. She is intolerant of falsehood and pretense. In the spiritual life, she is the one who drives us forward, provided we are sincere in our perseverance. She will never leave us until we have attained our goal.

Her form is beautiful. She is described as being as fair as the white lily, the moon, or the garlands formed by snow crystals. She is clad in spotless white garments. The white garments show that her form is that of pure *shuddha tattva* (purest element), the first emanation from the Brahman. Thus she is formed entirely of *sattva guna*, the pure, spiritual thread of nature. Her *sattvic* nature dissociates her from the mud of existence, including the sap of fertility to which many of the other goddesses are closely related. Her motherhood is metaphorical. She gives birth to ideas and inspirations. She is said to have an ascetic nature and grants boons to those who perform *tapas*. Therefore she is not a goddess of the householder or the farmer but of the intellectual, of the ascetic, of the student and the artist.

She is normally shown seated on a white lotus. This shows her transcendence. Although having its source in the mud, the lotus lifts its head and opens itself to the glorious sun, untouched by the muddy waters below. Saraswati inspires human beings to transcend their physical limitations and enter the realm of the arts and thus reach for the heavens.

Her vehicle, the swan, also points out her uplifting nature, far removed from the impurities of the natural world with its rhythms of growth and fertility. The swan is a symbol of spiritual transcendence in Hinduism. It is said to have the power to separate milk from water. So also great *yogis* have the power to separate the milk of immortal life from the water of material life. Such *yogis* are known as *paramahamsas* or great swans. Saraswati glides over this tangible universe of energy that we see, seated on her white swan, pointing out to us a different dimension of human existence, above the physical world of the senses. Her realm is one of perfection, beauty, culture, and grace.

Saraswati has four hands. One carries the *veena* (lute) that produces the vibration of life. The sound of the *veena* is the origin of the Sama Veda. One who has the ears of wisdom will be able to hear the whole world vibrating to the sound of her *veena*. In fact, the whole world of objects is nothing but the material manifestation of the sound of her lute. We know that the visible world is made up of forms and all forms have names and all names are only a combination of sounds. Thus out of sounds come names, or *nama*, and from that is created form, or *rupa*.

In another hand she carries the Vedas. The Vedas signify the totality of all knowledge, of both things that can be known as well as those that lie beyond thought. This suggests that Saraswati holds all knowledge in her hands, both material as well as transcendental.

In another hand Saraswati holds the spotless crystal *japa mala* (rosary), indicating the necessity for continuous spiritual practice or *sadhana*. Thus she stands for both the theory and practice of *yogic* knowledge. As every aspirant knows, continuous practice is essential for success in *sadhana*. The fourth hand shows the *abhaya mudra*, the sign of grace or fearlessness.

Saraswati is at once the origin and the conclusion of the evolutionary process of the *jiva* from ignorance to enlightenment. But it must be remembered that she gives us not only material knowledge but also supreme wisdom. The *jiva* in its entanglement with matter gets enmeshed in the goddess's role as Maha Maya. But at the end of its evolutionary cycle, when the *jiva* longs to trace its journey back to the source from which it came, it has to worship Maha Saraswati, for she is the giver of Brahma Jnana or knowledge of the supreme. This circle of existence projects the *jiva* from knowledge to ignorance and back to knowledge. Maha Saraswati is both the origin and the conclusion of this process of evolution. The seeker of knowledge as well as the seeker of enlightenment must look for her grace.

By reading the scriptures regularly we are worshipping Saraswati, for she is present in word form in every book. By speaking the truth and by speaking sweetly we are worshipping her, for her *veena* has no discordant tones. For Navaratri, the nine-day festival celebrating the Divine Mother, the tenth day is called Vijayadasami—the day of victory, when the aspirant finally cuts the knots of ignorance that have bound him to the mundane world and gains victory over his ego and is united with the supreme. This day is dedicated the goddess Saraswati.

Goddess of wisdom, who appears as syllables,
Words, sentences and understanding,

Goddess in whom all meaning inheres
From beginningless time, grant me your grace.
Goddess who purifies and enriches the soul,
You who are the treasurer of intelligence,
Please accept these words, my humble offering!

—Saraswati Rahasya Upanishad

Thus ends the twenty-second chapter of *Shakti,* known as "Saraswati," which describes the goddess Saraswati.

Aum Aim Hreem Kleem

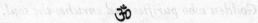

Aum Sri Radhayai Namaha!

23

Radha

O Devi Radhika! Your color is like the white champaka
    flower.
Your face is like the autumnal full moon;
Your body shines with the splendor of ten million moons,
Your eyes are as beautiful as the autumnal lotus;
Your lips are as red as the bimba fruit;
Your loins are heavy and decked with a girdle;
Your gracious face is sweetly smiling;
Your breasts defy the frontal lobe of an elephant;
You are ever youthful;
Your body is adorned with ornaments;
You form the waves of the ocean of erotic love;
You are ever ready to show your grace to all devotees;
Your hair is braided with jasmine;
Your body is as tender as a creeper;
You are seated in the middle of the rasa mandalam;
One hand shows the mudra of fearlessness and the other of
    granting boons;
You are dearer to Krishna than his life.
O Parameswari! The Vedas reveal your true nature.

—SAMA VEDA

Lord Krishna, the Purushottama or the supreme personality of God, is well known to the world. But the esoteric significance of Radha, his soul mate, has not been fully understood.

Radha's life is inextricably connected with that of Krishna, and she is hardly ever mentioned by herself. She was the daughter of a herdsman called Vrishabhanu and was born in the little village of Barsana, close to Vraja, where Krishna spent his childhood. Krishna was the son of Vasudeva, a nobleman of the Yadava clan. However, because he feared Kamsa, the king of their clan, his father brought the baby Krishna to the village of Vraja and exchanged him for the baby girl who had just been born to the village headman, Nandagopa, chief of the cowherders (*gopalas*).

Krishna's foster parents, Yasoda and Nandagopa, fully believed him to be their son, and he was brought up like any other *gopala* boy. In the village of Vraja and later in the woods and glades of the nearby forest of Vrindavana, the boy Krishna performed many miracles that are sung about by bards to this very day. The *gopis* (women of the *gopalas*, or milkmaids) doted on Krishna as a baby and as a child. But their interest changed to passionate longing for him when he grew older. None of them, even married women, were able to resist his beauty and charm. Though he was only twelve years old at that time, Krishna's appeal was irresistible. Everyone and everything was drawn to him—the cows, the herdsmen, the trees, and the boys. What wonder that the *gopis* felt as if they could not exist without him? There were hundreds of *gopis*, and all of them felt that Krishna alone was their lord and master. Nothing could deter the mad rush of their hearts toward him.

The young *gopis* performed forty-one days of adoration and worship of the Divine Mother in her form as Kartyayini, the virgin goddess, and begged her to enable them to achieve their hearts' desire and get Krishna, son of Nandagopa, as their husband.

> *O Kartyayini, [the virgin goddess]*
> *O Mahamaya! [the great deluder]*
> *O Mahayogi! [the great yogi]*

O Yateeswari, [goddess of all renunciates]
O Devi! Please grant me the boon that I will get
the son of Nandagopa,
As my husband.

—BHAGAVAD PURANA

In the beginning of spring, the *gopis* bathed in the cold waters of the river Kalindi in the predawn hours and, using an idol made out of river sand, worshipped the goddess with the *mantra* above. Finally, on the last day of their worship, while they were bathing naked in the river, the lord of their hearts arrived, looking like a veritable Cupid. He decided to teach them the most important lesson in the life of any true devotee. With a teasing glance in their direction, he took away the clothes they had left on the banks and perched himself on the branch of a tree. He hung the clothes on different branches and told them to come out of the water and get their clothes one by one. They begged and pleaded with him, but he was adamant.

"How did you get into the water?" he asked them. "You must have left the clothes on the banks and jumped in naked. If you felt no shame being with each other, why should you feel shame with me? Don't you know that I am the Paramatman and you are part of me? There is nothing about you that I don't know."

At last they came out of the water one by one and received their clothes from his hands. He then blessed them and promised them that he would satisfy their desires on the full-moon nights of the autumn season.

This is one of the most misunderstood scenes in the life of Krishna. But it has a deep esoteric significance that has to be understood before we can proceed on the path of devotion. There are many bonds that separate the *jivatman* from the Paramatman. The main bond is the one of the body. Considering ourselves to be the body alone, we willfully cut ourselves off from our inner reality. As long as this sense of separation exists we can never attain union with the supreme. The *gopis* have been eulogized as the greatest examples of pure *bhakti* or devotion to

God, without any trace of selfishness. Though this was true, they still had one bond left, and that was the one to their body. Krishna had to remove this final attachment before he could grant them the fulfillment of their desires, which was union with him, who was the embodiment of the supreme reality. This was the reason he asked them to come naked and receive their clothes from him without shame—without the feeling of separateness.

The highest *yogis* in Hinduism are known as *avadhutas* or those who wear no clothes. These great souls have cast off their attachment to their body, and as a symbol of this detachment they have discarded their clothes. Before he could give them the ultimate experience, Krishna had to transform the *gopis* into *avadhutas*.

The famous episode, known as the Rasa Lila, in which Krishna danced with the *gopis*, took place in the forest of Vrindavana on the night of the full moon in the month of Kartika (mid-October to mid-November). The lord took his stance under a tree in the forest at night, just as the moon started to rise, and played on his celestial flute. The notes were heard in far-off Vraja and brought thrills of delight to the hearts of the *gopis*. It is said that in the mad rush of their hearts toward him, who was the beloved of the whole of creation, the *gopis* forgot all their external bonds—their duties to their husbands, parents, and even children. Leaving all their unfinished chores, hundreds of them ran to the forest, totally oblivious of everything except the call of their divine beloved. This was the enticing call of the Paramatman, the supreme soul, to the *jivatman*, the embodied soul encased in the gown of the body. How could they resist it? All the duties of a normal Hindu woman were forgotten.

The human being has only one basic duty, and that is to attain union with God. Until we realize this, we are bound to perform all the other duties imposed on us by society and by our own nature and desires. But the moment this supreme duty becomes paramount in our minds, all other duties can be forgotten. We have no more duties to perform because we expect nothing from the world. Our entire dependence is on God alone. This was the state of the *gopis* of Vrindavana, and that is why they are worshipped to this day as the greatest examples of devotion.

In their eagerness to reach their beloved the *gopis* had forgotten to put on their makeup or even to dress properly. None noticed the state in which the others were, since their minds were concentrated totally on their beloved. The state of their mind was that of a meditating *yogi*, single-minded and fixed on Krishna. He tenderly attended to the perfection of their toilette before leading them to a clearing in the woods that was perfect for the dance that is known as the Rasa Lila.

In this dance every *gopi* found herself to be partnered by a Krishna, so that there were hundreds of Krishnas and hundreds of *gopis*. There was yet another Krishna in the middle of the circle who was playing the flute and supplying the music for their dance. This setup is an allegory of the dance of life that the Paramatman plays with each *jivat-man*. Each one feels that God is her very own, just as every *gopi* felt that Krishna belonged to her alone. Then, however, ego reared its ugly head in the breasts of the *gopis*, and they felt that they had conquered Krishna by their charm and beauty. At that moment it is said that the lord disappeared from their midst and they were left bereft.

The only *gopi* who had no ego was Radha, and for this reason she was Krishna's favorite. She lived in a world peopled by Krishna alone (Krishnamayam Jagat). Some books say that she was married. Regardless, she cared not for any worldly ties. For a few short years she lived in blissful companionship and love with her beloved Krishna.

Radha is the supreme model of love for Krishna. Radha's love and therefore her fame are far greater than that of his wives. Why this illicit love has been extolled in the life of Krishna is a pertinent question with deep esoteric significance. A wife gives up nothing to go to her husband. The marital ties are supported by society and she has nothing to lose. In fact, she gains the security of a husband and a fair name in society and may look forward to a protected life and an old age supported by her husband and the children to come. On the other hand, a woman who steals out in the middle of the night to meet her lover is despised by society and has no rights over her lover. He might desert her at any moment. But she cares not for these material things. She is prepared to sacrifice everything for the sake of her love. She gives up her fair name and her chastity and demands nothing in return. She gives up everything that is precious to a woman without any thought of recompense. This is the height of selfless love! A wife's love can never compete with this. This is why the Bhagavad Purana extols the illicit love of the *gopis* as the highest of all loves.

Only the soul who is prepared to give up everything for the sake of God will be accepted by him as his very own. Hence was Radha so dear to Krishna. The frenzy and ecstasy of their union was heightened by the constant threat of separation. At last the inevitable happened and Krishna left Vraja, never to return. But his love for Radha never diminished, nor did hers for him, for theirs was the union of the *jivat-man* with the Paramatman, and physical distance could never separate them. Krishna's love for Radha is depicted as being as deep as or even deeper than hers for him. The love that God bears for his devotee is far stronger than what the human heart can feel for God. Hence all the great poems written in India about their amazing love affair stress Krishna's love for Radha as being equal to hers for him.

In Hindu philosophy the devotee is allowed to approach God in many ways. In the *shanta bhava* or the contemplative mood, God is considered to be transcendent. In the *dasya bhava* or the attitude of the servant, God is the master. In the *vatsalya bhava* or the attitude of a parent, God is thought of as a child. In the *sakhya bhava* or the attitude of a friend, God is considered to be a friend. The culmination of all devotional moods is said to be *mathurya bhava* or the mood of ecstatic love, in which God is considered to be one's lover. This was the case for the *gopis* and, most particularly, Radha.

The relationship between Radha and Krishna typifies the pinnacle of devotion and is a graphic metaphor for the human-divine love affair. This relationship is what every devotee wants to achieve with her own *ishta devata* or favorite deity. However, we rarely experience such intense love in our lives. We are never true to ourselves. How, then, can we be true to God? We are all mediocre devotees, with weak bodies, frail minds, and raging emotions that cannot be controlled. The fire of supreme love cannot be contained within our weak frames. It is a mystery that the ordinary human mind just cannot fathom.

The Puranas say, "Speech and mind turn back from that which they are not supposed to express or understand." Human beings have a certain mode of thinking that they are not prepared to change even for the purpose of attaining God. We fear losing the approbation of the society as well as losing our individuality in the ocean of love that God offers. We are bound by the shackles of the society that divides us into men and women, rich and poor, good and bad, Indian or American. Until we strip ourselves of these false values, like the *gopis* did, and stand naked before God, we will never be able to understand the mystery of the love of Radha and Krishna. God is beyond all relationships. He demands nothing short of complete abnegation of the individual ego from the one who wants to be his beloved. All our pride and prejudices have to melt before God, the super-relational being. This melting of the human individuality is *bhakti* (complete devotion). This is what Krishna demanded of the *gopis*. There was nothing halfhearted or mediocre in their love for Krishna. And Radha's love for him surpassed the consummation of all other loves.

In later poetical works and especially the love poems of twelfth-century writer Jayadeva, called the *Gita Govinda,* the picture of Radha is clearly drawn. The Bhagavad Purana gives the play of Krishna with the *gopis* a festive, joyful appearance, like that of a carnival. In the *Gita Govinda,* the stress is on the sorrow felt by the woman (Radha) when she is separated from her lover. This sadness, known as *viraha dukkha,* is an emotion felt by all lovers of God when he fails to manifest himself even after years of constant prayer and supplication. This anguish of separation is something that has been experienced by every ardent devotee. The *Gita Govinda* portray in full the deep sense of despair and loneliness that the soul experiences when separated from the cosmic beloved. All Jayadeva's poems are written from the point of view of Radha, and they take place in the secrecy and stillness of night in the woods. They explore the interior landscapes of a mind obsessed with the love of God, in this case Krishna. But the sentiments they explore would apply equally well to any devotee who has felt this sense of desolation and sorrow at the separation from God. The pathos in these poems will bring tears to the eyes of a loving reader.

Radha's illicit love for Krishna is also the central theme in the poetry of Vidyapati (1352–1448) and fourteenth-century poet Chandidasa. Vidyapati describes Radha as a woman of a noble family and Krishna as a common villager in order to show the extent of the sacrifice that Radha was prepared to make in order to consummate her love.

Radha plays a prominent role in the Vaishnava cult, which considers Krishna to be the supreme incarnation of God. The superiority of illicit love is given great stress in all the schools of Vaishnavism. As has been mentioned before, married love has its basis on rights and obligations in which both partners have specific demands and duties. They may easily stop loving each other if either partner does not live up to these expectations. Even their physical love is characterized by selfish desire, known as *kama,* being for the gratification of their sexual lust. There are no obstacles in the path of their love, and thus it tends to become monotonous and boring.

The relationship between Radha and Krishna, however, is based on *prema* or unselfish love. The impediments that Radha has to face only increase her love and longing. Her love is faced with risk and filled with insecurity. The long periods of separation help enhance her feelings and augment the thrill of union. This is why this type of relationship has been extolled as the highest in the human-divine love affair. The devotee's affair with the cosmic beloved knows no waning or boredom. God is the perfect lover, and the devotee has to be always on guard, always keeping her mind on him alone. God does not tolerate any adulterous behavior on the part of the perfect devotee. She cannot have partial love for the world and partial love for him. If she does, then like Krishna deserted the *gopis* she will find that God has deserted her. Then like Radha she has to weep and beg and pray incessantly until he deigns to reveal himself again. The lord plays a game of hide-and-seek with the devotee. He is always free to come and go, and the devotee often has to spend long periods in painful separation from him.

Radha is the paradigm of complete devotion. Her mind is obsessed with Krishna and cannot forget him even for a moment. Her total absorption in him is contrasted to the fleeting glimpses of the lord that meditating sages and ascetics attain after arduous spiritual exercises. In many sects of Vaishnavism, especially in Bengal, Radha herself is worshipped. Krishna has many powers or *shaktis* within himself; the most essential of these is the *aahladini shakti* or the power of bliss. This *shakti* is the most sublime and refined essence of God. Radha is supposed to be the embodiment of this *shakti*. In this aspect, God's sport with her is an expression of his dalliance with himself—the supreme, reveling in his own bliss.

The Devi Bhagavatam identifies Radha with Mula Prakriti or the original cause of this universe. Radha is the presiding deity of *prana* (the life breath or force) and Durga of *buddhi* (intellect). These two *shaktis* guide the whole world. Liberation cannot be obtained without satisfying them. The six-syllabled *mantra* of Radha is *Sri Radhayai Svaaha* (I invoke Sri Radha). Radha is Krishna's *prana*. She is the queen of Vraja and the chief participant in the Rasa Lila. During worship she is to be seated on a golden throne along with Krishna and worshipped as Mula Prakriti. Thus we find that over the course of history, Radha's role has changed from being the supreme devotee of Krishna to being considered a goddess in her own right. This shows us that God elevates his pure devotees to his own status.

> *O friend, I cannot tell you*
> *Whether he was near or far, real or a dream.*

Like a vein of lightning,
As I chained the dark one,
I felt a river flooding in my heart,
Like a shining moon.
I devoured that liquid face,
I felt stars shooting around me.

—Vidyapati

Thus ends the twenty-third chapter of *Shakti*, known as "Radha," which describes the greatness of Radha, the goddess of love.

Aum Aim Hreem Kleem

ॐ

Aum Vrindavanyai Namaha!

24
Tulasi

Namastulasi kalyani,
Namo Vishnu priye shubhe,
Namo moksha prade devi,
Namah sampad pradayini.

Salutations to Tulasi, the auspicious,
Salutations to the propitious beloved of Vishnu,
Salutations to the goddess who gives liberation,
Salutations to the one who gives all prosperity.

Tulasi had been a *gopi* in Goloka, the celestial abode of Krishna where Radha is queen. She had incurred Radha's displeasure and been cursed by her to be born in the world as a human being. Tulasi had only one desire in her mind, and that was to be united with Lord Krishna, the supreme incarnation of Vishnu, known as Narayana.

She was born on Earth as the daughter of King Vrishadvaja and the celestially beautiful Madhavi. The queen had become pregnant due to the blessings of a *deva*. She carried the baby for a hundred years and at last gave birth to a baby girl on a most auspicious day, the day of the full moon in the month of Kartika, at a time when all the planets were in favorable positions. The baby, named Tulasi, was an incarnation of Lakshmi, the

226

consort of Vishnu. She was a most enchanting infant with all auspicious signs. She remembered her past life perfectly, and as soon as she reached the age of puberty she decided to go to the most ancient and spiritual spot in the Himalayas, known as Badrikashrama, to do *tapas* in order to get Lord Narayana as her husband. Nothing and no one could deter her determination, and she practiced austerities for many years, subsisting for a long time only on fruits, then on leaves, then on air alone. At last Brahma manifested himself and told her to ask for a boon.

Tulasi informed Brahma that her only desire was to have Lord Narayana as her husband, and she had done *tapas* only with this aim. Brahma declared that getting Narayana as a husband was not such an easy thing, and before she achieved her desire, she would have to go through a period of time as the wife of another person, called Shankachuda, who had been practicing penance for many years in order to get Tulasi as his wife.

Brahma gave Tulasi an outline of Shankachuda's previous life. He had been a *gopala* called Sudama who had been a close friend of Krishna in Goloka. Radha had cursed him to become a demon because he had become enamored of Tulasi. Brahma told Tulasi that she would have to marry this *asura* since he was also a devotee of Krishna and had set his heart on marrying her. After many trials she would get the blessings of Lord Vishnu and be changed into a plant known as *tulasi*. This plant would be beloved by Narayana. No *puja* (ritual) of his would be complete without the offering of *tulasi* leaves. She would be born in the forest of Vrindavana and would also be known as Vrindavani. All devotees of Krishna would have to offer *tulasi* leaves at his feet in order to please him. She would be as dear to Krishna as Radha. Thus Radha's curse would really be a blessing to the whole world, since the *tulasi* plant would have great medicinal properties. Tulasi was very happy to hear this and continued to live in Badrikashrama, contemplating the lotus feet of Lord Narayana.

In the meantime, the *gopala* Shankachuda, who had been turned into an *asura* by Radha's curse, had been doing severe penance at the only holy spot dedicated to Brahma, known as Pushkara. Brahma appeared to him and told him to proceed to Badrikashrama, where he would attain his heart's desire. When Shankachuda reached Tulasi's hermitage and saw her, his love for her overwhelmed him. He ran to her and knelt at her feet and begged her to marry him.

Tulasi told him that it was most unbecoming to talk of marriage to a young girl without getting the permission of her parents. Then Shankachuda reminded her of their connection in a previous life: "I was a *gopala* named Sudama, a close friend of Krishna, and I was born on earth due to Radha's curse. I fell in love with you in Goloka but could not associate with you for fear of Radha. But now I have been given the opportunity of marrying you, so will you consent to be my wife?"

Tulasi gladly agreed, since his words tallied with what Brahma had told her. Just then Brahma appeared on the scene and gave Tulasi in marriage to Shankachuda. Since it was a marriage of mutual consent, no formalities, rites, or priests were necessary. The couple continued to live in the hermitage in perfect harmony and love. At last, when they tired of their solitude, Shankachuda took Tulasi back to his own kingdom. Soon, however, he began to display his *asuric* tendencies and fought with the gods, dispersing them from heaven.

The despondent gods, headed by Indra, went with their eternal complaints to Brahma. He professed his helplessness in this matter. They proceeded to Kailasa, the abode of Shiva, who told them that Vishnu was the best person to deal with this issue, since Shankachuda had been his devotee in his previous life.

When they came to him, Vishnu narrated to the gods the history of Shankachuda's previous life:

O *devas!* As you know, Shankachuda was my favorite attendant in Goloka. He is fully protected by the armor that I gave him when Radha cursed him. As long as he wears this armor he is invincible, so first I will have to go to him in the form of a Brahmin and beg him for his armor. Brahma has also given him the boon that he can be killed only if his wife commits adultery. Since his wife, Tulasi, is dear to me and has done much austerity in order to procure me as her husband, I will personally approach her and tempt her. When she falls, as she is bound to do, Shiva will easily be able to kill him.

Shiva promised to help the gods and sent a messenger to Shankachuda asking him to return the heavens to the gods or come and fight with him. Shankachuda laughingly told the messenger to return to his master and ask him to get ready for battle. He then informed Tulasi of the impending encounter. She wept when she heard this and begged him not to go, for she had seen many ill omens.

Shankachuda said, "Be not afraid, O beauteous one! Everything happens due to the will of Maha Devi. I have satisfied my desires with you, and now it remains for you to fulfill your desire. You will certainly get Narayana as your husband, so be not afraid. Everything that is meant to happen will happen with the turning of the wheel of time."

In the morning, Shankachuda bathed and prayed to Lord Krishna and set out for battle with Shiva. It is said that the battle went on for many days without any fatigue on either part. It was then that Vishnu took the form of a Brahmin and came to the battlefield and begged Shankachuda for his armor. The *asura,* who was noted for his great generosity, immediately took it off and gave it to the Brahmin. Vishnu then took the form of Shankachuda and arrived at the palace. He went to Tulasi and took her in his arms. She thought that her husband had returned to her and complied with his wishes.

At this precise moment Shiva hurled the fatal trident at Shankachuda. When Shankachuda saw the spear coming, he immediately sat in his chariot in the *yogic* posture and fixed his mind on Krishna. The world-consuming trident turned to ashes both the chariot and its occupant. To the amazement of all, the *asura* took the form of a *gopala* and got into a celestial car that had come for him. It is said that Shankachuda's bones were turned into conches, which are considered most auspicious in Narayana's *puja.* (Lakshmi resides in conch shells, and the water from all the holy rivers flow from these shells, so bathing a deity with water poured from them is considered most holy.)

In the meantime Narayana assumed his real form and gave Tulasi a vision of his beauteous countenance, blue in color, with lotus-petaled eyes. When she saw him, Tulasi was grief-stricken and said, "O master magician! Why have you betrayed me? In order to help the gods you have cheated me and allowed your devotee to be killed. Your heart is like a stone, so I curse you to take the form of a stone!"

The lord spoke gently to her:

O Tulasi! For many years you performed *tapas* in the mountains to get me as your husband. Now that I have accepted you, why have you changed your mind? Shankachuda also performed great austerity to get you as his wife. Such rigorous penance cannot go unrewarded. Both of you have achieved your heart's desire. Divine ways are strange and inexplicable. Your husband, who is a true *yogi,* knew this. He has already gone back to Goloka and is residing in splendor and happiness with Krishna. You have a further role to play in the world. You will have to give up your earthly body, which will turn into a river known as Gantaki. Your hair will turn into a plant called *tulasi.* The leaves of this plant will be considered most sacred in all the three worlds and will be used in all *pujas* done to me. All holy rivers will reside at the foot of the *tulasi* plant, and all places where you are cultivated will become pure and holy. I myself with every one of the other gods will remain at your feet and await the falling of a single leaf. I will get more pleasure from the offering of one *tulasi* leaf than I would get from the offering of countless gems and holy waters. *Puja* done in the month of Kartika, when you were born, will be even more effective. One who drinks *tulasi* water at the time of death will be freed from all sins. He who wears a string of *tulasi* beads around his neck will get the same benefit as one who has conducted a horse sacrifice.

As for me, I will become the stones in the river Gantaki, in compliance with your curse. These stones will be known as *saligramas,* and each will have a mark of Vishnu inside them. My devotees will adore these stones. They will bring auspiciousness to the household in which they are kept and worshipped. The best way to venerate them will be to pour Ganga water over them and offer *tulasi* leaves. The devotee who does this will receive great prosperity and liberation at the end of his life.

Thus Narayana pacified Tulasi, further telling her, "O Tulasi! All my devotees will worship you. Everyone will keep you on his or her head. I myself will keep you on my breast, for you are a partial incarnation of Lakshmi." Thus saying, he took his leave of her. Tulasi gave up her life and became the river Gantaki as well as the sacred plant *tulasi*. In these forms she continues to bless all devotees of Lord Krishna. And Lord Vishnu became the *saligrama* stones that are found only in the Gantaki River.

Devotees of Krishna or Vishnu perform *tulasi puja* on the day of the full moon of the month of Kartika, the day on which Tulasi was born on earth. One who worships her with devotion will attain the feet of Narayana and will attain liberation from the mundane world.

> *A bliss lived in her heart too large for heaven,*
> *Light too intense for thought and love too boundless*
> *For earth's emotions in her skies of mind,*
> *And spread through her deep and happy seas of soul,*
> *All that is sacred in the worlds drew near,*
> *To her divine passivity of mood.*
>
> —*SAVITRI* BY SRI AUROBINDO

Thus ends the twenty-fourth chapter of *Shakti*, known as "Tulasi," which describes the greatness of Tulasi, the goddess of the sacred plant.

Aum Aim Hreem Kleem

Aum Vasundharayai Namaha!

25
Sita

> Sita is all creation and the gods of creation,
>   She is cause and effect, saints and demons, the elements,
>   souls;
>   She is supreme virtue and supreme beauty,
>   The worlds are illumined by her form as the sun;
>   She adorns herself with lightning;
>   She is the evolving wheel of the cycles of time;
>   Merely by opening her eyes, she calls the worlds into being.
>   As her beautiful eyelids flutter closed,
>   The universe collapses.
>   She is the power of enjoyment, the tree of plenty,
>   The wish-fulfilling gem.
>   In two hands she bears fragrant lotuses,
>   Another hand signals the granting of boons,
>   While the fourth gestures, "Don't be afraid";
>   She is the goddess Lakshmi, seated in yoga posture
>   On her lion throne.
>   All the beauty you see around you is hers alone,
>   Yes, hers alone.

—Brahma in the Sita Upanishad

Rama, the seventh incarnation of Vishnu, was the prince of the king-dom of Kosala. He was the upholder of all *dharmas* in all fields of life. He is depicted as the perfect son, perfect brother, perfect husband, perfect king, and perfect man. His life shows that a person holding a high political position should always put his loyalty to his subordinates before his personal interests.

Rama married Sita, princess of the country of Videha. Sita was the model of wifely devotion and loyalty. Her love for Rama, unlike that of Radha, was based on strong marital ties. She is one of the most popular heroines in Hindu mythology and is always given as an example of the perfect wife to all young girls.

Whenever Vishnu takes an *avatara,* his consort Lakshmi also takes on a bodily form to be with him. Thus Sita was an incarnation of Lakshmi, though she is also said to be an incarnation of another of Vishnu's wives, Bhudevi, or the earth deity.

The word *sita* means "furrow," and we find that there was a female deity called Sita who was known prior to the story of Rama and Sita. She was associated with agriculture and fertility. The heroine Sita described in the sage Valmiki's epic Ramayana may have been named after this deity, for we find that her origin is the earth. In one of the Vedic hymns addressed to the lord of the fields, the goddess Sita is invoked:

Auspicious Sita, come near,
We venerate and worship you,
That you might bless and prosper us,
And bring us abundant fruits.

In the *Kausika-sutra,* Sita is depicted as the wife of Parjanya, god of rain. She is said to be the mother of gods, mortals, and creatures and was invoked for growth and prosperity. In the *Paraskara-sutra* Sita is depicted as the wife of Indra, god of rain and fertility. In the *yajnas* or Vedic fire ceremonies, she, along with the other gods, was offered cooked rice and barley. In the *Vajasaneyi Samhita,* Sita was invoked by the drawing of four furrows on the sacrificial field. And the Purana known as Harivamsa gives Sita as one of the names of the goddess Arya, the earth goddess. Thus we notice that in the Vedas and Puranas, the goddess Sita has always had a close association with the earth and all its bounties.

Sita's role is to make us aware of the necessity of a male power to awaken the fertility of the plowed earth and arouse and inseminate it. The beautiful interaction between divine and human is brought out in all the ancient stories concerning Sita. The fertility of the earth is the result of the interaction between sky (god) and earth (man), between male and female, between the latent powers of the field and the inseminating effects of the plow, which opens the earth for the insertion of seeds into her fertile interior. The esoteric meaning of this play is that human endeavor and noble actions are needed to ensure an unfailing supply of crops from the earth. If humans do not have this goodwill, the earth deity will withdraw all her goods into herself.

However, Sita was not a very significant deity prior to the Ramayana. In the Ramayana she is depicted as the daughter of Janaka, king of Videha. When taking part in a royal ritual in which he had to plow a sacrificial field, he found a baby girl in one of the furrows. Hence she was given the name Sita (furrow). She was the personification of the earth's fertility, abundance, and well-being. Thus Sita was no mere human being. Her birth was supernatural and her abilities and appearance are exalted throughout the text. She was called *ayonija* (not born from a womb). She was deeply associated with the primordial powers of the earth.

Even as a child Janaka was astounded by Sita's strength. She was able to lift a huge bow that normally could be lifted only by a hundred men. Janaka vowed that he would give her in marriage only to one who could lift and string the bow. When she came of marriageable age, it was found that only Rama, the prince of Kosala, was capable of this stupendous feat. He broke the bow and married the celestially beautiful Sita, who had already given her heart to him. Theirs was a love story beyond parallel. Rama's love for Sita and hers for him has been the theme song of many bards from that day to this.

Despite their great love for each other, Sita and Rama's story is one of sorrow from beginning to end. Thanks to the machinations of his stepmother, Rama's father exiled him to the forest for fourteen years on the very eve of his coronation. Rama, being a noble soul, was unperturbed by his father's command and prepared to go to the forest by himself. However, both his brother Lakshmana and his wife Sita insisted that they should be allowed to accompany him. When Rama pointed out the dangers of the forest to one as delicately nurtured as she, Sita replied that to a chaste woman, her husband was her god, and apart from him she might as well be dead:

> For a woman, it is not her father, her son, her mother, her friends, or her own self but her husband who, in this world and the next, is ever her sole means of salvation. If thou dost enter the impenetrable forest today, O descendent of Raghu, I shall precede thee on foot. I shall happily live in the forest as I lived in the palace of my father, having no anxiety and reflecting only on my duties toward my lord. Ever subject to thy will, docile, living like an ascetic, in those honey-scented woodlands, I shall be blissfully happy, for you will be near me, O illustrious lord!

When Rama pointed out to her the dangers and rigors of forest life, her reply was, "The hardships described by thee will be transmuted into joys through my devotion to thee. Separated from thee I should immediately yield up my life. Which woman can live without her consort? Thou canst not doubt this truth where I am concerned. O Rama! I shall remain sinless by following piously in the footsteps of my husband, for thou art my god!"

For twelve years Rama and Sita led an idyllic life in the forest. In their thirteenth year of exile Sita was abducted by Ravana, the demon king of Lanka, and taken to his island kingdom. There she was severely tried by Ravana, who wooed her diligently. However, he dared not touch her, since he had been cursed that if he took a woman without her consent he would be struck dead.

With the aid of Sugriva, king of the monkeys, and his able general, Hanuman, Rama found out the whereabouts of Sita and went to Lanka. He defeated Ravana and rescued his beloved wife. But her trials were far from being over. Rama accused her of infidelity, and in order to prove her chastity, he asked her to undergo the ordeal of fire. Personally he had no doubts about her purity, but he knew that peoples' tongues would wag and question the chastity of his queen, who had stayed for one full year in the Ashoka forest, which belonged to the notorious Ravana.

Sita was shocked at this accusation. She commanded Lakshmana to make a pyre for her. After having been publicly denounced by her husband, she felt it would be better for her to die. When the fire was blazing, she circumambulated Rama and prepared to jump into the flames.

She addressed Agni, god of fire, thus: "If my heart has never ceased to be true to Rama, do thou, O witness of all beings, grant me thy protection! As I am pure in conduct, though Rama looks on me as sullied, do thou, O witness of the worlds, grant me full protection!"

With these words she jumped into the blazing pyre, but because of her innocence and faultless purity, Agni refused to harm her and brought her out unscathed. Even her flower garland remained unwithered in the flames. Rama and Sita returned in triumph to Ayodhya, capital of Kosala, where the citizens were waiting with great joy to welcome them back.

All Puranic stories have esoteric meanings. In this particular story, Sita is the individual soul captured by the overpowering demonic forces of the material world. However, she never forgets her divine beloved. This play demonstrates that God will always protect a soul or *jivatman* that remains faithful to the Paramatman throughout the temptations of life and refuses to surrender to greed, lust, and power. He will rescue the *jivatman* and carry it back to its own world. God loves every soul as passionately as Rama loved Sita.

The union of Sita and Rama represents the interplay between a powerful and virtuous king with a woman who symbolizes the fecund forces of the earth. She was literally the child of the earth. The result of this auspicious relationship between kingly virility and earthly fertility was the kingdom of Rama, known as Ramarajya. His reign was characterized by harmony, longevity of the people, order, and abundant crops. Social, political, and economic virtues dominated this society where the ruler was the epitome of *dharma* and his wife the personification of womanly virtues.

Unfortunately for Sita, despite his passionate attachment to her, Rama placed his duty to his people and adherence to *dharma* before his duty as a husband. One was for the good of his country and people, whereas the other was for personal gratification. The welfare of his people was always held above his own pleasure. In one of his incognito expeditions through the streets of Ayodhya, Rama heard his wife being maligned. He recalled the old saying, "As the king, so the citizens." It was the duty of the ideal king to set a perfect example to his people. When the people heard that he had taken back as his wife one who had lived in the court of another for a whole year, they were tempted to follow his example. Such behavior would lead eventually to the degeneration of the moral consciousness of the society. As the upholder of *dharma*, Rama was forced to banish Sita to the forest, even though he had just learned of her pregnancy. This bitter decision to part from his beloved wife was made for the sake of his subjects. He commanded Lakshmana to take her to the forest and leave her there.

Sita knew nothing of his decision and went joyfully with Lakshmana to the forest. She had desired to be taken for a while to the hermitage of the sages where she had spent so many happy years with her husband. Just before he left her, Lakshmana gave her the unhappy news that she had been banished by the king, her husband. Even when she heard of this bitter decree, Sita did not blame Rama. She sent a message to Rama through Lakshmana: "O Raghava, you know that I am truly pure. You have renounced me for fear of dishonor, because your subjects have reproached and censured you. I am not distressed on my own account. It is for you to keep your fair name untarnished. The husband is a god to a wife. He is her entire family and her spiritual preceptor. Even at the price of her life, she must seek to please her lord!"

Sita found protection in the hermitage of the sage Valmiki, author of the Ramayana, and there she gave birth to twin sons. Rama lived a lonely life in the palace and refused to take another wife, though both his priests and his subjects urged him to do so. He remained faithful to Sita in body and mind and refused to follow the trend of the age, in which kings were allowed to take numerous wives. When his sons were twelve years old, Rama once again considered taking Sita back. Valmiki urged Rama to meet with her. Rama was eager to do so, but yet again he asked her to undergo a public ordeal that would convince his subjects once and for all of her innocence.

However, Sita was fed up with life on this earth. She could bear no more, and she begged the earth, her mother, to take her back to her bosom: "If in thought, word, or deed I have ever dwelt on my husband Rama alone, may the earth goddess Madhavi receive me."

As she said these words, the ground shuddered and split open. A throne twined with all the creepers and plants of the earth rose up from the ground. On this was seated the earth deity. Sita ran to her and was clasped to her bosom. The throne sank into the earth and the crack closed over it before the horrified eyes of the beholders. Rama ranted and raved and angrily demanded the earth to return his beloved to him, but the ground remained silent and closed.

Rama lived for many years after this as a recluse, though he continued with his duties as the perfect king and ruler. His life was lived in sorrow and he never took another wife, for Sita's image was enshrined in his heart forever. He made a golden effigy of Sita and used it in her place in all the religious rituals that demanded a wife.

Sita's steadfast loyalty to her husband makes her the model of the ideal wife. Her life was inextricably bound with that of her husband. Throughout the Ramayana, her only thought was of Rama's welfare. Thus Sita represents all the good qualities of a chaste woman and an ideal wife. Although other goddesses like Parvati and Lakshmi express many of these qualities, Sita is by far the most popular and beloved as the paradigm for wifely devotion, forbearance, and chastity. The

Ramayana is well known in every Hindu household, and Hindu ideals have been modeled on the examples given in this book.

The Hindu tradition teaches a woman to emphasize those points in her character that would make her a model daughter, mother, and wife. She is supposed to succumb to the demands of society and not impose her own demands on it, as the modern woman does. From childhood, women are taught to cultivate an attitude that subordinates their welfare to the welfare of others, especially that of their husband and children. This, of course, ensures an integrated society, since it produces a strong family unit that is the basic block of any social structure. The Hindu community in this manner is instructed by a mythology that provides numerous models and images to which the individual may aspire. In the case of a Hindu woman the model is condensed to just one character, and she is Sita.

> *The wedding of the eternal Lord and spouse,*
> *Took place again on earth in human forms;*
> *In a new act of the drama of the world,*
> *The united two began a greater age.*
> *In the silence and murmur of that emerald world,*
> *And the mutter of the priest-wind's sacred verse;*
> *Amid the choral whisperings of the leaves;*
> *Love's twain had joined together and grew one.*
> *The natural miracle was wrought once more;*
> *In the immutable ideal world,*
> *One human moment was eternal made.*

—*SAVITRI* BY SRI AUROBINDO

Thus ends the twenty-fifth chapter of *Shakti,* known as "Sita," which describes the greatness of Sita, the model of womanhood.

Aum Aim Hreem Kleem

Aum Savitryai Namaha!

26

Savitri

A power dwelt in her soul too great for earth,
A bliss lived in her too large for heaven,
Light too intense for thought and love too boundless,
For earth's emotions lit her skies of mind
And spread through her deep and happy seas of soul,
All that is sacred in the world drew near,
To her divine passivity of mood,
A marvellous voice of silence breathed its thoughts,
All things in Time and Space she had taken for her.
In her they moved, in her they lived and were,
The whole wide world clung to her for delight.

—*SAVITRI*, BY SRI AUROBINDO

In the Vedas the most famous goddess connected with the sun is Ushas, goddess of dawn. Some of the most beautiful hymns of the Rig Veda are addressed to her. She is described as the daughter of the sky. Night is her sister. At times she is spoken of as the wife of Surya, god of the sun. Ushas is said to travel in a shining chariot, drawn by ruddy horses or cows. The *rishis* of the Vedas describe her in the most poetic terms. She is a beautiful girl dressed by her mother, a dancing girl covered with

240

jewels, and a gaily attired wife appearing before her husband. She is like a fascinating damsel coming out of her bath; smilingly she unfolds the irresistible power of her attraction and lowers the cloth covering her bosom. Her quiet modesty is like that of a shy maiden, conscious of her beauty, ushered into society by her mother.

She dispels not only the darkness of the night but also the darkness of ignorance in the minds of human beings. She illumines everything, including the darkest recesses of the mind. She is the giver of both life and health. She causes the birds to fly from their nests, and like a housewife she sends forth all creatures to attend to the needs of their day's routine.

She is eternally young, since she is born anew every day. Yet she is immeasurably old, since she is immortal. She wears out the lives of successive generations, which disappear one after the other while she continues, undying. The souls of the departed are said to go through her and pierce the orb of the sun.

> *Hail Ushas, daughter of the sky,*
> *Borne upon thy shining car,*
> *By ruddy steeds from realms afar,*
> *And ever lightening draws nigh,*
> *Thou sweetly smiling goddess fair,*
> *Disclosing all thy youthful grace,*
> *Thy bosom bright, thy radiant face,*
> *And luster of thy golden hair.*
>
> —Rig Veda, *Hymn to the*
> *Goddess of Dawn*

The Gayatri *mantra* is a famous hymn to the sun god from the Savitri Upanishad. Actually *gayatri* is the name of the meter in which the *mantra* is written. But the meter is conceived of as a goddess, called Gayatri. In looks, she is something like the Vedic goddess Ushas. Repetition of the Gayatri *mantra* is compulsory for all Hindus, not just

Brahmins, though the Brahmins were the custodians of this *mantra* for centuries. Even though it appears to be a hymn addressed to the sun, it is actually addressed to the supreme consciousness and is a prayer for enlightenment. It is universally applicable. It is nothing but a prayer for spiritual light addressed to the Almighty as *tat savitur,* "that sun of supreme consciousness," which lights up everything, including the physical sun. The word *savitur* is masculine and refers to the sun. The feminine counterpart is the goddess Savitri. This hymn has been regarded as the greatest of all *mantras.* If there is one *mantra* common to all Hindus, it is this.

> *Aum bhur bhuvah svaha,*
> *Tat savitur varenyam,*
> *Bhargo devasya dheemahi,*
> *Dhiyo yo nah prachodayat.*

> Let us meditate on the supreme and his glory,
> Who has created this universe (earth, sky, and heaven),
> Who alone is fit to be worshipped,
> Who is the remover of all ignorance,
> May he enlighten us!

The *rishis* had a thorough knowledge of the subtle effects of sound, and they devised this *mantra* to have great mystic power and enable human beings to expand our consciousness and allow us to reach the supreme. Daily repetition of this mystical *mantra* with sincerity and devotion will help us attain our highest potential, both materially and spiritually. At dawn we should turn our face toward the rising sun, which is the visible manifestation of the supreme reality, and repeat this *mantra.* At midday we should think of the sun at its zenith and repeat the *mantra.* At sunset we should turn toward the setting sun and repeat it once more. It can be repeated as many times as one wishes.

The sun is the abode of the supreme Brahman. It is the first visible manifestation of the absolute. The Rig Veda glorifies the sun as Pratyaksha Devata or the divinity that can be seen before us. While scientists are aware of only the physical properties of the sun, the sages discovered its spiritual aspect, which is directly linked with the evolution of life and the expansion of intelligence. The *rishis* realized that the sun has an active spiritual field, which they called Surya Narayana. They found that the energy of the sun was born out of *rita,* the cosmic law of harmony, the pulsating rhythm of the deep spiritual laws of the supreme spirit. The sun is not just a huge mass of atomic energy but a radiant mass of life-giving vitality for all creation. The spiritual values inherent in the sun express themselves in various degrees through different creatures and reach their highest expression in the human being. The sun inspires us to push forward and evolve to the unconditioned freedom of the absolute. The Gayatri *mantra* throbs with this intense yearning on the part of the human race to evolve toward its highest potential.

Thus *savitur* is nothing but the supreme itself. Hence the Gayatri *mantra* is not just a hymn to the sun god but a paean of praise to the supreme Brahman. The goddess Savitri is the presiding deity of the Surya-mandala or the solar orb along with its aura. She is said to be the mother of the Vedas. Brahma in his role as custodian of the Vedas was the first to worship her. The story of how she came to be born on earth is told in the Puranas.

Once there was a king of the solar dynasty called Asvapati. He had a highly spiritually minded queen named Malati. Though they wanted children they had none, so their *guru,* Vasishta, advised Malati to worship the goddess Savitri. She went to the holy lake of Pushkara and did *tapas* for many years with no result. Dejected, she returned to the palace. Her husband told her not to worry and that they would perform austerities together. They did severe *tapas* for a hundred years. At last a celestial voice announced, "Repeat the Gayatri *mantra* ten *lakhs* of times and your wish will be fulfilled."

At this time the great sage Parasara appeared on the scene and told the king of the glory of the Gayatri *mantra*. "O King!" he said. "If you repeat the Gayatri *mantra* just once, all that day's sins will vanish. One hundred repetitions will take away the sins of one year. One *lakh* destroys the sins of this birth and ten *lakhs* destroys the sins of other births. If a thousand *lakhs* are done, liberation is attained."

Parasara then instructed the king on the type of *japa mala* or rosary to be used in counting: "The *japa mala* should be made of the seeds of the white lotus or of crystal. It should be purified by being dipped in milk or Ganga water and consecrated at the feet of one's favorite deity. If a person repeats ten *lakhs* of *mantras* on such a *mala,* he or she will receive the vision of the Devi Savitri."

The king performed the rites as commanded by the *rishi* on the fourteenth day of the black fortnight of the month of Jyesta for fourteen years. He offered fourteen different types of fruits, flowers, and incense to the goddess and distributed wealth to fourteen Brahmins. He used the following *mantra* to invoke her: "I meditate on that Savitri, the mother of the Vedas, who has the nature of *aum,* and whose color is that of burnished gold. Thou art effulgent like the rays of the noonday sun and adorned with many jewels and ornaments. Thou art the bestower of happiness and liberation, the consort of the creator. May thou be gracious unto me."

After repeating this *mantra* and performing the prescribed rituals for fourteen years, King Asvapati and his queen received a vision of the goddess. She said, "O King! I know your desire. Your wife wants a daughter and you want a son. You will both get what you want." Thus having blessed them, the goddess returned to the celestial regions.

Soon after, the king received a most beautiful daughter, whom he called Savitri, after the goddess. When Savitri came of age, the king brought many proposals for her, but she would have none of them. She had already seen the man she would marry in one of her excursions into the forest. He was called Satyavan, and he was the son of the blind king Dyumatsena. The king had been deposed from his kingdom and had gone to the forest, where he lived the life of a sage, accompanied by his faithful wife and son. Asvapati was not happy with his daughter's choice, even though he knew that Dyumatsena was a noble man, and he had heard that his son was the soul of truth and honor. At this time, sage Narada came to Asvapati's court and gave him another distressing bit of news. Looking at Savitri's palm, he told the king that her husband would die after just one year of marriage. The king was grief-stricken and exhorted his daughter to give up her scheme of marrying such a man. But she was adamant and prayed to her mother goddess Savitri to give her the courage to keep to her decision and also to give her a long life as the wife of Satyavan.

At last the king agreed and gave Savitri in marriage to Satyavan, who took her back to his hermitage in the forest. For one full year Savitri prayed with all her heart to the goddess Savitri to grant her the life of her husband. On the concluding day of her vow, which was supposed to be Satyavan's last day on earth, she insisted on accompanying him to the forest when he went to cut wood. As the day wore on, she noticed that Satyavan became more and more exhausted. At last he lay down with his head on her lap. Just at that time Yama, the god of death, approached and took away Satyavan's life in a noose. With her perception sharpened by her austerities, Savitri was able to see all these happenings. She kept the lifeless body of her husband gently on the ground and followed Yama.

Yama saw her following him and asked her, "O Savitri! Why are you following me? No mortal can come with me to my abode. If you want to come with me you will have to shed your body. The time has come for the death of your husband and that is why I am taking him away, but your time has not yet come and you will not be able to follow me to the nether regions. It is only due to your great austerities that you are able to see me at all. The time of birth and death of each being is decreed by his or her *karma*. No one can go against *karma*."

Savitri then asked Yama to explain the nature of *karma* and how it could be overcome. Yama said, "*Karma* is produced by the actions of individuals and is of two kinds, good and bad. Those actions that do not go against the dictates of *dharma* are considered good and will result in beneficial *karma*. Actions done for the sake of God without expectation of reward increase devotion to God and lead to liberation. Now, Savitri, return to your home and look after your aged parents. This is your *dharma* at the moment."

Savitri said, "A wife's *dharma* is to follow her husband wherever he goes. Where shall I go, leaving my husband? Pray instruct me, for you are the greatest of all teachers." Yama said, "O Savitri! You are a portion of the goddess and hence you are precocious beyond your years and filled with knowledge. Ask three boons from me and I shall grant them."

Savitri immediately said, "Let me have a hundred sons by my husband Satyavan. Let my father-in-law get back his eyesight and his kingdom, and let my father have many sons."

Yama agreed to this, and swiftly Savitri said, "O gracious Lord! How will I get sons from Satyavan unless you give back his life?"

Yama was pleased by her presence of mind, perseverance, and deep devotion to her husband, and he said, "My child, I am pleased with your devotion and intelligence. Worship the Devi Savitri, who is none other than Mula Prakriti, and all happiness shall be yours. Take your husband and return to your home and live happily with him. Undertake the Savitri vow for fourteen years, which is what your parents did, and you will certainly attain liberation, along with your husband." Saying this, Yama blessed Savitri and told her to go back to the spot where she had placed the corpse of her husband.

When Savitri returned to the tree under which she had kept her husband's body, she found him getting up as if from deep sleep. He had no memory of what had happened and thought he had fallen asleep. She told him the whole saga and they rejoiced at his miraculous return from the land of the dead. They returned to the hermitage and repeated the wonderful tale. Soon after, Dyumatsena got back his eyesight and his kingdom, and Savitri and Satyavan went back to their land and worshipped the goddess as advised by Yama. Savitri's parents also got many sons, as promised by Yama. All of

them attained liberation from their mortal coils after many blessed
years spent conducting the affairs of the kingdom, worshipping the
goddess Savitri, and repeating the Gayatri *mantra*.

> *She pressed the living body of Satyavan;*
> *On her body's wordless joy to be and breathe,*
> *She bore the blissful burden of his head,*
> *Between her breasts, warm labour of delight,*
> *The waking gladness of her members felt,*
> *The weight of heaven in his limbs, a touch*
> *Summing the whole felicity of things,*
> *And all her life was conscious of his life,*
> *And all her being rejoiced enfolding his,*
> *The immense remoteness of her trance had passed;*
> *Human she was once more, earth's Savitri,*
> *Yet felt in her illimitable change.*

—*SAVITRI* BY SRI AUROBINDO

Thus ends the twenty-sixth chapter of *Shakti,* known as "Savitri,"
which narrates the story of the goddess Savitri and her descent to the
earth.

Aum Aim Hreem Kleem

Aum Kalaratryai Namaha!

27

Shivaduti

Ati saumyathiraudrayai nathasthasyai namo namaha!
Namo jagatpratishtayai devyai krtyai namo namaha!

We prostrate before her who is at once most gentle and most
terrible.
We salute her again and again.
Salutations to her who is the support of the world.
Salutations to the devi who is of the form of volition.

—DEVI MAHATMYAM, CHAPTER 5

The symbology of gods and goddesses in the Hindu pantheon covers
an infinite array of forms. Some are ravishing, some provocative, some
kind and compassionate, and others grotesque and barbaric. Some sug-
gest spiritual powers and some material gains. In every case the depic-
tion is elaborately detailed and designed to evoke a certain response
within the consciousness of the aspirant. The symbology is based on the
eternal archetypal structure of human beings' collective unconscious.
These depictions or *mandalas* are intended to draw out these arche-
types from our unconscious as a magnet draws out iron filings. We
have delineated a few of the benign forms of the Maha Devi, and now

248

we have to outline the characteristics of some of her fierce forms. She has two sides that portray the dual-faced visage of creation. To present the good and beautiful alone would be to give a lopsided picture of life. Hinduism insists that both sides should be confronted and accepted before we can be enabled to gain a vision of her supreme form, which is beyond all duality.

Tantric images of gods and goddesses often go beyond the boundaries of the rational. Some forms have sixteen hands and three eyes, some are naked and drink blood, while others are shown carrying weapons of mass destruction. Apart from their symbolic significance, these forms are the Tantric way of asserting that life can never be fitted into one mold. To attempt to do so would simply denigrate the diversity of life. We have to experience life in all its multifaceted, contradictory aspects before we can live it fully.

Many of the violent forms we shall discuss in this chapter are mentioned at various times in both the Devi Mahatmyam and the Devi Bhagavatam as well as other Puranas. One of the fierce goddesses referred to in the Devi Mahatmyam is Shivaduti. In the episode of the battle with the two *asura* brothers called Shumbha and Nishumbha, Shiva told Chandika to kill all the *asura* hordes that had been sent by Shumbha and Nishumbha. At this there issued from the body of Chandika an exceedingly fierce and horrific *shakti* who came out howling like a hundred jackals. Turning to Lord Shiva, she ordered him to go as her emissary to the court of Shumbha and Nishumbha: "Tell those two haughty *asuras* and all those assembled there that they have to give back to Indra the three worlds that they stole from the gods. They will then be allowed to return to the netherworld, which is their rightful domain. But if out of pride they refuse to obey my command, let them come for battle and allow my jackals to feed on their flesh!"

Since that *devi* appointed Shiva himself as her ambassador, she came to be known as Shivaduti. She is a common figure on battlefields and other scenes of destruction.

Another group of fearsome goddesses mentioned in the Devi Mahatmyam are the Sapta Matrikas (seven mothers). When the *asuric* armies of Shumbha and Nishumbha approached Chandika, the male gods who were watching the episode with eager interest from the sidelines created *shaktis* or female counterparts of themselves to aid her. Seven such *shaktis* were created, and they resembled the male gods by whom they were produced. They had the same ornaments, vehicles, and weapons as their masculine counterparts. These were the Sapta Matrikas, known as Brahmaani (from Brahma), Maheswari (from Shiva), Kaumari (from Skanda), Indrani (from Indra), Vaishnavi (from Vishnu), Vaarahi (from Vishnu's incarnation as Varaha), and Nrisimhi (from Vishnu's incarnation as Narasimha). Along with Kaali and Shivaduti (Durga), the Sapta Matrikas devastated the demon hordes (see chapter 13). After the battle, they danced and rioted, intoxicated with the blood of their victims. Despite their names and appearances they are to be understood not as the divine consorts of the male divinities but rather as forms of the *devi* herself.

In the Vamana Purana this fact is made even clearer, since the Sapta Matrikas are seen to arise from different parts of Maha Devi's body and not from the male gods. In the Matsya Purana Shiva commands the Sapta Matrikas to defeat the demon Andhaka. After killing the demon, the bloodthirsty *shaktis* proceed to devour the gods, demons, and people of the world. They refuse to listen to Shiva and go on a rampage. Shiva then summons Narasimha, Lord Vishnu's *avatara* as the man-lion, and he creates a host of benign goddesses who calm down the terrible Matrikas.

The Sapta Matrikas act never by themselves but only as a group, and they share many characteristics. The Puranic accounts show them as Maha Devi's assistants who help her in combating demons, but their wild, bloodthirsty characters are undiminished whatever the role they play. Their characteristics are meant to portray those demonic traits in the human mind that refuse to be subjugated even with constant example and advice.

The Bhagavad Purana links the Sapta Matrikas with other malevolent beings like *rakshasas* (giants of darkness and evil) and other spirits of darkness. The *gopis* made charms for the baby Krishna against the evil effects of these malicious beings. The Purana also gives instructions on how to overcome their evil effects.

The Mahabharata describes the Sapta Matrikas as the mothers of Skanda, in which role they seem to be connected in some way with the six Krittikas who nursed the infant Kartikeya. They are known for the atrocities they wreak upon pregnant women and small children. There is a cult in many villages that recognizes their power and worships them in order to ward off their baneful effects. Though in most cases the Matrikas are seven in number, in some cases there are more; up to sixteen are mentioned. On the whole the Sapta Matrikas are given importance only because of the sinister role they play in the field of difficult pregnancies, infant mortality, the joys of childhood, and the mystery with which this joy and horror are intermingled. The issues they stand for are relevant to all life; hence they are found in some form or other in all the different sects of India.

As we have seen, Maha Devi manifests herself in a great variety of forms. Another group of goddesses given prominence in Devi temples are known as the Mahavidyas: Kaali, Smashan Tara, Bhuvaneswari, Bagala, Dhumavati, Kamala, Matangi, Shodashi, Chinnamasta, and Bhairavi. They are ten in number, and they may be the Shakta version of the ten *avataras* of Lord Vishnu who appear from time to time when *dharma* declines. Some texts even claim that Vishnu's *avataras* originally came from the Mahavidyas. For example, Kaali is supposed to have become Krishna and Chinnamasta to have become Narasimha. This is only a theory. In actual fact, the Mahavidyas differ quite radically from the *avataras* of Lord Vishnu.

The Mahavidyas' first appearance is connected with Daksha's *yajna*. As we have seen in chapter 14, Shiva was not invited to this *yajna* and at first he refused to let Sati, his wife, attend. In her fury at his refusal, it is said that she multiplied herself into the ten forms known as the

Mahavidyas. In order to show the superiority of Sati (the incarnation of the Maha Devi), the Devi Purana portrays Shiva as being frightened by these fearful forms that surrounded him, and he gives in to Sati's wishes and tells her that he can't prevent her from going if that is her wish.*

Kaali, as we have seen, has a fierce countenance, is naked, dwells in the cremation grounds, and holds a severed head in one hand and a bloody sword in the other. Her body is gaunt, with her ribs sticking out. She has thin, drooping breasts and a cavernous belly.

Smashan Tara's nature is similar to Kaali's, though she differs somewhat in her form. She is the color of collyrium, stands on a funeral pyre with her left foot on a corpse, and wears a girdle of arms, a tiger skin, and a garland of severed heads. Her hair is braided in a single matted plait. She is fully pregnant and has full breasts. *Smashana,* the Sanskrit word from which her name derives, means "burning *ghat.*" Smashan Tara's function is similar to Kaali's. Her devotees are Aghoris who worship her at midnight in burning *ghats* where the dead are creamated.

Bhuvaneswari has a light complexion and a smiling face. She is said to nourish the three worlds. Her breasts are large and ooze milk, and she carries a piece of fruit in one hand. In her other hand she carries a goad and a noose.

Bagala has the head of a crane and is yellow in color. She is seated on a throne of jewels. With one hand she appears to be beating an enemy with a club and with the other pulling out someone's tongue.

Dhumavati is tall and pale with a stern, unsmiling face. She is toothless, her nose is large and crooked, her breasts are long and pendulous, and her hair is disheveled. She is dressed in dirty clothes and looks like a widow. She holds a winnowing fan in one hand and her vehicle is the crow. She appears to be afflicted with hunger and thirst.

Kamala is a beautiful young woman with a golden complexion.

*The story is different in the Shiva Purana, which seeks to portray Shiva as superior to all other gods and goddesses. The Shiva Purana avoids any mention of Shiva being afraid.

Elephants stand on either side of her, pouring pitchers of water over her. She is seated on a lotus and holds a lotus in each hand. She looks like the goddess Lakshmi. In fact, one of Lakshmi's names is Kamala.

Matangi is black. She appears to be always intoxicated and reels about like an impassioned elephant. She has red, rolling eyes.

Shodashi is a young girl of sixteen. She is red in color and is shown sitting astride the prone body of Shiva, with whom she has obviously been having intercourse. They lie on a bed whose legs are upheld by the gods Brahma, Vishnu, Rudra, and Indra. Sometimes Shodashi is identified with Tripurasundari, and hence the reference to the bed upheld by the gods.

Bhairavi has a reddish hue and her eyes roll as if she were intoxicated. She wears a garland of severed heads. She has four hands; one holds a *japa mala* (rosary), another holds a book, a third is held in the gesture of fearlessness (*abhaya mudra*), and the fourth is held in the symbol of conferring boons.

Chinnamasta is depicted stark naked. She carries in her left hand her own head, which she has seemingly severed herself with the sword held in her right hand. Three streams of blood spout from the stump of her neck. One falls into her own mouth and the other two into the mouths of the two *yoginis* (female yoga practitioners) who are on either side of her. She normally holds the head on a platter, as if to make an offering of it. Beneath her feet lie Kama, the god of desire, and his wife Rati, who are joined together in the act of love while stretched out on a lotus.

Even though a few of the Mahavidyas appear to have appealing forms, on the whole they are meant to be ferocious deities. With the exception of Kaali, they are not known to be warriors but are meant to project certain esoteric truths, which the *sadhaka* (one who studies a spiritual discipline) is supposed to find out for her- or himself. Most of them play a part in Tantric rituals. Their powers are meant to subdue the enemy by various methods. These powers include *maarana* (the ability to destroy the enemy), *ucchatana* (the ability to force a person to stop whatever he or she is doing), *kshobana* (the ability to cause emotional disturbance), *mohana* (the ability to cause delusion and infatuation), *draavana* (the ability to cause people to run in terror), *jrimbhana* (the ability to cause people to become lazy and keep yawning), and *stambhana* (the ability to cause paralysis). All the conditions these powers can initiate are not just physical maladies but also psychological and emotional ones, and they can affect our spiritual life and spoil our *sadhana* (spiritual practice). The Mahavidyas can be invoked to get rid of these emotional ailments and give us *moksha* (liberation).

Creation and destruction are part of the cosmic process. The economy of the universe is kept in balance by a harmonious alternation of giving and taking life. The ever bountiful figure of Annapurna (Lakshmi in her form as the giver of food) giving food shows only one aspect of the process—that of giving. Kaali shows us the picture of the goddess severing the heads of others and demanding their blood as nourishment. In fact, demons often sacrificed their own heads to the goddess. This represents the truth that the forces of the cosmos as depicted by the goddess require regular nourishment. Since we have received life from her, we are obliged to give it back to her. Life can be maintained only by the ingestion of the corpses of other beings.

Chinnamasta conveys the same message but reverses the roles. She gives her own blood to herself and to her two devotees. Instead of taking the heads of her victims and drinking their blood, she takes her own head and drinks her own blood. She is nourished not by death but by the copulating couple beneath her. This is one of the most dramatic pictorial representations of the stark reality of life. It points out that life, sex, and death are all part of a closely interrelated system. None of them can exist alone. The whole scene, ghastly though it might appear to the casual viewer, becomes clear to the *sadhaka* who strives for a deeper meaning to reality.

This striking spectacle points out many of the truths that we tend to cloak with a weak sentimentalism to mask our inherent inability to face the gory aspects of life. As far as nature is concerned, the sole necessity for sex is to propagate life, which in turn will decay and feed another life at another time and in another place. In other words, life feeds on and is nourished by death. The copulating couple pump the goddess with their own life-giving energy, which she in turn offers back to herself and to her children or devotees by the sacrifice of cutting off her own head. Life is portrayed by the copulating couple, death by the decapitated goddess, and the renewal of life by the *yoginis* drinking her blood.

The uninitiated may be shocked at the number of gruesome female goddesses depicted so realistically in Hindu mythology. To the initiate, however, the two types of goddesses only display the two sides of life, as we have seen again and again. Lalitha is worshipped on full-moon days for she represents consciousness at its most beautiful—full and resplendent like the moon. Kaali and all her counterparts are worshipped on new-moon days when the sky is dark and nature herself appears in her most foreboding aspect. The analogy is to human consciousness, which is still unawakened and cluttered with material desires and longs to be freed from this dark hold. Kaali extinguishes desire and Lalitha replaces the vacuum with liberating knowledge. Kaali typifies *sunyata* or void, while Lalitha is *purnata* or fullness. But what we should remember is that there is only one moon, whether waxing or waning, new or full. Thus both Kaali and Lalitha are one and the same, pointing to the same truth from different viewpoints.

> *The harmony of a rich culture's tones,*
> *Refined the sense and magnified its reach,*
> *To hear the unheard and glimpse the invisible,*
> *And taught the soul to soar beyond things known,*
> *Inspiring life to greaten and break its bounds,*
> *Aspiring to the immortal's unseen world,*
> *Leaving earth's safety, daring wings of mind,*

> *Bore her above the trodden fields of thought,*
> *Crossing the mystic seas of the beyond,*
> *To live on eagle heights near to the Sun.*

—*SAVITRI* BY SRI AUROBINDO

Thus ends the twenty-seventh chapter of *Shakti* known as "Shivaduti," which describes the seven Matrikas and the ten Mahavidyas.

Aum Aim Hreem Kleem

Aum Adi Shaktyai Namaha!

28

Adi Shakti

Indriyanam adhistatri bhutanam chakhileshu ya,
Bhuteshu sathatam thasyai vyaptidevyai namo namaha!

She who governs the senses of all creatures,
And who is present in the elements,
To the goddess of all pervasiveness, hail! All hail!

As has been mentioned before, the Shakta cult is one that affirms the ultimate reality to be a duality of masculine and feminine—Shiva and Shakti, with greater accent on the feminine or Shakti. Tantra is the practice of this cult; it is an esoteric teaching handed down from *guru* to *shishya* (disciple). Even though Shaktism accepts the presence of an all-pervading reality, it insists that this reality has a dual aspect of consciousness and energy. Shiva is consciousness, and Shakti is energy. Shiva is the static principle, which remains as pure unconditioned consciousness. It is only at the behest of Shakti that Shiva is motivated to action. Shiva and Shakti are complementary to each other at every level. If he is Shambhu, she is Shambhavi; if he is Maheswara, she is Maheswari; if he is Rudra, she is Raudri.

The Shakta cult probes and analyzes the nature of ultimate reality as feminine. However, Shakti is the kinetic power of the divine, so we

257

find that even Vaishnavites (followers of Vishnu) and Shaivites (followers of Shiva) worship Shakti or the goddess as power. The expression *shakti* thus denotes not only the great goddess Maha Devi but also the energizing power of any particular divinity. Unfortunately, Shakti worship has been misunderstood by many people, including Indians themselves. Shakti worship is the worship of God's glory. Devi belongs to all sects, for she is the conscious power of the *deva* or of God. The Upanishad says, "Parashakti, the supreme power of God, is the nature of God manifesting as knowledge, strength, and activity." In fact, we can say that everyone in the universe is a Shakti worshipper, for none can go without all these things. Physicists and scientists have proved that everything is pure imperishable energy. This energy is nothing but the divine Shakti who exists in every form of existence.

What are the vital aspects of the theory and practice of the Shaktas? Shaktism is dynamic Hinduism. It reconciles and amalgamates all aspects of Hindu philosophy. In the Puranas, Devi is known as the sister of Vishnu and the wife of Shiva, the mother of Ganesha and Kartikeya. Thus she is the center of all the great deities who are worshipped in India. The Puranas are considered to be among the authorities of the Shakti cult. The Brahma Vaivarta, the Skanda, and the Kalika are the main Puranas that inculcate the worship of the supreme as feminine. But the principal rites, rituals, and incantations of this sect are found in a different source: the *bija mantras* that are used in Shakta rites are all derived from the Tantras.

The Tantras are therefore the main books for the worship of the goddess as Shakti. Adi Shankaracharya asserts that the books on Tantra are sixty-four in number. The authorship of these books is attributed to Lord Shiva. It is said that the saintly sons of Brahma—Sanaka, Sananda, Sanatana, and Sanat Kumara—begged Lord Shiva for a simpler method of *sadhana* (spiritual practice) than is given in the Vedas, and so Lord Shiva taught them the secret doctrines of the Tantras.

Another and more popular theory is that Shiva taught these esoteric doctrines to Parvati. She asked him for an easy means of liberation for human beings who are born in this Iron Age of Kali, and he answered that Tantra was the easiest method of release. He disclosed this esoteric doctrine to Parvati, and Vishnu confirmed it. The Tantras are therefore collectively known as the Agamas, since they issued from the mouth of Shiva, were heard by the mountain goddess Parvati, and were sanctioned by Vishnu. (There are three syllables in the word *agama*.)

In the Shiva Tantra, Shiva says, "The five scriptures [the four Vedas and the Tantras] issued from my five mouths. They correspond to the five directions—east, west, north, south, and above. These five are known as the paths to final liberation. There are many scriptures, but none are equal to the one 'above' [meaning the Tantras]."

In the Tantras we find that Brahman is synonymous with Shakti. Brahman stands for the formless ultimate or Turiya Brahman that is ever united with Mula Prakriti or fundamental nature. Shakti is another name for Mula Prakriti united with Turiya Brahman. Brahman cannot exist without Shakti, nor can Shakti exist without Brahman. Brahman is static Shakti and Shakti is dynamic Brahman. In Tantric books, Shiva stands for this Turiya Brahman, which is pure unconditioned consciousness.

The excellence of Tantra lies in its emphasis on *sadhana* or spiritual practice. There can be no *siddhi* (spiritual perfection) without *sadhana*. Complete knowledge of anything can come only by becoming that thing; to know Brahman (the supreme), we must become Brahman. Tantra is popularly known as *mantra shastra* and *sadhana shastra*, for it is a practical science that makes use of *mantras*. This *sadhana* is meant not merely for transcendental but also for material benefit, for the Tantrists consider the material world to be the foundation that upholds the spiritual structure. One has to start from the base to reach the summit. The Vedic *vac* or creative word becomes the *adya spanda* or primal throb that develops into the seed sounds or *bijaksharas* used in Tantric *mantras*. These sound vibrations take us to their ultimate cause or original throb that is the supreme.

The Tantras give a set of rituals, *mantras*, and *yogic sadhanas* that supplement the Vedic *sadhanas*. These are meant to give the fastest results if practiced properly. They are open to all castes and both sexes, unlike the Vedic *sadhanas*, which are meant only for initiates, mainly Brahmin males. Thus we find that especially in Bengal and southern India, Tantric rituals have superseded the Vedic fire ceremonies. Tantra offers the means by which the undying reality within oneself can be uncovered through *yoga*, ritual, selfless service, art, study, and total dedication to the goddess in whatever form you conceive of her.

The meaning of the word *tantra* is found in the word itself. It is a combination of two words, *tanoti* ("expansion") and *trayati* ("liberation"). It is a method of expanding the mind to its fullest capacity in order to attain liberation. Expansion of the mind allows us to experience a reality that lies beyond the realm of the five senses. The knowledge derived through the senses is sadly restricted to the boundaries of space, time, and causality. But if we know the technique of turning the mind inward, it will go beyond these boundaries and expand into the cosmic mind. When this happens the apparent differences between matter and energy disappear. Just as a river loses its limitations when it enters the ocean, so the individual mind becomes a receptor and transmitter of cosmic truth when it expands into the ocean of the infinite mind. There is an explosion of energy, and the apparently small individual consciousness is freed from the thralldom of matter. It is only in this modern age that physics has accepted the fact that matter and energy are interconvertible. Over two thousand years ago, however, Tantra went one step further and asserted that matter, energy, and consciousness are all interconvertible. Modern science is slowly and reluctantly coming to the same conclusion. Today Tantra stands as the only spiritual tradition that has kept the sphere of practical application alive and uses it as a scientific treatment for the human mind and consciousness.

The ancient *rishis* dissected the human personality and made different sciences that would raise each aspect of the personality to its highest potential, thus creating a holistic and complete human being. Ayurveda is a method of maintaining a perfect physical body, while

Tantra is a mental science, a meta-psychology, a method of exploring the mind and developing the range of one's perceptions. In fact, it is the science of personality. Tantra declares that the path of liberation is open to every type of nature—sensual or spiritual, atheistic or theistic, weak or strong. It helps one discover one's own path. All human emotions, from passion and love to fear, hatred, and anger, are energy forces. If controlled, they can enable one to experience higher realities.

The universe possesses all possible qualities and attributes, and each creature within the universe possesses a limited number of these qualities and attributes. The human psyche is itself a field of all possibilities, though we don't make use of it. The personality of an individual depends on his or her identification with a certain set of attributes. The supreme, according to Shaktism, is Adi Shakti and possesses the ultimate personality, the supreme expression of the totality of manifested existence. Illness, according to Tantra, lies in having a limited, nonintegrated personality. Health is derived both from internal balance as well as from harmony with the environment. On the physical level, our body's immunity lies in the number of white blood cells and antibodies that it has; similarly the strength of the mind lies in the degree of its personality integration. The aim of Tantra is to replace the limited human personality with an unlimited, permanent one. Anyone who continues to live with a limited personality can be considered to be diseased. Only those who choose to go beyond the three limiting factors of time, space, and causality can be said to be in harmony with the cosmos and, therefore, truly healthy.

Tantrists use certain types of medicinal plants, metals, and gems in their practices. They discovered the obscure secret of mercury, which has an infinite number of uses. The Tantrists also searched for the philosopher's stone, which would change base metal into gold, but esoterically speaking, the change they sought was the transmutation of the individual's limited personality to the gold of enlightenment, a state of unlimited consciousness.

One area of Tantric research lies in seeking methods of prolonging life, since that would give a practitioner more time for integrating the personality and attaining harmony with creation. A Tantric practitioner may fail to gain immortality in one lifetime, but it is very possible that he or she would gain *siddhis* (extraordinary powers). Wisely used, *siddhis* can accelerate one's spiritual evolution. But if they are commercialized, as they very often are by foolish Tantrists, they will only bind one down more firmly to the wheel of cause and effect.

Though Tantra may seem too complex for the ordinary person, one cannot fail to be filled with awe at the amazing thoroughness and attention to specific details that the ancient sages displayed in this science. Thankfully it cannot be exploited, for only one who can practice it in its every detail would be qualified to teach it, and such practitioners are rare.

As has been mentioned before, there is no *siddhi* or perfection without *sadhana* or spiritual practice. The *sadhanas,* which make use of *mantra* and *yantra,* are essential for the procurement of any *siddhis.* A *mantra* is a particular vibration of the original creative throb of the cosmos and represents the seed sound of a particular godhead in the structure of consciousness. *Mantras* are chanted during rituals in order to invoke the appropriate deities. All gods have their own *mantra,* which has the ability to conjure up the form of the deity when used repeatedly in the prescribed fashion. *Yantras* are a particular arrangement of the original light emanating from the absolute. They represent the form pattern of a god. *Yantras* are normally diagrams drawn on bark, crystal, or copper plates. They can also be drawn on the ground with different-colored powders or sand; this is done before the commencement of a *yajna* (fire sacrifice) or *puja* (ritual). In other words, *mantra* is the seed sound of the deity and *yantra* the form pattern. In this way the *rishis* captured the nameless and the formless in sounds and forms!

Tantra insists that no worship of a deity is complete without the worship of the deity's body in a material image like an idol or a *yantra* or *chakra*. Inner worship leads one to the path of knowledge, but for the full development of both the spiritual and the material aspects of life, outer worship is necessary. Outer worship is more powerful; it intensifies devotion and stabilizes the inner realization to the outer conditions. When practiced in an automatic and lifeless manner outer worship will have no results, but when done with knowledge it can open up the body and mind of the aspirant to the heights of consciousness and delight. If offered to the higher force within oneself, any act, however mundane it may be, becomes a medium through which one can expand awareness.

Tantra teaches that through the name and form of any deity it is possible to attain the nameless and formless Brahman. *Mantra,* the sound, and *yantra,* the form, are both used in the path mapped out by Tantra. Therefore *mantra* and *yantra* are both necessary to obtaining *siddhi. Mantra* is the energy that moves the vehicle or *yantra* according to the path as described by Tantra. The best *yantra* is said to be the human body. The divine is already resident within this body, and through the practice of certain Tantric rites the individual will be able to reach his or her full divine potential. The highest self is said to be a priceless gem locked in a chest that is buried in mud. Tantric disciplines consist of cleaning away the mud of our petty desires and negativity and opening the treasure box in our brain to expose the gem of self-awareness within.

Tantric *sadhanas* are divided into three different types to be used by different types of personalities. The *pashu* type is the *tamasic* individual whose life is akin to that of an animal inasmuch as he lives only for the sake of externalized enjoyments. Such an aspirant should perform external worship in its grossest form to control these urges. The *divya* or divine type has a *sattvic* temperament and tends to be introverted. Such a person need not bother with external rituals, even though he or she may continue to practice them with devotion and knowledge. The *vira* or heroic type is *rajasic* in nature and likes activity. Such a person can perform both external and internal rituals. He or she is capable of giving complete attention to every detail of the ritual, which is an important point in all Tantric rites. The true *divya* and *vira* types consider every act of daily life to be a ritual. Every breath is an offering to Adi Shakti. Their whole life is an offering to the supreme. Their goal is to awaken the inherent feminine Shakti or energy within in order to attain union with the supreme consciousness known as Shiva. Every act of theirs is geared toward this consummation. Without awakening this energy, one can never attain the supreme.

Tantra insists that there can be no *mukti* (liberation) without *bhukti* (experience). Though Tantra affirms the existence of the transcendental Brahman, it also affirms the existence of the universe as a manifestation of the divine Shakti. So everything that takes place in the universe is divine, and every experience that comes to the individual, whether good or bad, has to be accepted gratefully. The Tantrist does not mind regarding the world as *maya* so long as it is understood that this *maya* is nothing but the Divine Mother herself. Tantric *sadhana* is used for procuring not only spiritual benefit but also material goods, for they are the foundations on which the whole spiritual structure stands. The *sadhaka* depends totally on the magnanimity of the goddess to protect and provide.

The Tantric attitude toward life differs greatly from that of some of the other schools of Indian philosophy. Advaita Vedanta or monism, for example, the philosophy of a nondual Brahman, proclaims that Brahman alone is real and the world is unreal. If the world is unreal, then our view of the world is clouded. The world is considered to be the source of pain and sorrow, for it is evanescent. Adi Shankaracharya, the founder of Advaita Vedanta, viewed the world from the transcendental point of view and thus concluded that it was unreal. Tantra, on the other hand, takes the standpoint of the *jiva*. To the *jiva,* the world is real and Iswari, the goddess as creator of the universe, is also real. It is her *shakti* that brings forth creation out of herself, like the spider spinning the world of its web out of itself. The Tantrists consider the goddess to be Anandarupini, pure blissful consciousness. From this they derive the idea that the universe is not only real but also joyful in character and meant for enjoyment. However, because of our desires for transitory things we are unable to enjoy this life as it is meant to be enjoyed.

Tantric rituals are sacrificial rites. Though herbs, minerals, and sometimes even animals are used as offerings, they are only secondary to the true offering, which is the sacrifice of one's limited self into the fires of penance. Contrary to popular belief, Shaktism, like other schools of Hinduism, affirms that a healthy physical and moral life is absolutely essential to the practice of Tantra. One who has not refrained from evil acts and has no peace of mind and self-control cannot attain God by any means.

Tantra is divided into two main branches: the Dakshina Marga, or the right-hand path, and the Vama Marga (sometimes called the Kaula Marga), or the left-hand path. The Dakshina Marga is meant for those who seek steady progress with reduced danger of setbacks. The Vama Marga is described as fast, terrible, and intense. On this path the chances of a fall are great unless one has the protection of a powerful *guru*. The sexual rituals that have made Tantra notorious are part of this path. There is much misunderstanding about this path even today. The Vama Marga is the most esoteric teaching of Tantra and, as has been said, should never be practiced without a competent *guru* who has mastered the art and is capable of leading the aspirant step by step through this walk on the razor's edge, where the slightest fall could lead to death or insanity.

The Dakshina Marga or right-handed path devotes itself to the worship of the goddess in her most benign form, while the left-handed path worships her in her most terrible and base forms. With the typical fearlessness of Hinduism, Shaktism insists that worship of the goddess should reconcile all aspects of the deity, both good and so-called evil. Since she is Adi Shakti, she encompasses everything, so there is nothing that can be considered beyond the pale. This is one of the reasons why Tantric practices have been a closely guarded secret. There is a great danger of them being misinterpreted and falling into the wrong hands. One should never practice classical Tantra without a *guru* because there are no Tantric texts that give accurate information about the rituals. All the texts either omit an essential step or give false information so it is only through the *guru* that the esoteric information can be received. It is always handed down from teacher to disciple.

One of the first steps in Tantric practice is *tattva shuddhi,* the purification of the elements that make up our material body. These elements are earth, water, air, fire, and ether. By continuous practice we can divine these elements in our body so that they are seen not as gross matter but as forms of the divine Shakti, who is nothing but the supreme consciousness. To achieve harmony these elements must be purified, and to experience pure consciousness we have to go beyond the matter these five elements comprise. *Tattva shuddhi* releases and transforms the energy that is locked in matter. The universe, including our own bodies, has evolved out of Shakti or pure energy. Her cosmic counterpart is Shiva or pure consciousness. Although Shiva and Shakti have momentarily separated to give rise to the whole of creation, they are forever striving to unite in the human body in order to reexperience the cosmic unity from which they evolved. The whole object of Tantra is to attain this cosmic union.

Panchamakara is one of the many Tantric rituals that aim at *tattva shuddhi,* sometimes called *bhuta shuddhi.* Its name, *panchamakara,* denotes the five offerings of the ritual, whose names all start with the Sanskrit letter *ma*: *madya* (wine), *matsya* (fish), *mamsa* (flesh), *mithuna* (sex), and *mudras* (mystic gestures) Sometimes parched grain (grain that cannot sprout) is used as the fifth offering in place of *mudras.* These five have different meanings according to the type of aspirant who practices the ritual. The *pashu* or *tamasic* type alone is meant to follow the verbal meaning of the *panchamakaras,* or five offerings. The intensity of these five articles of worship, like the eating of fish, meat, wine, and parched grain and having controlled sex, is supposed to overwhelm the dullness of the *tamasic* person and stimulate his or her brain. If the aspirant has been properly taught by a competent *guru,* this increased mental energy can help to hasten his or her spiritual evolution. A half-baked aspirant, on the other hand, will be overcome by this stimulation and descend into debauchery of the worst type.

Rajasic or *vira* types have active minds that must be properly channeled. They need less stimulation and more control. So they use ginger instead of meat, radish instead of fish, boiled rice instead of parched grain, honey instead of wine, and flowers instead of sex in their *panchamakara* rituals.

The *divya* or *sattvic* types are naturally balanced and harmonious and do not require external aids to worship. For them meat is their own flesh that is eaten through fasting and silence. Fish is breath control through the practice of *pranayama;* breath flows through the two nostrils like fish swimming upriver. Grain is the use of concentration techniques. Wine is the intoxication obtained from God, and sex is the union of one's limited ego with the absolute.

Esoterically speaking, *madya* is the nectar flowing from the *sahasrara chakra. Matsya* and *mudra* stand for the two *nadis* (tubes of astral matter that carry psychic energy) of *kundalini:* the *ida* and *pingala. Mithuna* is, of course, the joy of union of the *atman* with the Paramatman in the *sahasrara chakra* at the crown of the head.

Panchamakara is a fast, intense way to achieve *tattva shuddhi.* Each of its five offerings represents one element. Meat stands for earth, fish for water, wine for fire, grain for air, and sex for ether. By the correct use of this ritual we can balance these elements in our body and thus achieve perfect harmony with the universe, which in turn gives us the perfect physical health that is so necessary for spiritual practice.

The doctrine of *kundalini* and the *chakras* is also closely connected with the five great elements. When the elements have been thoroughly purified in an individual, Kundalini Shakti, the embodiment of *kundalini* that is the individual equivalent of the cosmic Adi Shakti, has a free path upward through the *chakras* and is able to meet and unite with Shiva in the *sahasrara chakra* in the brain. Each of the five lower *chakras* is the seat of the subtle form of one element. As each one is purified and harmonized, Kundalini Shakti can free herself from their grasp and rise upward. Many methods like the *panchamakara* are advocated in order to enable this psychic force to rise. The chanting of the Lalitha Sahasranama, a listing of the thousand and one names of Lalitha, with an understanding of its esoteric meaning as a description of the rise of Kundalini Shakti, is one of them.

The wonderful hymn of Brahma to the goddess in the Brahmanda Purana gives us a clue to the form of the goddess worshipped by the Shaktas. It is addressed to the goddess Adi Lakshmi or Kamakshi, who is said to be the mother of the Trimurtis (the Hindu trinity). She has the glorious form of light and shines in the hearts of all. She is Jaganmata (mother of the universe) as well as Tripurasundari (most beautiful in all the three worlds). She creates, preserves, and destroys the universe, but none can really know her. She is known only to herself. She is to be meditated upon by Brahma, Vishnu, and Shiva as well as by Indra and the other deities. She is *jnana shakti,* and it is at her command that the sun and moon light the earth and fire burns brightly. She is the immanent soul of all souls.

> *There was no mind there with its need to know,*
> *There was no heart there with its need to love,*
> *All people perished in its namelessness,*
> *There was no second; it had no partner or peer.*
> *Only itself was real to itself.*

—*SAVITRI* BY SRI AUROBINDO

Thus ends the twenty-eighth chapter of *Shakti,* known as "Adi Shakti," which describes Tantra, the cult of the Shaktas.

Aum Aim Hreem Kleem

ॐ

Aum Bhadrayai Namaha!

29

Maha Maya

Srishti sthiti vinashanam,
Shaktibhute sanathane,
Gunashraye gunamaye
Narayani namosthute!

Salutations to thee, O Narayani, the eternal,
Who is the power behind creation, maintenance, and
    destruction,
Who consists of and abides in the three qualities of
    primordial matter.

Maya is the external garb of the universe. She is like a well-dressed, heavily made-up woman who appears beautiful and enticing. It is only when you remove her makeup that you discover her real form. The green color and sour taste of a fruit are not its permanent state; soon it will become yellow, ripe, and sweet. The green state is an impermanent one. So it is the case with *maya*. Her external garb is made up of the three *gunas* or esssential qualities of primordial matter. It is only when you strip her of these adjuncts that you see her beauteous form as Maha Devi.

She is also known as Shakti, since her projection of this universe is dynamic. Shakti is the energy that emanates spontaneously from the supreme. Pure energy in any form is dangerous if not controlled. In Tantric philosophy it is Shiva who controls and conditions Shakti. He is the male aspect of the supreme Brahman. He is depicted as having three eyes. Maya is his Shakti and contains the essence of duality, which is space, time, and causation. As long as Shiva keeps his third eye closed, Maya can have full play. Shiva's two eyes, like ours, see only duality, and when he keeps them open the world exists. However, with his third eye, the eye of transcendent wisdom, he can see only unity. So when he opens his third eye, the cosmos, which can exist only in duality, will return to the plenum from which it was projected. As long as Shiva's third eye is opened, nothing can exist. There is only *pralaya* or dissolution, the undifferentiated consciousness of absolute reality. When he closes his third eye, Shiva becomes subject to duality once again, and Maha Maya appears in the forefront and the cosmos rises up.

The special sect of Tantra known as Aghora belongs to the Vama Marga, the left-hand path mentioned in the previous chapter. In Hindu tradition the left hand is used for performing inauspicious actions like cleaning the lower orifices. Shakti controls the left side of our body. A man's wife is always seated on his left when they perform rituals together. In Tantra the supreme deity is the Divine Mother, and she stands always on the left side of the devotee to help him, so Aghora is indeed the left-hand path in more ways than one.

The word *aghora* means "deeper than the deepest" or "filled with light." The aim of Aghora and Tantra is *laya,* or dissolution of the individual consciousness, which is a return to the state of undifferentiated consciousness. It gives many methods of achieving this *laya,* or the union of the individual with the supreme. In this, it is not at variance with the rest of Hindu religion, which also aims at the union of the *jivatman* with the Paramatman. The difference lies only in the methodology and words used to describe this union. In Tantra this union is described by sexual metaphors. The personalized ego is considered to be feminine and the absolute to be male.

Due to the use of sex in its rituals, there is a lot of misunderstanding about Aghora. But actually it is only under special circumstances that a sexual ritual is employed to hasten spiritual progress. Even this has to be under the strict supervision of an enlightened Tantric practitioner or *guru*. Aghoric practices include not just sex but also necromancy, intoxicants, and other dangerous types of rites. This has given Aghora a bad reputation. The truth is that Aghoris try to overcome all mental differentiations between auspicious and inauspicious events and actions and deliberately perform actions that might be considered inauspicious by most people. Everything is favorable to the Aghori, since everything comes from the Divine Mother. Sincere Aghoris depend totally on the power of the goddess to protect them. This protection is given only if the practitioners have developed absolute internal purity, take up the practice only for the sake of spiritual progress, and shun every other type of power or *siddhi* that might come to them. Those who take to this way without the necessary purification of mind and body (*tattva shuddhi*) and without renouncing all sensory gratification are bound to suffer tremendous repercussions, which might lead to madness or even death.

Commercialization of the *siddhis* or special powers that might come to a practitioner as a result of these practices will lead to his downfall. Hence you find that even in India there are very few true Aghoris, for most people are incapable of making the incredible physical and mental sacrifices that the cult demands. It is truly a most dangerous path for the unwary—the razor's edge. Due to the difficulties on the course most people are quite frightened to take it up. So thankfully it cannot be commercialized like so many other paths in the Hindu religion.

Westerners brought up in the conservative tradition of Christianity who first came to India condemned Aghora as a sect steeped in sinful indulgence. They cannot be blamed for this, for their denunciation was based on ignorance. Aghora is far from being a type of indulgence. On the contrary, strict renunciation is the prerequisite for initiation.

Only when personal purity is perfect is the aspirant allowed to perform rituals that to the ignorant observer might appear hedonistic or sinful. Aghora is not a path of indulgence but a forcible transformation of the darkness of the individual consciousness to the luminescence of the absolute. Renunciation is itself renounced when you reach the absolute state of perfection, for there nothing remains to be renounced. Before they reach this luminescence Aghoris are expected to plunge into the worst types of darkness that the human mind can conceive of. Only then can they shake off the darkness and emerge into the sunlight of a supramental consciousness.

Aghoris are not content to sip the wine of the sweetness of life. They are determined to explore the very dregs of this cup. The Aghori is like the lotus flower that revels in the mud in which it was born, but when the time for blossoming comes, it shakes off the mud and raises its beautiful visage to the golden orb of the morning sun. Why dabble in such unsavory things when Hinduism offers such sublime paths to the same goal? The answer given by Aghoris is that it is the fastest path to liberation—as well as to destruction!

The popular picture of an Aghori is that of a wild-eyed ascetic with long matted hair, smeared with ashes from the burning *ghats,* skulking in cremation grounds, fighting with jackals over human carcasses. But the fact of the matter is that the true Aghori may well look like an ordinary person. His practices are kept strictly private and his internal purity is unbelievable, but such a one will not be interested in exposing himself to the curious gaze of the public. He practices in secret, at the dead of night in cremation grounds where none dare approach.

One of the immutable tenets of Aghora is that death is to be personified and deified. Shiva is known as Mahakaala, or death in the form of time. It is not physical death that the Aghoris crave but the destruction of all human limitations. Once he sets out to undertake the difficult rituals of the sect, the Aghori is prepared either to succeed or to die in the attempt. There is no middle course and no retreat. One who fears death should not embark on this path. It is meant only for those who have totally given up all fears, especially the fear of death.

Many Aghori rituals are conducted at midnight in burning *ghats* and cemeteries. These rites are done in a state of intoxication, next to a blazing funeral pyre, with flames shooting up into the blackness of the night. Most of the rites will remain incomprehensible to the normal mind brought up with the prudish ideas of a conservative religious background. But lack of understanding should not make us condemn the practice.

Western philosophers once experimented with the science of alchemy, by which they sought to change the dross of base metals into gold. Aghora has a similar pursuit, but the base metal it seeks to change is the animal-born mind of the human being. Aghora is one of the great discoveries of the Hindu religion. It has dared to explore every facet of the human mind and find out methods of transmuting every aspect, even the basest, into the gold of enlightenment. It is one of the highest spiritual sciences that India has produced. Aghora is a mysterious practice and only those who are capable of laying aside their cultural clothing and plunging deep into the depths of their psyche will be able to discover the pearls within. It is not a path for the cowardly who want easy and safe methods of enlightenment. It is meant only for those who can leave the standard paths, which have few pitfalls, and take to the path of the razor's edge, who dare to renounce their very lives if necessary, to find the jewel of enlightenment. Hinduism offers many safe paths to enlightenment in which the practitioner can lift himself up if he falls and restart his journey. But in Aghora it is "do or die." If you fail, you fall into the deepest pits of hell; if you succeed, you are the master of the universe. Nothing can harm you. You can roam about as you like, eating anything you like, drinking anything you like, for you are a walking corpse. Why should a corpse care what it eats or drinks? Nothing can harm it. The cosmic Shakti is in possession of your body and you are like a *yantra*. She plays through you and with you and allows you to enjoy the bliss. But of course this is the final stage, and the Aghori has to pass through many treacherous and highly dangerous disciplines before reaching it.

Aghora is the path of no return, a highly personal creed that stakes all on the love of the Divine Mother. The true Aghori is prepared to relinquish every earthly pleasure for the sake of her love. He or she is not bound by the worldly bonds in which *maya* binds the ordinary mortal. He or she is intoxicated with love for Maha Maya. The devotee's own identity is totally merged in hers so that he or she, as the personalized ego, no longer exists. *Mantra, yantra,* and Tantra are used to create the form of the deity in the aspirant's consciousness. After this the devotee and the goddess are expected to keep strictly to the type of relationship that suits him or her best: mother/son, lover/beloved, child/mother, or just friends. This melting of the devotee's personality into that of the deity is known as *tanmayata.* The devotee has to continue his or her worship in this fashion until the relationship is fully stabilized. Eventually all traces of the devotee's original personality will be effaced and only the deity's personality will remain. This is known as *tadrupata,* or attaining the same form.

The Aghoris also practice the *panchamakara* ritual, which is basic to all Tantric rites. A couple who wants to practice this ritual correctly must first perfect the *shiva lata mudra,* or mystical gesture in which all traces of animal desire are completely eliminated. The male identifies himself with Shiva and the female with Shakti. Aghoris say, "Only one who has become Shiva will be able to worship Shiva." Thus the couple should attain *tanmayata* with these deities before starting the ritual.

In the *shiva lata mudra,* the man places his wife on his left thigh and cups her left breast with his left palm. The woman holds his penis with her right palm and clings to him like a creeper (*lata*). They practice *japa* (repetition of *mantras*) with the appropriate *mantras.* The man holds the *mala* or rosary with his right hand, and the woman holds it with her left. Soon they are so immersed in the repetition of the *mantra* that they both forget their individual personalities. She sees him as Lord Shiva and he worships her as the cosmic Shakti. They should be able to retain this attitude for at least three hours without any sexual excitement. There should be neither erection nor dilation!

This can happen only when self-identification with the deities (*tadrupata*) is complete. Their concentration must be intense and the identification absolute. In fact, the couple will soon go into a state of *bhava samadhi* (superconsciousness), in which they forget the mundane world and identify themselves wholly with Shiva and Shakti.

Only couples who have successfully practiced the *shiva lata mudra* many times can successfully perform the *panchamakara* ritual in its purest form. Of course this is not always the case, and many half-baked *yogis* perform the ritual and bring ruin on themselves and a bad reputation for the practice.

As we have seen in the previous chapter, the word *panchamakara* denotes the five types of offerings that are used in the *panchamakara* ritual, all of which start with the Sanskrit letter *ma*. These are *matsya, mamsa, mudra, madhu,* and *mithuna,* which stand for fish, meat, parched grain and certain hand postures, wine, and the sexual act. To the couple that has become adept in the *shiva lata mudra,* the partaking of these articles is no longer an act of indulgence but a sacrament. Since they have attained *tadrupata* with the deities (their physical bodies have attained total identification with these divine beings), the deities are the ones performing the rite and directly partaking of the offerings. Ordinary sex is for the gratification of the lust of the couple concerned, but in this Tantric rite the partners have totally submerged their personalities with that of their chosen deities and offer themselves for the gratification of these gods alone. Tantric rituals are sacrificial rites like the Vedic *yajnas* (fire sacrifices). In this ritual the female is the fire into which the male offers his semen, just as ghee is offered into the *yajna kund* (sacrificial pit) in orthodox methods of fire worship.

Aghoris also use herbs, minerals like mercury, and sometimes even animals as offerings. But it must be remembered that these are secondary to the true offering of one's limited self into the sacrificial fire of penance. It is a very difficult path to pursue, and the chances of a fall are legion. This is one of the reasons that Tantra has always been such a closely guarded secret.

The body of the Aghori must always be kept in a state of perfect health, since it is the *yantra* or vehicle that will enable him to reach his goal. His mind must be fearless and free of worries. He must be careful of what he eats and what he thinks while practicing these esoteric rites. The *bhuta agni* is the fire of austerity that enkindles the *jatara agni* or the fire of digestion. When the mind is weak and worried, the *bhuta agni* is weakened, which in turn weakens the *jatara agni*. This results in indigestion and disease. So the spiritual person must try to preserve his *bhuta agni* or spiritual digestion, which will give him both mental and physical health. The best way to do this is to eat less. This is why all religions insist on some type of fasting, which will improve health. As one's bodily hunger decreases, one finds an increased hunger for spiritual things. Sleep and sex dull both the *bhuta agni* and the *jatara agni*.

Alcohol is generally considered to strengthen the fire of digestion, but it also has the effect of clouding the *bhuta agni*. Aghoris ingest alcohol and drugs only because they can keep their minds under control and use these intoxicants in the appropriate dosage needed to produce a heightened feeling of consciousness that will further their spiritual practices. If the intoxicant overcomes them, as it does most people, it is of no use and will end in downfall. Another reason why Aghoris use intoxicants is because Shiva is said to use them, and they think it will help them identify with the deity. It is only when they reach the height of their *sadhana* that they come to understand that Shiva is always in an intoxicated state of the bliss of the Brahman and not in the temporary state of euphoria produced by drugs and alcohol. The Aghori who wants to emulate Shiva's example has to gingerly tread this path of fathomless pitfalls and hang on to his Shakti, depending only on her to support him and stop him from falling.

When Aghoris take intoxicants, they must do so in the proper way. They must invoke the proper *mantra* before ingesting any of them. Then the ingestion becomes a rite and is no longer an indulgence. Again, this is a very dangerous path since the mind has a thousand ways in which it can fool itself. Taking an intoxicant without the appropriate *mantra* will ruin the *bhuta agni* and consequently the mind. This is because a lot of *karmas* are involved in taking intoxicants. Intoxicants can be useful in *sadhana* or they can severely damage your psyche. It all depends on how you use them.

Even with all these precautions, the body will deteriorate with the constant use of intoxicants, because the mind becomes partially free from the constraints of the body. So in all ordinary forms of *yoga* you will find that the taking of any type of intoxicant is strictly forbidden. Even in Aghora there is the constant pitfall that the practitioner may become addicted to the intoxicant and unable to withdraw himself from it even after it has served its purpose.

Advaita Vedanta declares *Brahma satyam, jagat mithya*—"Brahman alone is real, the world is an illusion." Aghoris claim that *jagat* or the world is equally real. The world is a direct expression of Maha Maya, who is an emanation from the Brahman, which is the absolute reality. So the world, which is a product of the creator Brahma's Shakti, who is known as Saraswati, must also be real. The world and Brahman form parts of a harmonious whole; they are interdependent. The world may not be absolutely true, but it has its own reality that is based on the falsehood of impermanence. It is as real as we are. Enlightenment does not mean that you enter into some white light. It is not something that comes from the outside but the natural state of your mind. What enlightenment means is that you have lightened yourself of your burden of *karmas* and debts that you have been carrying for many births. This lightening process is done through *sadhana* and of course by the grace of your *guru* and the Divine Mother.

The Vedic religion is the religion of light—the light of all lights, the supreme light of consciousness by which even the sun is lit. Aghora, on the other hand, is the religion of darkness—utter, absolute, abysmal darkness. Can anyone define light or truth? Similarly, can anyone define darkness? All we can say is that it is an absence of

light. The deepest darkness is the darkness of a mind shrouded in ignorance. The light is the light of one's own consciousness. Aghora teaches
you to embrace impurities, to embrace darkness, for it is the veil of
Maha Maya. You have to catch her by the hair and drag her to you and
force her to push you through the darkness to the light within. All normal people are dreadfully frightened of Maya because they are totally
enmeshed in her web. Maya is the projection of the Shakti of Shiva into
the outside world, and they fear her because they cannot control her.
The Aghori, however, identifies himself with Shiva, the supreme within
him, and thus controls Maya. From the mortality of earthly existence he
propitiates the destroyer Mahakaala (Shiva) and thus becomes immortal. Having controlled Shakti, he becomes luminent like Shiva.

The Vedas say, "Lead us from the unreal to the real, from darkness to light, and from death to immortality!" This is also the goal of
Aghora. But the difference is that Vedanta tells us to proceed from the
semidarkness in which we exist and follow the path of self-inquiry into
the nature of the "I" until we reach the light of the absolute. Aghora,
however, tells us to find out the nature of our darkness first and inves-
tigate both aspects of duality, the negative and the positive, until we go
beyond both into the state of nonduality.

Nothing is inauspicious to the Aghori, whose initiation has been in
the burning *ghat* amid the corpses, ghosts, and spirits that roam there.
The first fear that he is taught to conquer is the fear of death. He must
totally give up attachment to the body. If he clings to the body and fears
death, he cannot perfect even the preliminary lesson in Aghora. To be
an Aghori he must go beyond all limitation, and the greatest limitation
is that of the body. He must embrace death while alive. When he has
given up attachment to the body, he has nothing to lose and nothing
to fear, for the greatest fear is the loss of the body through death. His
mind must be absolutely firm. Even if the most beautiful spirit comes
to tempt him, he must remain firmly concentrated on Shiva. Ghosts
and ghouls can throw hot coals on him in the cremation grounds, but
he must be able to watch his skin burn with detachment and uncon-

cern. It is only one who has controlled himself to this extreme extent who can succeed in Aghora.

Three things bind us firmly to the body: food, sleep, and sex. If you want to die while remaining in the body, you have to restrict all three. The more you get of these, the more you want. Gratifying them can eliminate other desires, but these three will keep increasing in intensity the more you give in to them. The more you eat, the more you want to eat; the more you sleep, the more you want to sleep; and the more you indulge in sex, the more you crave it. Unless you learn to curb these three, you can never make any true spiritual progress. Too much food makes you sleepy and sex exhausts you. Aghoris cannot afford to indulge in any type of relaxation. They have to be alert all the time. If you fall asleep in the cremation grounds while practicing some rite, you become psychically weak and any passing spirit will be able to enter your body and use it for its own purposes.

To die while remaining alive means that you have to eliminate all involuntary stimulation of the senses. You cannot salivate if you see a tempting dinner. You cannot become aroused if you see a beautiful man or woman passing by, not even if that person comes close and winds his or her arms around your neck. You cannot even dwell on such things in memory and get a vicarious pleasure from them. When you no longer react to this type of stimuli, you are as good as dead. Your body has dried up. The juicy thoughts that keep you bound to the body and perpetually produce desires no longer exist. Only such a person is fit to imbibe the real juice of life—the nectar of immortality. As such a person you may perform many things physically, but they will not affect you, since you are totally unaffected by them mentally. You no longer react to physical stimuli.

To die while still alive means to extinguish duality altogether. The absolute is one, not two, so all perception of duality has to be eliminated—pleasant and unpleasant, boring and exciting. A corpse does not care about any such distinctions. We are conditioned to think that corpses, skulls, menstrual blood, and feces are filthy and must be avoided at all cost. The very thought of using such things for rituals is nauseating to the common person. But the Aghori makes use of all these things and is prepared to eat even human flesh from the cremation grounds if it will help him or her gain a goal. Aghoris hang around cremation grounds and wait for the skull of a corpse to burst. They then swoop on the body, scoop the brain from within the skull before it is burned, and consume it. The brain is supposed to have special properties that will help them in their *sadhana*. The goal of *sadhana* is to be able to accept everything in the world, both enticing and disgusting, with equanimity, because everything in the world is part of Maha Maya. Genuine Tantra is therefore the nonrejection of all things and not the indulgence.

The Bhagavad Gita declares that the enlightened soul is one that can see no difference between a clod, a stone, and a diamond. All are different forms of matter; the diamond should not have more appeal though it has greater material value. Similarly, to the perfect Aghori, a chocolate pudding, a clod, and a lump of feces should have the same value. All are different forms of matter and should be treated as such. The only truly valuable thing on earth is the supreme. Everything else is of equal value. It is the ignorant mind that places different values on different things. The man of wisdom does not accept these differences, even though he may be aware of them.

Have you ever paused to reflect on the number of murders, rapes, robberies, tortures, and other heinous crimes that are being committed every moment in some part of the world or other? Who is responsible for all this? No doubt it is each person's *karma* that brings such things within his or her orbit, but even so, why cannot an omnipotent God stop such atrocities? As has been discussed before, the absolute Brahman does not concern itself with the running of the universe. Parashakti (Maha Maya) enacts both the stage and the drama of the world, and she forces each person to take full responsibility for his or her actions. Ignorant fools, without a thought of the dreadful consequences of their appalling deeds, continue to commit one crime after another. But she knows it all, and none can gainsay her! Can you imagine the amounts of *karma* people accumulate? No wonder that the *jnanis* (men of wisdom) who are aware of the consequences of each *karma* try to avoid actions altogether.

The Aghori recognizes the pitfalls of *karma* but forces himself to go beyond the fear and to see that everything is part of the whole. Everything moves according to Maha Maya's divine plan. Every murder and every rape has its significance. You have to love everything that takes place in the universe if you want to go beyond duality and reach unity. When you see one in all and all in one, you lose all fear. Fear exists only in duality. When you see only the *atman* in everything and yourself as part and parcel of it, then who or what should you fear? Once you drop fear, the whole world is open to you because you have no demands. You have gone beyond anticipation and expectation. You anticipate nothing and expect nothing. You know only to give because you have so much and nothing that belongs only to you! You are the possessor of everything. The devotee sleeps like a baby in the lap of his Divine Mother, absolutely certain that everything will be be provided for him. When death ceases to have a hold over you, then both time and causality cease to hold any fears.

Now you will realize that Aghora is a path that is suitable only for a very special type of temperament. Not everyone can practice it. Not only does the Aghori strip off his clothes, but he also strips his mind of every preconceived notion that society, culture, and the environment have clothed him in. He plunges himself into every possible type of so-called sin known to man, knowing that he has the power to draw himself out of it. He does this by complete surrender to the Divine Mother. He is certain that she will draw him out after having purified him in the fire of his austerities. However, he is prepared to be tested at every moment, for that is part of her *lila*.

After having indulged in all types of intoxicants, after having eaten all types of flesh, including human flesh, offal, and feces, without the slightest trace of disgust, the Aghori comes to realize that the greatest narcotic, the greatest delicacy, the greatest bliss, is the name of God alone. He realizes that the best drama is being enacted on the stage of his body and he himself is the main actor dancing the macabre dance of death with the destroyer himself, to the tune called by the divine Shakti. What joy can the world offer him? All the eight *siddhis* (extraordinary powers) will be at his command. The Divine Mother can deny him nothing, but now he wants nothing but her. He clings to her like a child, and she in turn leads him to the supreme from which she has emanated. Such is the final state of the perfect Aghori, for whom the material world is but a toy that his Divine Mother has given him to play with. He cares not for such trifles, for his body is aflame with desire for the cosmic beloved and he knows no other bliss but that of union with her.

In his highest state the Aghori becomes the greatest devotee. He is prepared to sacrifice everything in order to attain union with his deity. He is prepared to go to any lengths to attain the goal of his *sadhana*. No ordinary devotee can be as intense as an Aghori. The Aghori burns the candle of his life at both ends. It might not last through the night, but while it does, it casts a lovely light!

> *Life became a sure approach to God,*
> *Existence a divine experiment;*
> *The world a conception and a birth,*
> *Of Spirit in Matter, into living forms.*
> *Nature bore the Immortal in her womb,*
> *That she might climb through him to eternal life.*

—SAVITRI BY SRI AUROBINDO

Thus ends the twenty-ninth chapter of *Shakti*, known as "Maha Maya," which describes Aghora, the left-hand path of Tantra.

Aum Aim Hreem Kleem

ॐ

Aum Chakrarajayai Namaha!

30
Sri Chakra

Lakshmi, lajje, mahavidye, shraddhe, pushtiswadhe,
*   dhruve,*
Maharatri, mahavidye,
Narayani namosthute!

O Lakshmi! O modesty!
Of great knowledge, faith, prosperity, O firm one!
O great night, O great knowledge,
O Narayani! Praise be to you!

Yantra means an instrument, a machine, or a storehouse of power. All forms of creation are nothing but energy, and a *yantra,* due to its mathematical precision, is a powerhouse of inherent energy. Within its concrete form it encloses the uncontrollable power of the deity. It limits the limitless within a figure of crisscrossed lines that bind and channel the form of the deity. It creates a field of power that lives, breathes, and moves with life and within which the power of the divine can be invoked. *Yantra* images exist within us, but in order to perceive them we must develop a new way of seeing and sharpen our inherent faculty in which these images are stored. These images are pulled out of the vast ocean of consciousness that holds within it all conceivable forms.

As our awareness penetrates into deeper levels of consciousness, our inner experiences also change. They become more abstract. The forms we see in nature are only their gross representations, which rest on their abstract subtle forms, and these are what the *yantra* represents. The *yantra* is the original form of everything in nature. Every image in nature can be represented by its linear dimension, which is the *yantra*.

A *yantra* is composed of a combination of the basic primordial shapes: the *bindu* or point, line, circle, square, and triangle. The focal point of a *yantra* is always the center or *bindu*. It represents the nucleus or seed from which creation has evolved and into which it will return—the process of creation and dissolution. It also represents the union of the two dual principles of the universe, Shiva and Shakti, consciousness and energy. The *bindu* represents the state of their union preceding creation. In the human body this focal point is found at the top back portion of the head. You will find that the Brahmins in India cover this spot with a tuft of hair.

Space cannot be circumscribed by anything less than three lines, so the triangle is considered to be the first form to have emerged out of creation. In its inverted (downward-pointing) form it represents Mula Prakriti or the matrix of creation; the upward-pointing triangle represents Purusha or Shiva or pure consciousness. In the Sri Chakra we see an intersection of the upward-pointing triangle with the downward-pointing one, which represents the downward thrust of energy that is met with an upward thrust of consciousness.

The circle represents the cycle of timelessness, which has no beginning and no end. It denotes eternity and implies the process of birth, life, and death as an eternal cycle of events. The square is the substratum on which the *yantra* rests and denotes the physical or terrestrial world that has to be transcended.

Chakras are a type of *yantra*. They are always in the shape of a wheel, representing constant movement. The *chakra* signifies the constant and dynamic circulation of the power of the infinite. The *chakra*, like the *yantra*, can lead us to the direct perception of the divine. The perfect lines of beauty, harmony, and symmetry with which the Master Mathematician designs the universe are caught in the *chakra*. Like *yantras*, *chakras* are drawn with lines, triangles, circles, and squares. They frequently employ the lotus motif.

The *mandala* is always represented within a circle. Any form that is pictorially created within the consciousness can form a *mandala*. Tantric iconography is filled with *mandalas* of the deities. These are often not the forms that are visible to the gross vision but the forms that are seen by the inner eye. An object can be visualized from both the outside and the inside, but the difference is that when you visualize inwardly, you catch a glimpse of what lies beyond the form. The *mandalas* that you create will depend on your level of consciousness. The more evolved your mind, the more universal will be the *mandalas* you create. The Tantric *mandalas* were created by those who had transcended the material plane and become enraptured in some supracosmic ecstasy.

Every civilization has its own *mandalas,* and these give us a clue as to the level of consciousness of that society. These *mandalas* are created in the subconscious abyss of the mind, and hence they have a profound influence on the minds of those who look at them, even though they may not be able to understand what they see. They can influence generations of people long after they were made. That is why Tantric *mandalas* have such a strong impact on us even today. All the ancient temple art of India was in the form of *mandalas,* since the artists were inspired by their inner vision, and that is why the art has withstood the test of time and exists as immortal and eternal ideas.

Even today *mandalas* are drawn in various colors in front of houses and for special rituals. The *mandala* that is normally drawn before the commencement of any Tantric ritual is not a mere decorative image. It actually provides a potent and graphic focus for the operation of subtle forces both internally and externally. Each deity has his or her own *mandala*. Concentration on the *mandala* awakens the deep-rooted instincts within us and reveals unknown mysteries, in the form of dreams and visions. This is a psychologically subtle way of dispensing with a fearful enemy for which you have no outward defense. These *mandalas* are always aesthetic and are able to capture and direct our imagination, which is our link with our higher mind.

The Vedas speak of the supernal ether or *akasa* as the abode of *vac* or sound. Tantra calls this ether *mahakaarana* or the cause of all causes. It is the storehouse of all sounds and is the permanent place of the light of all lights. From this mass of formless light emerge the rays that fashion all forms during the course of evolution. *Deva* means "the shining one," and the gods or *devas* are also emanations from this light. The formless radiance emits rays of definite forms and weaves them into the forms and features of the various gods. These lines of light that make the form-patterns of the gods are known as *yantras* and *chakras*. We can contemplate the absolute as a mass of ineffable light, but if we want to see the auspicious form of our favorite deity, this light has to be codified into a definite pattern of rays, and this codification results in the *yantra* or the *chakra*. Tantra says that by worshipping the *chakra* or *yantra* of a deity, we can immediately visualize the deity's form and thus enable the god to manifest in front of our physical eyes. There is a wonderful passage in the Isavasya Upanishad that says:

> The face of truth is covered with a brilliant golden lid;
> That do thou remove, O fosterer of the law of truth, for sight;
> O fosterer! O sole seer, O ordainer, O illumining sun!
> O power of the father of all creatures!
> Marshal thy rays, draw together thy light;
> The light, which is thy most blessed form, that in thee I behold.
> The Purusha there and there,
> He am I.

Esoterically, this verse is a plea to the ordainer asking him to mass the rays of his eternal light in a special formation so as to enable us to see the glorious form of the godhead.

The circle represents that principle that has no beginning and no end and is perfectly symmetrical and equidistant from the center. It stands for the radiations from the one divine center to the circumscribed field of action of the world. The *bindu* or dot in the center normally denotes the supreme. Triangles represent the triple worlds of creation—three lower and three higher. Each triangle enfolds the *yoni* or womb, which is the origin of everything and which stands for the Divine Mother. Both equilateral and isosceles triangles are used. A triangle with its apex turned up indicates the single-pointed aspiration of the *sadhaka* that raises her from the broad-based depths of her being to the heights of the divine. The triangle with its apex pointing downward corresponds to the *shakti* or grace of the Divine Mother that immediately responds to the efforts of the seeker. The figure formed by two triangles intersecting each other is known as the *shatkona* or six-cornered figure; it represents the rising aspiration of the *jivatman* that is being enfolded in the responding grace of the Divine Mother. This figure, which forms the base of the Sri Chakra, represents the ascent of the inner power, which is encouraged by the higher power, which descends to welcome it. When the supreme Shakti of her own volition takes on the form of the universe and turns her gaze on her own pulsation, the *chakra* comes into being. The Sri Chakra is thus a master plan for the manifestation of the universe drawn by the divine architect on the board of the infinite.

The lotus is a flower that responds only to the call of light. It raises its head when the sun rises and closes its petals when it sets. The flower opens petal by petal, corresponding to the gradual unfolding of the latent spirituality in us. That is why the lotus plays such a significant part in all *chakras*. The centers of psychic consciousness in the human being are also known as *chakras*, and a lotus flower diagrammatically represents each of them.

The *yantra* known as the Sri Chakra is considered to be the king of all *chakras*. It is called Chakraraja in the Lalitha Sahasranama and constitutes the chariot of Lalitha. It is the most potent and famous of all *yantras*. It is the eternal abode of Maha Devi as Tripurasundari and the supreme storehouse of all felicity. The Lalitha Sahasranama says, "The *japa* of the king of *mantras,* the worship of the king of *chakras*, and the recital of the occult names are the fruits of no little *tapas!*"

The Sri Chakra is the king of all *chakras* for another reason also: it contains all other *chakras* within it, in the same way that the Divine Mother contains and sustains all other gods and goddesses. Therefore it is said that by using the Sri Chakra one can worship any god or goddess. The vibrations that emanate from it are so positive that even a person who sits near it is subtly influenced by it without his or her knowledge. Hence it is present in many centers of worship. Adi Shankaracharya is famous for having installed the Sri Chakra in all the temples that he visited or established all over India. Modern mathematicians are astounded by the beauty and symmetry of this amazing figure, the secret of which they have not been able to fathom. The lines and angles are delicate and sharp. The curves and petals are round and smooth. Its intricate pattern defies all intellectual analysis.

The universe is a projection of the Paramatman, who creates it in order to know himself and to see himself. The goal of life is a conscious and voluntary return of the *jivatman* back to the Paramatman. If the divine consciousness were only the inaction of unmanifest bliss, there would be no universe and no creation. In contrast, the supreme manifests himself so that he might become conscious of himself. The first manifestation is of light. This light contains within it the seed of an unformulated desire to manifest. This seed desire or *vimarsha,* as Tantra names it, is the original Shakti or Mother Goddess. Whereas the color of the light is pure white, the color of the desire or Shakti is red, since it presupposes the activity of *rajas*. This seed is the digit of desire. At this time the goddess is known as Kameswari (giver of desires). This desire creates a throb or *spanda,* which concentrates itself into a spot, or *bindu.* It contains the seed of the entire creation. When it gets into the mood to create further, it emanates as sound and is known as Sabda Brahman. Sabda Brahman contains both Shiva and Shakti, which projects into three points. These three points stand for *iccha shakti, jnana shakti,* and *kriya shakti,* or the powers of desire, knowledge, and action, without which the universe could not have been created. The three points also stand for the three *gunas* (*sattva, rajas,* and *tamas*), which are the qualities of primordial matter. They also denote the three states of consciousness—waking, dreaming and deep sleep. The three points form the primary triangle of the Sri Chakra. The *bindu* or dot in the center denotes the *turiya* state of pure consciousness.

The original *bindu* is the point of contact between the creator and his creation. It is the drop that swells into the ocean of consciousness. It is the cipher by which everything else is deciphered. The *bindu* is the navel of the Sri Chakra, from which the whole of creation originates.

This *bindu* becomes the triangle, and the triangle expands into the eight-edged figure, then to a ten-cornered figure, and so on. Thus the *bindu* of the primary triangle transforms itself through a series of

The Sri Chakra

lines, triangles, circles, and squares to the fully formed shape of the Sri Chakra. When the great goddess subjects herself to the division of the three *bindus,* she is known as Tripurasundari. She is both the transcendent point in the middle of the primary triangle and the three points that form the triangle.

The figure of the Sri Chakra actually contains nine *chakras.* The shape on the extreme outside is a square traced by three lines, one inside the other. These lines are not joined, for they have four portals opening out to the four directions. This is the ground sketch representing the earth plane (*bhupura*). When we enter a portal we see three concentric circles, which are known as girdles. The space between the sides of the square and the girdles is a *chakra* in itself, which is known as the "enchanter of the three worlds" (*trailokya mohana chakra*). Sixteen lotus petals are arranged next to the three girdles, with their tips pointing to and touching the girdle and their bases resting on another circle. This *chakra* is known as the "fulfiller of all desires" (*sarvasya paripuraka chakra*).

Inside this circle is yet another circle. The space enclosed by these two circles is smaller than the space formed by the sixteen lotus petals. Inside this space are arranged another eight lotus petals, with their tips touching the centers of eight of the sixteen outer petals. This *chakra* is known as the "agitator of all" (*sarva sankshobhana chakra*).

Inside this final circle we come to the figure formed by the superimposition of five downward-pointing triangles with four upward-pointing triangles. This figure contains forty-three small triangles inside it. The outermost *chakra* consists of fourteen triangles and is known as the "giver of all auspiciousness" (*sarva saubhagya chakra*). The next figure consists of ten triangles and is known as the "accomplisher of all purposes" (*sarvartha sadhaka chakra*). Inside this is a ten-cornered figure known as the "giver of protection" (*sarva rakshakara chakra*). Next comes an eight-cornered figure, which is the "remover of all diseases" (*sarva rogahara chakra*). Inside this is the primary triangle with its apex pointing down, which is the "giver of all powers" (*sarva siddhiprada chakra*). In the heart of this is the dot or *bindu,* which is the seat of the Tripurasundari and is filled with unending bliss (*sarva anandamaya chakra*).

The Sri Chakra is thus formed out of the *bindu* and many intersecting triangles. The primary triangle, the eight-cornered figure, the two ten-edged figures, and the fourteen-pointed figures are known as Shakti *chakras*. The figures with eight and sixteen petals, the three girdles, and the three squares or *bhupuras* are known as Shiva *chakras*. Thus the Sri Chakra, which is the body of Shiva and Shakti, is formed with four Shiva *chakras* and the five Shakti *chakras*.

We have seen how the Sri Chakra's original formation is of nine *chakras,* five pointing downward and four pointing upward. The ones pointing downward are known as Shakti *konas* (triangles) and the four pointing upward are known as Shiva *konas*. The esoteric meaning here is that the dynamic Shakti is superimposed on the static Shiva. The amazing picture of Kaali dancing on the inert form of Shiva is a graphic representation of this.

The five Shakti *konas* also stand for the five elements and the four Shiva *konas* for *vidya, maya,* Maheswara, and Sadashiva (the eternal entity of Shiva, corresponding to Brahman). These four principles in combination with the five elements produce the universes inherent in the Sri Chakra. Thus every aspect of matter contains both Shiva and Shakti, in varying degrees of concentration. The Sri Chakra denotes both the microcosm and the macrocosm in the body of the two-in-one—Shiva/Shakti. This verse by Sri Kapali Sastriar, a disciple of Sri Aurobindo, describes this union: "His body is the dense sky, which she embraces secretly. Their breath of love spreads a hidden beauty all around. Their dance in space causes a series of universes and glittering stars as though they were the beads of perspiration caused by their intense bliss of union."

We have already mentioned that the *bindu* is the *kamakala* or the digit of desire of the supreme. It is the essence of love and bliss. So each *chakra* is a gradual development of that initial drop of love and bliss. Hence every aspect of life is meant to be filled with love and bliss.

The figure of the Sri Chakra also provides an esoteric path of return for the *jivatman* from the external world of matter to the point of unending bliss, or the *bindu*. The outermost *chakra,* as noted above, is known as the "enchanter of the three worlds," and the *jivatman* who has come under the spell of the goddess in this *chakra* can remain for many lifetimes enjoying her play of beauty and becoming. After indulging in this for an incredible amount of time, the individual hankers to possess and own all this. She fulfills this desire in the next *chakra,* known as the "fulfiller of all desires." But the more she possesses, the more she desires, so her mind is filled with agitation. And thus she passes to the next *chakra,* called the "agitator of all."

After staying in this *chakra* for many births of such agitations and unfulfilled desires, the *jiva* decides to penetrate further into the labyrinth of her own consciousness and discover the source of bliss. Now she comes to the *chakra* known as the "giver of all auspiciousness." From this point on progress becomes easier for the *jiva,* for divine grace is felt to be flowing toward her. All protection is given in the next *chakra,* and the disease and disharmony felt by the aspirant is removed. This in turn leads to all perfection and the attainment of powers or *siddhis.* From here it is but a step to reach the *bindu* or drop of bliss from which the whole journey started. Thus the *chakra* is a two-way map showing the descent of the divine into inert matter and the ascent of the *jivatman* back to the point of bliss from which it started its journey. The lesson the individual has to learn is that a perfect surrender to the Divine Mother will have the effect of pulling down divine grace.

The Sri Chakra can also be pictured in the human body. The *bindu* is contacted at the top of the spinal column in the *sahasrara chakra* on the crown of the head. The *trikona* or triangle is at the base of the spine in the *muladhara chakra.* The *kundalini,* which is the coiled energy of the Divine Mother in the *muladhara chakra,* travels upward until it attains union with Shiva in the *bindu.* The whole of creation is the outcome of the union of the *bindu* and the *trikona*—of Shiva and Shakti. All aspects of creation contain both these principles, the static and the dynamic. When the dynamic aspect is in the front, it is called Shakti, and when the static aspect is projected, it is known as Shiva.

Various formulas are given in ancient texts how the Sri Chakra should be drawn. In the Kaula tradition of the left-handed path of Tantra, the circle is drawn first and then the bases of the nine triangles. In the Samaya or right-handed tradition, the primary triangle is drawn first and the *bindu* placed inside, and then the sides are extended to form the rest of the figure. Both traditions employ the same method for drawing the outer petals, the three girdles, and the outer square. One important point to remember is that the petals should touch each other and no space should be left between them. Since the Sri Chakra is used with the intention of getting the most auspicious things of life and finally liberation itself, the color to be used in drawing it should be red. Saffron mixed with cow's milk is recommended for drawing this *chakra* for a *puja*. It can also be made on copper, silver, or gold plates and installed permanently in a house or *puja* room with the appropriate *mantras*. Then it acts as an armor of protection.

When the Sri Chakra is made in an upright form it is known as the Meru. Here the nine *chakras* are on different elevations and not on the same plane. This elevated figure is a representation of Mount Meru, which is considered to be the axis of the earth.

Many methods of worshipping the Sri Chakra are given, but one of the easiest is by reciting the thousand and one names of the goddess in the Lalitha Sahasranama. She is greatly pleased if *puja* is done with *vilva* or *tulasi* leaves or lotus flowers. Worship of the Sri Chakra on full-moon nights is highly recommended. If one worships the goddess on full-moon nights by using the Sri Chakra and reciting the Lalita Sahasranama, one attains the form of the goddess. This is the outer method of worship of the Sri Chakra.

When inner worship is done, the Sri Chakra is identified with the subtle centers or *chakras* in the body. One can meditate on it either in the *manipura chakra* situated in the navel or in the *anahata chakra* over the heart. After some deep meditation the *sadhaka* starts to hear the *nada* or sound that emerges from the cave of the heart. This turns into the radiance from which creation originally started. Very soon the small individual personality is shattered in this blast of light and dissolves into it. The *sadhaka*'s sense of identity with the body, mind, and intellect is completely dissolved, and he or she becomes filled with bliss and light alone.

> *While there one can be wider than the world,*
> *While there one is one's own infinity.*
> . . . .
> *The deathless Two-in-One,*
> *A single Being in two bodies clasped,*
> *A diarchy of two united souls,*
> *Seated absorbed on deep creative mood;*
> *Their trance of bliss sustained the mobile world.*
>
> —SAVITRI BY SRI AUROBINDO

Thus ends the thirtieth chapter of *Shakti*, known as "Sri Chakra," which describes the yantra known as the Sri Chakra.

Aum Aim Hreem Kleem

ॐ

Aum Kundalinyai Namaha!

31

Devi Kundalini

Manastwam, vyoma twam, marudasi, marutsarathirasi,
Twamapastwam, bhumistvayi, parinatayam, nahi param,
Twameva svatmaanam, parinamayitum vishvapurusha,
Chidanandakaaram, haramahishi-bhavena bibrushe.

O Devi Kundalini! You are mind, space, air, fire, water, and
   earth.
Nothing exists beyond you.
You have transformed your form of blissful consciousness,
And taken on the shape of the universe.

A quotation from the Vedas says, "Even if man acquires the capacity to
roll up the sky like a piece of leather, there would not be an end to sorrow unless he realizes the effulgent one within."

The supreme consciousness residing in the *sahasrara chakra* at the
top of the head is the effulgent one within. Kundalini Shakti embodies the cosmic energy of the Divine Mother that lies coiled up in the
muladhara chakra at the base of the spinal column. (The Sanskrit word
kundala means "coiled.") Her form is like that of a coiled serpent;
hence she is known as Mother Kundalini. She is the mystic fire of primordial energy. She is a fiery occult power, the force that underlies all

295

organic and inorganic matter. She is Parashakti, the subtlest and most potent form of energy.

The energy that Devi Kundalini embodies is not a physical energy like electricity but a spiritual potential. This cosmic power is found in all human bodies and lies dormant in the *muladhara chakra*. As a cosmic reality it has no form, but in the human body, as *yogis* have discerned, it has a coiled-up shape and can be made to rise upward by the use of certain techniques. Though all human beings possess this *shakti,* very few know that they have it, and even fewer know how to make use of it. Various rites and practices to awaken this force have been suggested by all the paths of *yoga* that are taught in Hindu philosophy. The Tantric method of awakening this dormant energy in us is called *kundalini yoga,* sometimes called *laya yoga. Kundalini yoga* is the culminating meditative experience.

When consciousness manifests as energy, it possesses the twin aspects of potential and kinetic energy. Kundalini Shakti represents a polarization of these two energies. The human body is the potential pole of the energy of the supreme. The latent energy of the goddess is stored in the *muladhara chakra*. It becomes dynamic only when it is stirred to action through different types of *yoga*. Then it moves upward from the *muladhara* in order to unite with the quiescent supreme consciousness in the *sahasrara*. These two are like the poles of a magnet.

Kundalini is primordial, cosmic power and cannot be trifled with. Attempts to rouse it without proper knowledge of the technique can cause great damage both mentally and physically. All Tantric *sadhana* aims at awakening Kundalini Shakti and making her unite with her lord, Sadashiva (Shiva).

The same amount of thought that Western scientists have given to probing the secrets of external nature have been given by the sages of India to discovering the secrets of our internal nature. The detection of this energy called *kundalini* is one of their most amazing discoveries. Using the laboratory of their minds they prized open the secrets of the universe and discovered that these secrets lay within themselves.

They underwent years of rigorous research and practiced intense self-denial and austerities before they discovered many amazing facts about *kundalini*. They described the details of the energy's path so minutely that we have to conclude that they describe their personal experience. Only after verifying these truths many times did they give the information to their disciples, who in turn confirmed it and thus made it into a purely scientific truth that could be verified in the minds and bodies of all human beings, provided they had the courage to set out on a voyage of this unchartered territory. Spiritual research needs more than physical courage. It needs the ability to control our animalistic tendencies of sex, gluttony, smoking, drinking, oversleeping, jealousy, cheating others, thinking ill of others, and doing harm to others. One needs to follow a strict code of ethical conduct for many years before venturing to practice these techniques.

Scientists have only a physical view of energy, and they think it to be a blind phenomenon without any mental characteristics. According to them all manifestation of energy takes place by accident. The seers, however, realized that physical energy is actually derived from pure consciousness or *chit,* an aspect of Shakti. *Prana,* or life force, is derived from *chit shakti.* All forms of physical energy and the very evolution of life are influenced by *prana.* It is only very recently that modern physicists have become aware of this energy. Max Planck, for one, talks about a force of the spirit that sets atomic particles in oscillation and concentrates them into minute solar systems.

Science is the result of the body-mind's perception of the phenomenal world. It gives us only one aspect of reality. It can never understand that other levels of reality exist outside of the perceptions of the five senses. Today, when the twenty-first-century human being is faced with horrifying Frankensteins of his own making, threatening to totally wipe out all his precious discoveries with, for example, the dropping of just one nuclear bomb, he is forced to pay heed to the words of wisdom uttered by India's sages more than five millenniums ago! Though our scientific discoveries have advanced in leaps and bounds, our spiritual

evolution seems to have become stagnant. We have learned to split everything including the atom, but we have not found a method for uniting
humanity into one civilized whole.

Modern thought, which is influenced by Western science, divides
life into spiritual and secular. This unnatural division gives a fragmented vision of life, and it is the main cause of our mental suffering and inability to find peace within. We are totally unaware of the
vast spiritual power that lies dormant in us. It is only by tapping this
source that the human being can evolve to his or her highest potential. Different fields of inquiry cannot be kept in watertight compart-
ments. At some point all of them have to merge, for life is a holistic
phenomenon. The ancient seers of India were well aware of this, and
they evolved an all-comprehensive vision of the ultimate unity of all
life in the universe.

The macrocosmos is inherent in the microcosmos. The human
being is a microcosm in which all the components of the macrocosm
are found in minute perfection. Whatever exists outside us exists in us.
All the *tattvas* (elements) that make up the macrocosm exist also in us.
The macrocosm is said to contain fourteen *lokas* or worlds, seven below
the earth and seven above; these are also found in the body of man.
Lokas are those astral regions in which the fruits of one's actions or
karmas can be experienced. The seven lower worlds have corresponding
locations in the legs of the human body. The seven upper worlds have
their corresponding locations within the seven *chakras* in the upper
body.

The *chakras* are lotus-shaped whorls of the spiritual energy of
Parashakti. Because they are centers of spiritual energy, they cannot be
seen by the physical eyes. They are situated in the astral body along the
nadi (tube of astral matter that carries psychic energy) known as the *sushumna,* which lies in the physical body within the spinal column. The first
six chakras can thus be found along the spinal column, with the seventh in
the brain. Starting from the base of the spine and moving upward, these
chakras are known as the *muladhara, swadhishtana, manipura, anahata,*

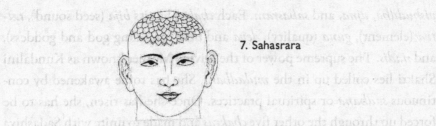

7. Sahasrara

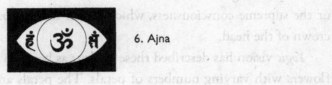

6. Ajna

5. Vishuddha

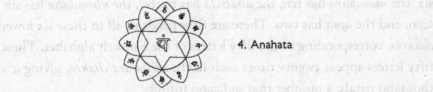

4. Anahata

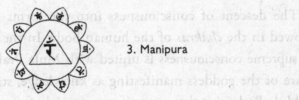

3. Manipura

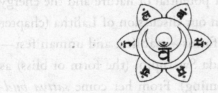

2. Swadhishtana

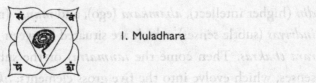

1. Muladhara

The seven chakras

vishuddha, ajna, and *sahasrara.* Each *chakra* has its *bija* (seed sound), *tattva* (element), *guna* (quality), *deva* and *devi* (presiding god and goddess), and *nadis.* The supreme power of the Divine Mother known as Kundalini Shakti lies coiled up in the *muladhara.* She has to be awakened by continuous *sadhana* or spiritual practices. Once she has risen, she has to be forced up through the other five *chakras* and made to unite with Sadashiva or the supreme consciousness, which lies in the *sahasrara chakra* at the crown of the head.

Yogic vision has described these *chakras* as being in the form of lotus flowers with varying numbers of petals. The petals are the *nadis;* each resonates to the sound of one letter of the Sanskrit alphabet, and each letter denotes one *mantra* of the Devi Kundalini. These sounds exist in the petals in latent form; they manifest and begin to vibrate only during intense meditation. The *muladhara* has four petals, the *swadhishtana* has six, the *manipura* has ten, the *anahata* has twelve, the *vishuddha* has sixteen, and the *ajna* has two. There are fifty petals in all in these six lower *chakras,* corresponding to the fifty letters of the Sanskrit alphabet. These fifty letters appear twenty times each in the *sahasrara chakra,* giving it a thousand petals, a number that indicates infinity.

The descent of consciousness into the forms of matter can be followed in the *chakras* of the human body. In the *sahasrara chakra,* the supreme consciousness is united with Mula Prakriti, which is the nature of the goddess manifesting as knowledge, strength, and activity. Mula Prakriti is the unmanifest potential of nature and the energy of the Divine Mother. As we saw in our discussion of Lalitha (chapter 7), she is capable of sustaining two forms—manifest and unmanifest—simultaneously. She is Satchidananda Swarupini (the form of bliss) as well as Bhavani (the form of becoming). From her come *sattva buddhi* (higher intellect), *ahamkara* (ego), and *manas* (mind) as well as the *indriyas* (subtle senses), which are situated between the *ajna* and *sahasrara chakras.* Then come the *tanmatras* or the subtle essences of the senses, which evolve into the five gross elements: *akasa* (etheric space), *vayu* (air), *agni* (fire), *apas* (water), and *prithvi* (earth).

All evolution proceeds from the subtle to the gross. Therefore what we call solid matter, including the body, actually emanates from the ethereal realm. Though the mind and the five elements pervade the entire body, there are certain centers where they are predominant. The *ajna chakra* is the center of the mind, and the five lower *chakras* are the centers of the five *tattvas* or elements. The human being is a microcosm in which the all-pervading spirit evolves into the form of mind and matter through the *tattvas*. Hence Tantrists insist that the first steps on this path should be *nadi shuddhi* and *tattva shuddhi*. They maintain that the final spiritual experience can be gained only after this purification. The path to perfection lies in retracing the way by which we have evolved—that is, from the gross elements to the subtle *tanmatras*, which in turn fold back into Parashakti, which is nothing but the Para Brahman.

As has been mentioned before, during the evolution of the cosmos, the universe unfolds and expands from the seed sound *hreem*. This vibrating mass of energy differentiates and expands in different wavelengths. By the fifth differentiation this energy evolves into the gross plane and creates the fifty articulate sounds or *varnas*. *Varna* means "color," and indeed, each sound has a corresponding hue. The universe of forms is created from the combinations and permutations of these fifty primeval sounds. Sound is potential form and form is manifest sound. In fact, experiments have found that predictable forms can be produced from sound: a specific note at a particular pitch from certain instruments can produce a specific geometrical pattern traced on a bed of sand. Underlying all the forms of the physical world are the oscillating wavelengths of the fifty primeval sounds in varying combinations. The alphabets of the Sanskrit language are directly derived from these primordial sounds.

The *chakras* are also the centers of *prana shakti* within us. *Prana* is the vital life force, a psychic energy. All life energy is manifested in the world through *prana*. Without it not even a leaf can move. Heat, light, electricity, and magnetism are all manifestations of *prana*.

Breath is the external expression of *prana*. By doing the *yogic* exercise called *pranayama* or control of the breath, one can influence the subtle *pranic* force. The mind cannot operate without *prana*. So control of the breath implies control of *prana,* which in turn leads to control of the mind. Within the human being, this *prana* assumes five different functions known as the *pancha pranas*, which control respiration, digestion, dreaming, evacuation, and blood circulation. These functions are linked to the different *chakras*. When we control the breath and direct it by the force of our will to different parts of the body, we can cure diseases and revitalize ourselves; this fact has been recognized in modern times and many people practice what is known as *pranic* healing. If we can control the *prana* within us, we can slowly learn the method of controlling the universal *prana*. This is how certain *yogis* perform miracles.

The physical body has certain plexuses that correspond to the location of the *chakras*. The *muladhara* corresponds to the sacrococcygeal plexus, the *swadhishtana* to the sacral plexus, the *manipura* to the solar plexus, the *anahata* to the cardiac plexus, the *visuddha* to the laryngeal plexus, and the *ajna* with the two lobes of the cerebellum. Above these lie the mind or *manas* in the middle cerebrum and finally the *sahasrara,* corresponding to the upper cerebrum, the function of which is still to be discovered by science.

The six lower *chakras* are thus vital centers of psychic energy that affect various essential physical functions within the body. They influence and govern the gross body outside the spinal column, which is coextensive with that section of the spinal column in which they are situated. The *muladhara* is the physical center controlling elimination. It is the subconscious center. The *swadhishtana* governs the generative organs; it is the sex center and controls the movements of greed and lust. The *manipura* governs the digestive organs. It is the center of the higher life forces and passions. The *anahata* is the seat of the cardiac and respiratory forces and controls the emotional center. The *visuddha* is the broadcasting system and is connected with the external mind.

The *ajna* is the control room of motor activity, the center of the will, inner mind, occult vision, and dynamic thought. The *sahasrara* is the master switchboard. It is the center of higher consciousness. It is the intuitive mind that can connect with the astral planes and the cosmic mind.

The body may be divided into two main portions. The head and trunk form the main part and the legs the other. The center of the body lies between these two, at the base of the spine. The spinal cord runs through the whole body and supports it; it can be seen as the axis of the body. The legs and feet are the grossest part of the body since they show less sign of consciousness. The head and trunk, together with the spinal column, which contains white and gray matter, are more highly developed. The body and legs below the center contain the seven lower or netherworlds or *lokas,* which are upheld by their respective *shaktis* or sustaining powers. From the spinal column upward, to the cerebral centers, consciousness manifests freely. The seven upper worlds or *lokas* are situated here.

The *nadis* are tubes of astral matter that carry psychic currents. They have no connection with nerves, arteries, or veins. (Again, though physical correlates are given to specify the whereabouts of *nadis* and *chakras,* it must be understood that they are situated not in the physical body but in the astral body. They are made of subtle forces that are not visible to gross perception.) The word *nad* means "motion" in Sanskrit. It is through these *nadis* that the *pranic* current or life force moves and flows and thus they have a vital role in *kundalini yoga.* All *nadis* spring from a place called the *kanda,* which is shaped like an egg and is located just above the *muladhara chakra.* The *kanda* is another great psychic center.

Out of the innumerable *nadis* in the body, the three that play a most important role are the *sushumna, ida,* and *pingala.* Of these the *sushumna* is chief. It extends from the *muladhara chakra* at the bottom of the spine to the *brahmarandra* orifice at the crown of the head. This *nadi* passes through the cylindrical cavity of the spinal column. Inside the *sushumna* is another *nadi* called the *vajra,* which is radiant like the sun and filled with *rajas.* Inside this is another called the *chitra,* which is pale like the moon and is *sattvic.* Within this lies the slender *nadi* called the Brahma *nadi;* when *kundalini* is awakened, its passage upward lies through the Brahma *nadi.*

The *ida nadi* lies on the left side of the *sushumna,* and the *pingala* on the right side. The *ida* starts from the right testicle and *pingala* from the left. They meet the *sushumna nadi* for the first time at the *muladhara chakra* and make a knot there. This is known as the Brahma *granthi* or the knot of Brahma. The three meet again at the *anahata* or heart *chakra;* the knot they form there is called the Vishnu *granthi,* or knot of Vishnu. They meet for the third and last time at the *ajna chakra,* where they make a knot known as Rudra *granthi* or knot of Rudra (Shiva). The Lalitha Sahasranama says that the goddess Lalitha herself is the one who cuts all three knots (the Brahma, Vishnu, and Rudra *granthis*); it is only after cutting these three knots that one can have access to Sadashiva, who resides in the *sahasrara chakra.* The *ida nadi* exits the body through the left nostril and *pingala* through the right. The *ida* is also known as the *chandra nadi* or the *nadi* of the moon and has a cooling effect on the body. The *pingala* is also known as the *surya nadi* or the *nadi* of the sun and is heating. The *ida* controls the nourishment of the body and the *pingala* the digestion of food. When the *nadis* are clogged with impurities, one cannot meditate and the body becomes unhealthy. One has to practice *pranayama* in order to purify them.

Muladhara means "root center." Four important *nadis* emanate from the *muladhara chakra,* giving it a four-petaled lotus shape. The petals are crimson in color. The Sanskrit letters corresponding to these four *nadis* are *vam, sham, shham,* and *sam.* This *chakra* is located at the base of the spinal column, between the reproductive organs and the anus. It is just below the *kanda,* the egg-shaped junction from which all *nadis* arise. The *tattva* or element of this *chakra* is *prithvi* or earth; it is found in the center of the lotus in a square *mandala* that is yellow in color. It resonates to the *mantra lam,* which is the *bija mantra* or seed sound of the earth element. This *chakra* corresponds with the Bhur *loka* or the earthly plane; the seven netherworlds lie below this *chakra*. The *swayambhuva linga* of Shiva is also to be seen in this *chakra*: Devi Kundalini lies facing downward at the mouth of the *sushumna nadi* with her face on the head of this *linga*. She is curled up into three and a half coils like a snake. The three full coils represent the three *gunas* of Prakriti—*sattva, rajas,* and *tamas*—while the half coil represents the *vikritis* or modifications of Prakriti. Ganesha is the presiding deity of this *chakra* and Dakini the goddess. The animal connected with this *chakra* is the elephant. The Brahma *granthi* or the knot of Brahma, where the *ida, pingala,* and *sushumna nadis* meet for the first time, is in this *chakra*. The *yogi* who concentrates on this *chakra* gets full knowledge of *kundalini* and the method of awakening it. Levitation or control over the gravity of the earth is one of the *siddhis* that can be obtained by concentration on this *chakra*.

The *swadhishtana chakra* is located on the *sushumna nadi* at the root of the reproductive organs. *Swadhishtana* means "one's own place." It corresponds to the Bhuvar *loka*. This *chakra* controls the lower abdomen, kidneys, uterus, and reproductive organs in the gross body. Six *nadis* emanate from this *chakra,* giving it the appearance of a six-petaled lotus. The color of the petals is vermilion. The vibrations of these *nadis* correspond to the letters *bam, bham, mam, yam, ram,* and *lam*. The *tattva* associated with this is *apas* or water, which is found in a space shaped like the crescent moon that is pure white in color. The seed sound of this *chakra* is *vam,* which is the *bija mantra* of Varuna, the god of waters. The presiding deity is Brahma and the goddess is Rakini (a form of Saraswati). The animal connected with this *chakra* is the crocodile. He who concentrates on this *chakra* will lose all fear of water and will even be able to walk on water.

The *manipura chakra* is located in the region of the navel corresponding to the solar plexus. *Manipura* means "full of rays." This *chakra* controls the liver, stomach, and spleen. Ten *nadis* emanate from this *chakra,* giving it the appearance of a ten-petaled lotus. The petals are dark purple in color.

The vibrations produced by these *nadis* correspond to the Sanskrit letters *dam, dham, nnam, tam, tham, ddam, ddham, nam, pam,* and *pham.* Its corresponding element is *agni* (fire), which is located in a deep red triangle with its apex pointing downward in the center of the *chakra.* Its *bija mantra* is *ram,* which is the seed sound of Agni, the god of fire. This *chakra* corresponds with the Swar *loka* or the heavenly region. The presiding deity is Vishnu and the goddess is Lakini (Lakshmi). The animal connected with this *chakra* is the ram. The *yogi* who concentrates on this *chakra* will have no fear of fire and will remain unscathed even if thrown into a blazing conflagration.

Next comes the *anahata chakra,* situated in the region of the heart corresponding to the cardiac plexus. *Anahata* means "soundless sound." Twelve *nadis* emanate from this *chakra,* giving it the appearance of a twelve-petaled lotus. The petals have a deep maroon color. The vibrations produced by these *nadis* correspond to the Sanskrit letters *kam, kham, gam, gham, gnyam, cham, chham, jam, jham, jnyam, tam,* and *ttam.* In the *chakra's* center is a hexagonal shape with a dark smoky aura; here resides the *vayu tattva* or the element of air. The *chakra* has the *bija mantra* of *vayu,* which is *yam.* It corresponds to the Mahar *loka.* The presiding deity is Isha (Rudra) and the goddess is Kakini (one of the forms of Kaali). The animal connected to this *chakra* is the antelope. The *nada* or sound of Sabda Brahman is heard from this *chakra.* In fact, the *yogi* in deep meditation can hear many astral sounds emanating from this *chakra.* This is the second place where the *ida* and *pingala nadis* meet the *sushumna* and form a knot; this knot is known as the Vishnu *granthi* or the knot of Vishnu. This *chakra* is full of *sattva* and one who meditates on it will find her heart overflowing with love for the whole of creation. She will also have control over the element of air and will be able to fly.

The *visuddha chakra* is located at the base of the throat, corresponding to the laryngeal plexus. *Visuddha* means "purity." The sixteen *nadis* that emanate from this *chakra* are smoky purple in color and give it the shape of a sixteen-petaled lotus. The vibrations they produce correspond to the leteres *am, aam, im, eem, um, oom, rim, reem, lum, loom, em, aem, om, aoum, um,* and *ah.* The related *tattva* is *akasa* or ether; it resides in the center of the *chakra* in a circle that is pure blue in color. The seed sound of this element is *ham.* This *chakra* corresponds to the Jana *loka.* The presiding deity is Sadashiva and the goddess is Shakini (a form of Durga). One who concentrates on this *chakra* will obtain knowledge of the past, present, and future.

The *ajna chakra* is situated in the space between the two eyebrows, known as the cavernous plexus in the physical body. *Ajna* means "command/order of a holy person." This *chakra* corresponds to the Tapo *loka.* The seed *mantra* here is ॐ *(aum)*, which is found in a pure white circle that is the seat of the mind. The *chakra* has two *nadis,* one on either side, that are pure white in color and give it the appearance of a two-petaled lotus. They vibrate to the sound of the letters *ham* and *ksham.* The element here is *avyakta,* the primordial cloud of undifferentiated energy and matter from which the five elements emanate. The presiding deity is Paramashiva in the form of a swan; the presiding goddess is Hakini (one of the forms of the Maha Devi). The *ida* and *pingala nadis* meet the *sushumna* for the final time at this junction and form a knot known as the Rudra *granthi* or the knot of Rudra. One who concentrates on this *chakra* will be able to destroy all the *karmas* of previous lives. She becomes fully liberated—a *jivan mukta.* She can acquire all the major *siddhis* or supernormal powers. *Yogis* consciously fix their *prana* here at the time of death.

Above these six lotuses we have the seventh, which is known as the *sahasrara* ("thousand-petaled"). All the other *chakras* are intimately connected with the *sahasrara chakra.* Situated at the crown of the head, it corresponds to the pineal gland in the physical body. One thousand *nadis* emanate from this *chakra,* giving it the look of a thousand-petaled lotus. Each of the fifty letters of the Sanskrit alphabet is repeated twenty times in these petals. This *chakra* corresponds to the Satya *loka.* It is the abode of Lord Shiva in his aspect as the Para Brahman or supreme consciousness. When Kundalini Shakti is united with Sadashiva in this *chakra,* the *yogi* enjoys supreme bliss and goes into a state of superconsciousness called *samadhi.*

The *brahmarandra* ("hole of Brahman") is an orifice at the crown of the head. The physical counterpart is the fontanel, which is very soft in an infant but hardens with age. The *jivatman* or the embodied soul enters the body through this opening at the time of birth. When a *yogi* departs from the physical body, he or she bursts open the *brahmaran- dra* and departs the way he or she came. *Prana* escapes through this opening, and thus the *yogi* attains immortality. The *prana* of ordinary individuals exits the body through one of its other orifices.

Thus Devi Kundalini is pure consciousness itself. She is Prana Shakti as well as Parashakti—the life force and the supreme force. It is through her that the world of matter exists. She is the subtlest form of energy. Creation, preservation, and dissolution are all found in her. She maintains both the individual body as well as the cosmos through her subtle *prana.* She is the dynamic working power of the universe.

The equilibrium of the universe is maintained by a polarity of positive and negative, of static and dynamic. In *kundalini yoga,* it is said that the static ground force or Shiva resides in the seventh *chakra,* known as the *sahasrara.* The dynamic feminine power or Shakti lies in the *muladhara* at the base of the spine. This manifestation of cos- mic power in the body, known as *kundalini,* is in a dormant, poten- tial state. In *kundalini yoga,* this divine power that lies asleep in every human being is aroused and pulled upward through the six *chakras* until it reaches the *sahasrara chakra,* which is the seat of Sadashiva, the supreme consciousness. This is the height of the meditative experience.

The static power of *kundalini* can be vitalized by *pranayama* and other *yogic* processes and made dynamic. When the energy is com- pletely vibrant, Kundalini Shakti rises and passes through the various *chakras* and finally unites with Shiva in the *sahasrara,* and the two poles become one. The *yogi* attains the state of consciousness known as *samadhi.* In this state, even though the body continues to exist, one appears inert, since the individual consciousness is no longer fixed on the body and the objective world but has been united with the supreme consciousness. *Yogis* have been known to stay in this state of suspended animation for many years. The question may be asked as to how such a body manages to sustain itself. The answer is that when this union takes place, there is a continuous dripping of nectar from the *brahma-randra* that sustains the whole organism for an incalculable period of time. When Devi Kundalini sleeps, the human being is awake to the world and clamors and frets for the objects of the world. When the goddess is awake, the individual no longer hankers for the world of the senses and is awake only to the supreme reality. He or she is asleep to the world of duality and enters into the state of unity. The so-called happiness of the world turns into an ecstasy beyond words. As the Bhagavad Gita says, "That which is night to the *yogi* is day to the ordinary man and what is day to him is night to the *yogi*."

In worldly-minded people given to purely physical pleasures and sexual enjoyments, this *kundalini* power is never awakened. It lies dormant throughout their lives. The power has to be stimulated through some form of spiritual practice and not through the acquisition of wealth or any other form of material control. When an aspirant seriously practices all the disciplines as given in the *shastras* (scriptures), under the guidance of a qualified *guru*, the layers of ignorance veiling *kundalini* begin to be cleared and are finally torn asunder and the energy is pushed upward through the *chakras*.

Even when it is awakened, *kundalini* does not proceed directly to the *sahasrara* except in the case of an exceptionally pure *yogi*. It must be moved forcibly from one *chakra* to another, which requires a great deal of concentration and patience. The energy may drop back at any time and have to be forced up again with great effort. When it reaches the *sahasrara* union takes place, but again the energy may not remain long in that state and can slip back. It's only after long and continuous practice that the adept experiences permanent union and final liberation. The speed with which *kundalini* is aroused depends entirely on the aspirant's longing for liberation, purification of the *nadis,* dispassion, and stage of evolution. In a course of time, the Divine Mother herself awakens the power and gives the *sadhaka* the knowledge as and when he or she is ready for it. Until the *sadhaka* is able to absorb this knowledge fully, nothing of importance will be revealed to him or her.

There are many methods for locating the *chakras*. They can be located both from the front and from the back. To locate them from the back, one's concentration has to move along the spinal cord from *chakra* to *chakra*. To locate them from the front, one's concentration has to move from the base of the spine to the navel, the heart, the throat, and so on. One's consciousness must be kept always alert so that it is receptive to the inner vibrations that denote an energy center. The *chakras* may also be focused upon by chanting *aum*. At the *muladhara, aum* must be chanted at the lowest pitch. As one moves up, the pitch has to be raised by one degree for every *chakra*. The *aum* sound gradually becomes imperceptible. Another method for locating the *chakras* uses the Indian musical scale. There is a strange relationship between the seven notes of the scale and the seven major *chakras*. *Sa* corresponds to the *muladhara, re* to the *swadhishtana, ga* to the *manipura, ma* to the *anahata, pa* to the *visuddha, da* to the *ajna,* and *ni* to the *sahasrara*.

The petals of the lotuses in these *chakras* are initially closed and drooping, but as Devi Kundalini pierces their centers, the blossoms lift their heads and bloom in all their glory, emanating a divine light and fragrance and revealing their esoteric secrets. The more *kundalini* advances, the more the *yogi* advances on the spiritual path. When *kundalini* reaches the *ajna chakra* the *yogi* gets a vision of his personal god. When it reaches the *sahasrara,* he loses his individuality in the ocean of *sat, chit,* and *ananda;* Shiva and Shakti become united and the *yogi* becomes a fully illumined sage or *jivan mukta*. Even the ignorant individual knows that he wants happiness. To get this he uses whatever means come to his command. Unfortunately, he does not realize that the happiness of the world is a pale reflection of the bliss that lies within him and that he could taste, if only he knew the method of finding it. *Kundalini yoga* is one such method.

As is the case for all other Tantric practices, the technique of awakening *kundalini* can be learned only after attaining ethical perfection. Otherwise it will lead to spiritual and physical downfall. Before starting this *yoga* one has to follow a strict discipline and cultivate the following qualities: nonviolence, celibacy, perseverance, patience, acceptance, sparse eating habits, humility, honesty, and selfless service to others. One must become detached from the lure of worldly pleasures and free from desire, anger, greed, and jealousy. The aspirant must have *deha shuddhi* (purified body), *nadi shuddhi* (purified *nadis*), *mana shuddhi* (purified mind), and *buddhi shuddhi* (purified intellect).

The necessity of a spiritual guide on this path cannot be overemphasized. As is the case for all Tantric practices, the pitfalls of *kundalini yoga* are many, and one has to be guided by a proper *guru*. *Kundalini* can be roused by different methods advocated in different *yogas*. *Hatha yogis* use *pranayama, asanas,* and *mudras. Bhakti yoga* advocates devotion and perfect surrender to one's personal deity. *Raja yoga* stresses concentration, meditation, and control of the mind. *Jnana yoga* supports the exercise of the analytical will, and Tantra advocates *tattva shuddhi* and the use of *mantras* and *yantras* in rituals. All these types of *yoga* have but one purpose, and that is the attainment of unity with the supreme consciousness. Every type of *yoga* is an attempt at the self-transformation of the base metal of the individual consciousness into the pure gold of supreme consciousness. The specific type of *sadhana* that one uses will depend on one's nature. Any one of these paths may be used with great success by a selected few. But for most people, a combination of methods might be most effective. Many of the ordinary paths of *yoga* can be followed safely by even an ignorant practioner, but *kundalini yoga* is an occult science. It can lead one to the heights in the shortest possible time, but it can also precipitate us to the lowest depths of darkness of the mind. It is a path filled with pitfalls, and for this reason a *guru* is essential.

The Yoga-Kundalini Upanishad is the eighty-sixth among the one hundred and eight important Upanishads. It is a most important work on *kundalini yoga*. It prescribes methods by which *prana* can be controlled and *kundalini* aroused and taken to its consummation in the *sahasrara chakra*. *Pranayama* and other *yogic* processes by which the state of *samadhi* can be attained are described in detail.

When *kundalini* travels from *chakra* to *chakra*, layer after layer of the mind becomes opened and the *yogi* acquires psychic powers known as *siddhis*. Many misguided people take to the practice only for the sake of attaining these powers. They use these powers to gain fame and wealth, and this eventually leads to their downfall. These powers are meant to be used for the benefit of the world and for furthering spiritual evolution, not for selfish ends.

As mentioned before, when *kundalini* sleeps the human being is awake to the joys of the world. When it awakes, the human being also awakes to the light within. Some of the signs of awakened *kundalini* are that the body becomes light as air. You begin to possess an inexhaustible energy and become divinely intoxicated. During meditation you will behold divine visions, tastes, smells, and sounds. But these are only the side effects. If you become deflected from the true purpose of the *yoga* and run after these tantalizing things that Devi Kundalini dangles before the unwary, you will never attain the goal. This is the time to be assiduous in the practice and never let up until you have achieved the final goal of unity with the supreme consciousness. In this state the *yogi* experiences cosmic love, peace, fearlessness, and harmony. When Devi Kundalini unites with Sadashiva, nectar starts to flow from the *brahmarandra* to the *muladhara chakra*, flooding both the astral and the physical body, satisfying the presiding gods and goddesses of the various *chakras* and thus filling the *yogi* with *paramananda* or supreme bliss.

What we have to understand from the study of the various Puranas and other scriptures is that a deep philosophy underlies all the traditional Hindu methods of worship and the various Puranic allegories. The path of spiritual *sadhana* is shrouded in a mystery that is not apparent even to the *sadhaka*. We may imagine that we are the ones who have started this *yoga* and who have been successful in it, but the fact is that even the heroism and strength that we put into it are the force of the Divine Mother working within us. A child may shake off his mother's restraining hand and run forward, secure in the knowledge that she is right there behind him. Similar is the case with us. Whatever intelligence we may possess and whatever extraordinary gifts and powers we might have are but a pale reflection of her mighty powers. She walks beside us and steers our course from within. Everything that is worthwhile in our existence we owe to her alone. Her watchful vigilance never falters even for a second. Those who have perfect faith in her can walk blindfolded on the path of life, for we can be sure that she is guiding our footsteps every inch of the way.

If we allow the cosmic mother to fill us with her love and beauty, our problems will vanish. As the child feels secure when holding the hand of his mother, so the devotee has no cares, for she knows that her beloved mother is always beside her. Every human being regardless of gender should try to develop motherly qualities. Only then will we be able to love the whole universe and all the people in it. We must not limit our maternal love to our children alone but must learn to look on everyone as our child. This is the only way in which humankind can attain peace. Most of us have experienced the glory of the unqualified love that a human mother can give. This is only a ray of the flooding sunshine of love that the Divine Mother can give us.

The wine that Chandika quaffs before her battle with Mahishasura is a divine nectar that she will give to all her devotees. May all taste of this divine beverage and attain the perfection that every human being is capable of. Chandika promises, "I will be present wherever my glories are sung and wherever I am worshipped with true devotion. My power destroys ill health and bestows prosperity. It protects and restores peace. By the mere remembrance of my name, one crosses over all troubles and sorrows. My devotees will always be protected from all types of fears."

> *I am the queen of the universe, the giver of all*
>   *wealth and fruits of works.*
> *I am intelligence and omniscience.*
> *Although I am one, through my powers I appear*
>   *manifold.*
> *I cause war for protection; I kill the enemy and*
>   *bring peace on earth.*
> *I stretch out heaven and earth.*
> *I have produced the father.*
> *As the wind blows by itself, so I produce all*
>   *phenomena by my own will.*
> *I am independent and responsible to none.*
> *I am beyond the sky, beyond this earth.*
> *My glory is the phenomenal universe;*
> *Such am I by my own powers.*

—Rig Veda 10, hymn 125

Thus ends the thirty-first chapter of *Shakti,* known as "Devi Kundalini," which describes the goddess Kundalini and the practice of *kundalini yoga.*

Aum Aim Hreem Kleem

APPENDIX ONE

Poems on
the Divine Mother
Verses Composed by Vanamali

Down the corridors of Time I fled,
With you in hot pursuit.
Along the sands of Space I ran,
With your breath hot on my back.
The whys and wherefores of Causality,
Held me in endless thrall.
Catch me as I fall
O Mother!
Catch me as I fall!

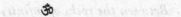

Give me a thousand tongues to describe thy glory,
Give me a million eyes to drink in thy beauty.
O thou Indescribable!
I have attempted the impossible,
Lakshmi! Enchantress,
Intoxicated am I by thy beauty,
Enchanted by thy glory,

Blinded by the compassion of thy loving glance,
Overwhelmed by the depth of thy infinite grace,
Bemused by thy moods, thy forms of play,
O Lakshmi, enchantress!
What can I offer thee,
Who has given me my all,
This alone I have to call my own,
And this I surrender with untold love,
My prostrations,
O Mother!
From now till infinity

Let me be a bird and build a nest in your heart.
Let me be a flower to be trampled by your feet.
Let me be the dewdrop glistening in your locks.
Let me be the moonbeam caught in your eyes.
Let me! O let me! O mother mine!
Let me be thine!
Let me be thine!

Why play hide and seek with me?
I care not for the game.
Between the rocks of infinity
You have eluded me,
Tossing me like a ball,
Between the rows of insanity.
Beguile me not with your beauty,
Disgust me not with your crudity,
I care not for this game.
Lift thy veil and let me glimpse
Thy sweet face of eternity

Far have I wandered,
Past heaven and hell,
Crossing the threshold of infinite time,
Arriving on planet Earth at last.
But where are you?
Why have you deserted me
In this barren waste of beguiling charms?
Charm me not, O charming one,
I care not for your sweets.
Reveal thyself, reveal thyself!
I want nothing else.

Caught am I in the strands of your hair,
Bewildered by thy ugliness,
Terrified by thy harshness.
Why the slap when all I asked for was a touch?
Wherefore the storm and the wreckage?
Wherefore the war and the carnage?
What lesson do you teach, O terrifier?
Is there no reprieve?
Call you this a game?
More terrifying than reality,
Release me, O Mother,
Release me from this game.

O Maya, Maha Maya,
Thou hast me in thrall,
Bound am I by thy beauty!
Caught by thy charm,

Thou hast me in thrall,
My sweet delight,
Enchantress of the three worlds,
Catch me if I fall.

Vishnu Maya! Maha Maya! Maha! Maha! Maha
    Shakti!
Greater than the greatest,
Beguiler of the gods,
Do you now seek to beguile me?
I'm already caught in your golden net,
Flapping like a helpless fish.
Show your strength and cut the strands,
Release me from these strangling bonds.

Why have you deserted me, O Mother?
Will a mother abandon her babe in the woods?
Will a mother kill her foolish child?
If not, then why have you forsaken me?
I stumble in a jungle called life,
I drown in a lake called tears.
Alone and helpless, an orphan am I,
Desolate on the sands of time,
Clinging to the creeper called death
Which in turn is upheld by thee!

Take me to the moon, the fair moon of thy face.
Take me to the sun, less brilliant than thy form.
Waft me to the stars, which swing from your hair.
O Sundari! Tripurasundari!

Reveal thyself!
Give the gift of divine sight,
Disclose to me thy exquisite face!

Why call me
If you didn't want me?
Why woo me
If you didn't love me?
But having wooed and having won,
Why thrust me to the darkness,
Groping like a blinded worm,
For something it knows not what,
Crying for one speck of light,
For one star, for one ray,
In the blinding darkness of a lonely night?

Have I not longed for you through many lives?
Have I not cried for you through countless births?
Where have I failed?
What have I left undone
That you should ignore me like this?
O Mother! Cut asunder the knots of my
ignorance,
Enfold me in your soothing arms.
Let me inhale thy sweet perfume,
Let me nestle in your soft bosom.

Bereft am I—desolate,
Cast on the lonely beach of life,
Prey of every passing wave,

Lashed by the relentless tide.
Will you not grasp my outstretched hand,
Rescue me from this friendless land?

Sing to me of eternity, O Mother!
Sing to me of glory!
Tell me those gentle tales
Of devotees you have helped.
Let me hear the music of the spheres,
Of astral worlds where live those fortunate ones
Who are beloved to thee,
That I may hear and perchance,
Learn to beguile thee!

Forgive this foolish one, O Mother!
Countless are my mistakes,
Courage have I none, yet
Dared have I to disclose the sweetness of thy tales.
Thy grace alone guided me, controlled me.
Can you forgive yourself?
For this poor scribe was but an instrument,
A note in the lute of fair Saraswati!

Divine Mother, I place these poems as a garland of wildflowers at your
lotus feet along with this book, which you alone have written. May
your blessings fall on all those who read it. May they be released from
this forest of *samsara* and attain thy supreme state.

Aum Aim Hreem Kleem

Hindu Scriptures

Agama Shastras	Scriptures for the formal worship of Vishnu, Shiva, and Shakti
Agni Purana	Scripture that extols Agni, the god of fire
Atharva Veda	One of the four Vedas
Bhagavad Gita	Holy song; advice of Lord Krishna given to Arjuna on the battlefield
Bhagavad Purana	Purana that extols Krishna as the supreme incarnation of Vishnu
Brahmanda Purana	Purana in which is found the Lalitha Sahasranama
Brahma Vaivarta Purana	One of the Maha Puranas
Brighu Samhita	Scripture designated to the sage Brighu; gives the astrological details of all the future generations
Chandi	Popular name of the Devi Mahatmyam
Devi Bhagavatam	Maha Purana that describes all stories of Shakti; most famous Shakta literature
Devi Gita	Advice given by the goddess to Himavan in the Devi Bhagavatam

Devi Mahatmyam	Scripture that glorifies Durga and her killing of the various demons; most powerful of the Shakta literatures
Devi Purana	Another name for the Devi Bhagavatam
Devi Suktam	Rig Vedic hymn to the goddess
Durga Saptashati	Another name for the Devi Mahatmyam
Harivamsa	Purana glorifying Vishnu
Isavasya Upanishad	Most famous of the Upanishads
Kumarasambhava	Poem by Kalidasa on the advent of Kartikeya, son of Shiva
Lalitha Sahasranama	Thousand and one names of the goddess as Lalitha
Lalithopakhyana	Portion of the Brahmanda Purana that deals with the story of Lalitha
Mahabharata	The epic story of the Kuru dynasty by Vyasa
Mahanirvana Tantra	One of the Tantric scriptures
Maha Puranas	The great Puranas, eighteen in number, attributed to the sage Vyasa
Markandeya Purana	Purana in which the Devi Mahatmyam or Chandi is mentioned
Matsya Purana	One of the eighteen Maha Puranas
Narada Purana	One of the eighteen Maha Puranas
Pancharatra	Agama dealing with the worship of Vishnu and his incarnations
Ramayana	Epic poem by the sage Valmiki on the life of the *avatara* Rama
Rig Veda	The oldest of the four Vedas

Sama Veda	Rig Veda chanted musically
Savitri Upanishad	Upanishad in which the practice of the Gayatri *mantra* is given
Skanda Purana	Purana that deals with the exploits of Skanda or Kartikeya
Sri Suktam	Rig Vedic hymn to Lakshmi
Tripura Rahasya	Poem that extols Lalitha
Upanishads	End portion of all the Vedas; deals with highly spiritual and philosophical matters
Upa Puranas	Subsidiary Puranas, eighteen in number
Vajasaneyi Samhita	Part of the Rig Veda
Vamana Purana	Purana eulogizing the *avatara* of Vishnu as the dwarf
Vayu Purana	Purana pertaining to the wind god
Vedas	Most ancient sacred revelations known to humanity; four in number: Rig, Sama, Yajur, and Atharva
Vishnu Purana	Maha Purana extolling Vishnu
Yajur Veda	One of the four Vedas
Yoga-Kundalini Upanishad	Upanishad dealing with the nature and practice of *kundalini yoga*

Names of Goddesses

Adi	"First"; name of the goddess
Adi Shakti	First emanation of the goddess
Aditi	Mother of the gods
Adya	Primordial earth goddess
Aindri	Female counterpart of Indra
Ambika	Female counterpart of Shiva; source of his power
Anandarupini	One whose form is bliss
Annapurna	Giver of food
Aparajita	The invincible
Aparna	Another name for Parvati; one who subsists on leaves
Arya	Another form of Adya; Sita's name in a previous birth
Ashtadevis	Goddesses who were guardians of the eight directions
Ashta Lakshmis	The eight Lakshmis; givers of all types of felicities to human beings

Atiguptarahasya	Secret police of Lalitha's army
Bagala	One of the Mahavidyas; has the head of a crane
Bala	Lalitha's daughter
Bhagavati	One who has all the six qualities or *bhagas*: omnipotence, ability, excellence, beauty, omniscience, and nonattachment; feminine of Bhagavan
Bhagirathi	Name of Ganga because she was brought to the earth by Bhagiratha
Bhagya Lakshmi	One of the Ashta Lakshmis; giver of fortune
Bhairavi	Feminine of Bhairava; one who brandishes a bloody sword
Bharata Mata	Mother India
Bharati	Another name for Saraswati
Bhavani	Parvati; becoming; feminine of *bhava* or being
Bhudevi	The earth goddess
Bhuvaneswari	Ruler of the earth
Brahmaani	Feminine counterpart of Brahma
Brahma Shakti	The power of Brahma; Saraswati
Chamunda	One of the names of Kaali; slayer of the two demons Chanda and Munda
Chandi	Short for Chandika; epithet of Durga
Chandika	Durga
Chinnamasta	One of the Mahavidyas; she holds her own decapitated head in her hand
Cybele	Goddess of ancient Phrygia
Dakini	Presiding goddess of the *muladhara chakra*

Dakshayini	Sati; daughter of Daksha
Dandanatha; Dandanayika	General of Lalitha's army
Demeter	Goddess of ancient Greece
Devi	"Goddess"; filled with light
Dhana Lakshmi	One of the Ashta Lakshmis; giver of wealth
Dhanya Lakshmi	One of the Ashta Lakshmis; giver of grain
Dhumavati	One of the Mahavidyas
Durga	Virgin warrior goddess; born out of the various powers of the male gods
Gaja Lakshmi	One of the Ashta Lakshmis; one who is seated on an elephant
Ganga	Goddess of the holy river Ganga
Gauri	Another name for Parvati; the golden-colored one
Gayatri	Goddess of the Vedic hymn to the sun (the Gayatri *mantra*)
Hakini	Presiding goddess of the *ajna chakra*
Hariti	Buddhist goddess
Indrani	Wife of Indra
Ishtar	Goddess of ancient Assyria
Isis	Goddess of ancient Egypt
Iswari	The goddess as ruler of the universe; feminine of Iswara
Jaganmata	Mother of the world
Jahnavi	Name of Ganga; daughter of the sage Jahnu

Jwalamalini	One of Lalitha's *shaktis* who makes a garland of fire to protect Lalitha's army
Kaali	Goddess in the form of all-devouring time
Kakini	Presiding goddess of the *anahata chakra*
Kalaratri	Another name for Durga; the great night of destruction
Kalika	Another name for Kaali
Kamakelitarangita	Another name for Lalitha; one who overflows with love and desire
Kamakshi	Another name for Lalitha; one with love-filled eyes
Kamala	Lakshmi; one of the Mahavidyas
Kameswari	Another name for Lalitha; giver of desires
Kartyayini	Virgin goddess to whom the *gopis* prayed
Kaumari	Feminine counterpart of Kartikeya
Kaushiki	Form of Parvati that came out of her bodily sheath or *kosha*
Kumari	Daughter of Lalitha; name for a young virgin or a goddess
Kundalini	The goddess as the embodiment of *kundalini*
Kundalini Shakti	Another name for the goddess Kundalini
Lakshmi	Goddess of auspiciousness and wealth
Lalitha; Lalithambika	Most benign and beautiful form of Maha Devi; born to destroy the demon Bhanda
Lolakshikamarupini	Another name for Lalitha; one with tremulous eyes
Madhavi	The earth goddess; another name for Lakshmi

Maha Devi	The Divine Mother; all other goddesses are her *shaktis* or powers
Maha Kaali	The great Kaali
Maha Lakshmi	The great Lakshmi, who is independent, not attached to Narayana
Maha Maya	The great delusion
Maha Medha	The supreme intellect
Mahamoha	The great deluder
Maha Nidra	The great sleep
Maha Prakriti	The great Prakriti or root cause of creation
Maharatri	The great darkness
Maha Saraswati	Saraswati as an independent principle
Mahasuri	The great demoness; appellation of the goddess who contains both good and bad
Maheswari	Feminine counterpart of Maheswara or Shiva
Mahishasuramardini	Name of Durga when she slew the demon Mahisha
Mantranayika; Mantrini	General of Lalitha's army
Matangi	One of the ten Mahavidyas
Maya	The delusory aspect of Maha Devi
Medini	Name of the earth goddess
Moharatri	The great night of delusion
Mohini	Incarnation of Vishnu as a female of great beauty in order to dupe the demons who had stolen nectar

Mula Prakriti	The transcendental feminine force that lies submerged in the Brahman
Narayani	One of the names of Durga
Navadurga	The nine aspects of Durga
Nrisimhi	Feminine counterpart of Narasimha, the man-lion incarnation of Vishnu
Padma	Lakshmi; lotus
Padmavati	Lakshmi; born from the lotus
Para Brahma Swarupini	The goddess who is no different from the Para Brahman or transcendental absolute
Parameswari	The supreme feminine power
Parashakti	The supreme feminine force
Parvati	Wife of Shiva; daughter of Himavan
Prakriti	The original force that emanates from the transcendental Mula Prakriti and produces this universe of forms
Radha	Beloved of Krishna; Prakriti incarnate
Rajarajeshwari	Queen of queens
Rakini	Presiding goddess of the *swadishtana chakra*
Ramya	Another name for Lalitha; the pleasing or beautiful queen
Rati	Wife of Kama, the god of love
Raudri	Feminine counterpart of Rudra or Shiva as destroyer
Rukmani	Princess of Vidharba; wife of Krishna
Sampatkari	General in Lalitha's army
Sandhya	Goddess of dawn and twilight

Santana Lakshmi	One of the Ashta Lakshmis; giver of progeny
Saraswati	Goddess of arts and sciences; wife of Brahma
Sarvavidya Swarupini	Saraswati; the embodiment of all wisdom
Satakshi	Another name for Maha Devi; one with a hundred eyes
Satchidananda Swarupini	The inherent form of the Brahman; existence, consciousness, and bliss
Sati	Wife of Shiva; daughter of Daksha
Savitri	Goddess of the sun; wife of Satyavan; famed for the power of her chastity
Shakambari	Another name for Maha Devi; one who carries a sheaf of corn
Shakini	Presiding goddess of the vishudha chakra
Shakti	Force; energy; power of the Maha Devi
Shankari	Feminine counterpart of Shankara (Shiva)
Shiva Shakti	The female energy of Shiva
Shivaduti	Fierce incarnation of Durga; one who made Shiva her ambassador
Shivani	Beloved of Shiva
Shodasi	One of the Mahavidyas; young girl of sixteen
Sita	Wife of Rama; princess of Videha
Smashan Tara	One of the Mahavidyas; found in burning *ghats*
Sri	Another name for Lakshmi

Sringararasapurna	Another name for Lalitha; one who is filled with the intoxication of beauty
Tamasi	Delusion; one of the names of Maha Devi
Tantrini	One of the chief attendants of Lalitha
Tara	Tibetan goddess; gentle in nature
Tirasankaranika	One of the *shaktis* of Lalitha who caused the opposing army to become blind
Tripurasundari	Most beautiful in all the three worlds
Tulasi	Wife of the demon Shankachuda
Uma	Another name for Parvati; "don't go"
Ushas	Vedic goddess of the dawn
Vaarahi	Female energy of Varaha, Vishnu's incarnation as a boar
Vac	Saraswati; the personification of the spoken word
Vagadeeswarees	Warrior goddesses of Lalitha's army
Vaishnavi	Feminine energy of Vishnu
Vamakesi	Another name for Lalitha; one with beautiful hair
Vamanayana	Another name for Lalitha; one with beautiful eyes
Vani	Saraswati; "sound"
Vara Lakshmi	One of the Ashta Lakshmis; giver of boons
Vidya Lakshmi	One of the Ashta Lakshmis; giver of knowledge
Vindhya Vaasini	Goddess who resides in Vindhyachala

Virya Lakshmi   One of the Ashta Lakshmis; one who gives courage

Vishalakshi   Another name for Maha Devi; one with large eyes

Vishnu Shakti   The feminine energy of Vishnu

Vrindavani   Another name for Tulasi

Yantrini   One of the chief attendants of Lalitha

Yashaswini   A *shakti* created by Lalitha

Yoga Nidra   Goddess in the form of sleep

APPENDIX FOUR

Names of Gods

Adi Shesha	Another name for Ananta
Agni	God of fire
Ananta	Serpent on which Lord Narayana (Vishnu) reclines; denotes endless time
Ardhanareeshwara	Single form of Shiva and Shakti; half male and half female
Aruna	Charioteer of the sun god
Bhava	Shiva; being
Brahma	Creator in the Hindu trinity
Brihaspati	Preceptor of the gods
Chandra	Moon god
Dakshinamurti	Shiva as the universal teacher
Ganapati	Master of the ganas
Ganesha	Son of Parvati; elephant god venerated by all sects of Hinduism
Hanuman	Monkey god; son of the wind god; chief helper of Rama in the Ramayana
Hara	Shiva; one who removes sins
Hari	Vishnu; one who removes sins
Hayagriva	The horse-headed incarnation Vishnu took in order to kill the demon Hayagriva

Indra	King of the demigods
Iswara	Divine as lord and ruler of the universe; personal god in all systems
Janardana	Name of Krishna; giver of all that people ask
Kalki	The tenth *avatara* of Vishnu, still to come
Kama	God of love and desire
Kameswara	Shiva
Kartikeya	General of the gods; son of Shiva
Krishna	Supreme incarnation of Vishnu
Kubera	God of wealth; king of the *yakshas*
Kumara	Another name for Kartikeya
Lakshmana	Brother of Rama
Madhusudana	Vishnu; slayer of the demon Madhu
Mahadeva	The great god; Shiva
Mahakaala	Shiva; god of destruction; lord of time
Maha Vishnu	Vishnu; the harmonizer and maintainer in the trinity
Maha Yogi	Vishnu; Krishna; lord of *yoga*
Maheswara	Shiva; the great lord
Mayan	Principal architect of the gods
Narasimha	The half-man, half-lion incarnation of Vishnu
Narayana	Lord Vishnu, who lies on the serpent Adi Shesha on the cosmic waters
Nataraja	Shiva as the cosmic dancer
Parjanya	Another name for Indra; giver of rain
Pradyumna	Son of Krishna
Pratyaksha Devata	Sun god; the form of the god as is visible before us
Purushottama	The supreme person; Krishna
Raghava	Lord Rama; born in the line of Raghu

Rama	Seventh incarnation of Vishnu; hero of the epic Ramayana
Rudra	The fierce form of Shiva
Sadashiva	The eternal entity of Shiva, corresponding to the Brahman
Savitur	One of the names of the sun god
Shambhu	Shiva
Shanmukha	Kartikeya; the six-faced one
Sharavanabhava	Kartikeya; born among the reeds
Shiva	The destroyer in the Hindu trinity
Shukra	Preceptor of the demons
Skanda	Another name for Kartikeya
Soma	Moon god
Subramania	Another name for Kartikeya
Sundaramurti	Shiva; the most handsome one
Surya	Sun god
Turiya Brahman	The absolute that is ever united with Mula Prakriti or the creative force
Uttama Purusha	The supreme person; Krishna
Vaasudeva	Krishna; son of Vasudeva; one who is immanent in all creation
Vamana	Fifth incarnation of Vishnu; the dwarf man
Varaha	Third incarnation of Vishnu as the boar
Varuna	God of waters; god of the sea
Vayu	God of wind
Vinayaka	Another name for Ganesha
Virabhadra	Incarnation of Shiva
Vishnu	The harmonizer in the Hindu trinity
Vishvakarma	Architect of the gods
Yama	God of death

APPENDIX FIVE

Names of Demons (Asuras)

Andhaka	Blind son of the demon Hiranyaksha
Balahaka	Seven brothers in Bhanda's army
Bhanda	*Asura* born out of the ashes of Kama
Chanda	General of Shumbha's army
Dhumralochana	General of Mahisha's army
Durgama	*Asura* killed by Durga
Durmada	General in Bhanda's army
Hayagriva	Demon who stole the Vedas; upon killing him, Vishnu in a horse-headed incarnation took his name
Hiranyaksha	Elder brother of Hiranyakashipu, Vishnu took the incarnation of the boar in order to kill him
Hiranyakashipu	Famed king of the demons; father of Prahlada, famous devotee of Vishnu
Kaitabha	One of the two demons born out of Vishnu's ears, whom he killed with the help of the goddess
Kamsa	Evil uncle of Krishna

Karambha	Demon who practiced austerities in order to get sons
Kuranda	Bhanda's best general
Madhu	One of the two demons born out of Vishnu's ears, whom he killed with the help of the goddess
Mahabali	Great demon who was slain by Vishnu in his incarnation as Vamana
Mahisha	Buffalo demon killed by Durga
Munda	One of the generals of Shumbha's army
Naraka	A demon who incarcerated many princesses in his dungeon; Krishna killed him and released the princesses
Nishumbha	One of the two *asuric* brothers killed by Durga in the Devi Mahatmyam
Raktabija	Friend and ally of Shumbha; every drop of his blood that fell onto the ground turned into a clone of himself
Rambha	*Asura* who became Raktabija in another life
Ravana	King of Lanka; he abducted Sita, wife of Rama
Shankachuda	Demon who married Tulasi
Shumbha	One of the two *asuric* brothers killed by Durga in the Devi Mahatmyam
Sugriva	Shumbha's minister
Taraka	Fierce demon to kill whom Kartikeya, son of Shiva, was born
Visunga	General of Bhanda's army

APPENDIX SIX

Alphabetical
List of *Mantras*

The *mantras* that appear elsewhere in this book have been listed here in alphabetical order to facilitate location of their translations.

Aum Adbhutacharitrayai Namaha!	Salutations to the one with amazing stories
Aum Adi Shaktyai Namaha!	Salutations to the the primeval force (power of the universal mother goddess)
Aum Aim Hreem Kleem	The three forms of Maha Devi (Saraswati, Lakshmi, and Kaali)
Aum Aim Hreem Kleem Chamundayai Vicchai Namaha!	the most auspicious nine-syllabled *mantra* of Maha Devi; the words *aum* and *namaha* are not counted in the nine syllables but are always repeated with the *mantra*
Aum Ambayai Namaha!	Salutations to the mother Amba
Aum Ambikayai Namaha!	Salutations to Ambika
Aum Bhadrayai Namaha!	Salutations to the giver of auspiciousness

Aum Bhavanyai Namaha!	Salutations to Bhavani (the form of becoming)
Aum Bhuvaneswaryai Namaha!	Salutations to the goddess of the universe
Aum Brahmanyai Namaha!	Salutations to the Brahman
Aum Chakrarajayai Namaha!	Salutations to the king of *chakras* (reference to the Sri Chakra)
Aum Chamundayai Namaha!	Salutations to the slayer of Chanda and Munda (Kaali)
Aum Chandikayai Namaha!	Salutations to Chandika (the fierce one)
Aum Devyayai Namaha!	Salutations to the goddess
Aum Durgayai Namaha!	Salutations to Durga (the remover of evil)
Aum Gangayai Namaha!	Salutations to Ganga
Aum Ishwaryai Namaha!	Salutations to the goddess
Aum Kalaratryai Namaha!	Salutations to the great night of delusion (Brahma's hymn to Adi Shakti)
Aum Kamakshyai Namaha!	Salutations to the goddess with eyes filled with love
Aum Kundalinyai Namaha!	Salutations to the goddess of *kundalini*
Aum Lakshmyai Namaha!	Salutations to Lakshmi (goddess of auspiciousness)
Aum Mahakalyai Namaha!	Salutations to the great Kaali
Aum Mahamayayai Namaha!	Salutations to the great deluder
Aum Mahashaktyai Namaha!	Salutations to the great power

Aum Maheswaryai Namaha!	Salutations to the great goddess
Aum Paramatmikayai Namaha!	Salutations to the one who is the form of the Paramatman
Aum Prakrityai Namaha!	Salutations to Prakriti
Aum Radhayai Svaaha!	the mantra of Radha
Aum Rajnyai Namaha!	Salutations to the queen
Aum Raudrayai Namaha!	Salutations to the wife of Rudra (the terrible one)
Aum Saraswatyai Namaha!	Salutations to Saraswati (the goddess of learning)
Aum Sarvabhuteshwaryai Namaha!	Salutations to the goddess of all creatures
Aum Sathyyai Namaha!	Salutations to Sati (the personification of truth)
Aum Savitryai Namaha!	Salutations to Savitri
Aum Shivaayai Namaha!	Salutations to the auspicious one
Aum Shivapriyayai Namaha!	Salutations to the beloved of Shiva
Aum Sri Ganeshaya Namaha!	Salutations to Lord Ganesha
Aum Sri Matre Namaha!	Salutations to the Divine Mother
Aum Sri Radhayai Namaha!	Salutations to Radha (beloved of Krishna)
Aum Tat Savitur Varenyam	I bow to that sun god Savitur (part of the Gayatri *mantra*)
Aum Vasundharayai Namaha!	Salutations to Vasundhara (the earth goddess)
Aum Vrindavanyai Namaha!	Salutations to the goddess Tulasi (also known as Vrindavani)
Aum Yoginyai Namaha!	Salutations to the female yogi

Glossary of
Sanskrit Terms

aahladini: Power of bliss, causing joy or delight

abhaya mudra: Sign of grace and fearlessness

Adi Shankaracharya: Founder of Advaita

Advaita: Philosophy of nondualism

Advaitin: One who practices this philosophy

adya spanda: Primeval throb of creation

Agastya: Great sage

Aghora: Extreme sect of Tantric philosophy

Aghori: Follower of Aghora

agni: Fire

ahamkara: Ego

ajna chakra: *Chakra* located between the eyebrows

ajnana: Ignorance

ajna shakti: Special forces of Lalitha in charge of wisdom

akasa: Ether; first of the elements

Akasa Ganga: Ganga flowing in the heavens; the Milky Way

akshaya patra: The pot of never-ending food

Alakananda: Tributary of the Ganga

amrita: Nectar of immortality

Amsuman: Bhagiratha's grandfather

anahata chakra: Heart *chakra*

ananda: Bliss

Ananga: Reincarnation of Kama; "the bodiless one"

Ananta: Serpent on which Vishnu sleeps; endless time

apana vayu: Pranic current controlling the lower portion of the body

apas: Water; fourth element

apsara: Celestial dancer

Arjuna: One to whom the advice of the Bhagavad Gita was given; the aspiring human being

Arundhati: Wife of sage Vasishta

Asamanjas: Great-grandfather of Bhagiratha

ashrama: Refuge; sanctuary

ashta shaktis: Eight forces of Lalitha

Ashwatthama: Son of Drona

Asikni: Wife of Daksha

astra: Missile

asura: Demon

asuric: Pertaining to an *asura*

Asvapati: Father of Savitri

Aswamedha Yajna: Horse sacrifice

Aswin: Seventh month of the lunar calendar, roughly corresponding to September/October

atman: Cosmic inner spirit, a contracted expression of the Brahman, containing the whole in a potential form and returning to the whole upon death of the body

aum: A mantra of primeval sound

avadhuta: Highest *yogi*; one who wanders naked and owns nothing

avatara: Incarnation of a deity

avidya: Ignorance; nescience; cosmic delusion

avidya maya: Veiling power of the goddess

avyakta: The unmanifest; primordial cloud of undifferentiated energy and matter from which the five elements emanate

Ayodhya: Capital city of Lord Rama

ayonija: Not born from a womb; describes Sita

Ayurveda: Science of medicine

Badrikashrama: Holy spot in the Himalayas; in modern usage Badrinath

Bana: Seventeenth-century poet; author of *Chandikashtaka*

bana linga: *Linga* found in the *anahata chakra*

Barsana: Birthplace of Radha

Bhagavan: One who has all six lordly characteristics

Bhagiratha: Prince of the solar dynasty who brought the Ganga to the earth

bhakta: Devotee

bhakti: Devotion

bhakti yoga: Yoga of devotion

bhand: An expletive

Bharata Varsha: Ancient name of India

Bhavabhuti: Eighteenth-century poet

bhava samadhi: State of superconsciousness

bhukti: Enjoyable experiences

bhupura: One of three lines forming outer squares in the Sri Chakra

Bhur: One of the astral worlds (*lokas*); the earthly plane or material world

bhuta agni: Fire of spirituality

bhuta shuddhi: Purification of the *bhutas*

bhutas: Spirits; the five primary elements

Bhuvar: One of the astral worlds (*lokas*), corresponding to the middle world of humankind; the world of becomings and desire that is the pivot for action

bija: Seed

bijakshara: Seed sound of a deity

bija mantra: Seed sound

bindu: Point; mystic point from which creation emanates

Bindusaras: Lake of drops

Brahma granthi: Knot of Brahma, formed by the junction of the *sushumna, ida,* and *pingala nadis* at the *muladhara chakra*

Brahma Jnana: Knowledge of the supreme

Brahman: The transcendental absolute; beyond thought and description

Brahma nadi: *Nadi* through which *kundalini* passes

brahmarandra: Orifice at the top of the skull

Brahmin: Member of the priest caste

Brighu: Famous sage; expounder of Brighu Samhita

buddhi: Intellect

buddhi shuddhi: Cleansing of the intellect

Chaitra: A lunar month, roughly corresponding to March/April

chakra: Lotus-shaped whorl of psychic energy

Chakraraja: King of *chakras;* another name for the Sri Chakra

Chandidasa: Fourteenth-century poet

Chandikashtaka: Eight verses on Chandika by the poet Bana

chandra nadi: Another name for the *ida nadi*

chaturyuga: Period of time comprising four *yugas*

chid: Consciousness

chidagnikunda: Eternal pyre in which all creatures are consumed

chintamani griha: Sanctum sanctorum of Maha Devi; made of the fabled
    jewel *chintamani*

chit: The force of pure consciousness; an aspect of Shakti

Chitrakarma: Sculptor who created Bhandasura

Chitrakuta: Hill on which Hanuman resided

chitra nadi: *Nadi* that encloses the Brahma *nadi*

chitta: Superconsciousness

daitya: Demon

Daksha: Father of Sati

Dakshina Marga: Right-hand path of Tantra

Dakshineswara: Famous Kaali temple in Bengal

danava: Demon

dasya bhava: Attitude of a servant

deha shuddhi: Purification of the body

Deva: Shining one; god

Devi: Goddess

Dhanya: Sister of Mena and daughter of Swadha

dharma: Law of righteousness

Dipavali: Festival of lights

divya: Pertaining to Deva or "the shining one"; the *sattvic* followers of Tantra are also known as *divya* since they are filled with light

Diwali: Another name for Dipavali

draavana: Ability to make people run in terror

dukkha: Sorrow

Durga Puja: Nine-day festival dedicated to Durga

Durvasa: Sage known for his anger

Dwapara Yuga: Third epoch

Dwaraka: Lord Krishna's capital

Dyumatsena: Savitri's father-in-law

Ganapatyas: Worshippers of Ganesha or Ganapathy

ganas: Shiva's entourage of goblins and spirits

gandharva: Celestial singer; marriage of mutual consent

Ganga: Ganges river; also the name of the goddess of that river

Gangashtakam: Eight verses to Ganga

Gangotri: Source of the Ganga

Gantaki: River in Nepal

Garuda: Eagle vehicle of Lord Vishnu

gayatri: Poetic meter in which the Gayatri *mantra* is written

Gayatri mantra: Famous mantra to Gayatri

Geyachakra: One of the chariots of Lalitha's army, driven by Mantrini

ghat: Safe place to bathe in the river; a "burning *ghat*" is a place on a riverbank where the dead are burned, after which bathing in the river is compulsory

ghee: Clarified butter

Gokarna: Famous temple town in south India; dedicated to Shiva

Goloka: Celestial world of Krishna

gopala: Cowherder

gopi: Milkmaid or woman of the *gopalas*

Goraknath: Famous Tantric sage; founder of the Nath

granthi: Knot

griha: Enclosure

guna: One of the three essential qualities (*sattva, rajas,* and *tamas*) of Prakriti and thus of all nature

gunatita: One who has risen above the *gunas*

gupta shaktis: Secret forces of Lalitha's army

guru: Spiritual preceptor

ham: *Bija mantra* of the element *akasa*

Haridwar: Pilgrim center on the Ganga in north india

hatha yogi: One who practices *hatha yoga,* a yoga of physical purification

Himavan: King of the mountains (Himalayas)

hreem: Esoteric mantra of the goddess

iccha shakti: Will to create; power of desire

ida: *Nadi* that lies on the left side of the *sushumna*

indriyas: Subtle senses that eventually locate in the gross *jnanendriyas*

ishta devata: Favorite deity

jagat: World

Jahnu: Ancient sage who drank the entire Ganga River

Jana: One of the astral worlds (*lokas*); the world of creative delight

Janaka: Sage-king of Videha; father of Sita

japa: Repetition of a *mantra*

japa mala: Rosary used for *japa*

jatara agni: Fire of digestion

Jayadeva: Author of the *Gita Govinda,* a series of love poems

jiva: The spark of life; individual soul that remains individualized upon death and is reborn within another human body

jivan mukta: Liberated soul; a fully illumined sage

jivatman: Embodied divine spirit that thinks itself separate from the whole

jnana: Spiritual knowledge

jnana shakti: Knowledge of the process of creation; the power of intelligence

jnana yoga: Yoga of knowledge

jnanendriyas: Five sense organs of knowledge: ears, skin, eyes, tongue, and nose

jnani: Man of wisdom

jrimbhana: Ability to cause people to become lazy and keep yawning

Jyesta: Lunar month, roughly corresponding to mid-May through mid-June

kaala: Time

Kailasa: Abode of Lord Shiva in the Himalayas

Kalaratri: The great night of destruction; also another name for Durga

Kalavati: Daughter of Swadha

Kalidasa: Great poet; devotee of Kaali

Kalindi: River in Vrindavana

Kali Yuga: The fourth epoch (in which we are living now)

kalpa: An epoch or age of Brahma the creator

kalpavriksha: Wish-fulfilling tree

kama: Selfish love; infatuation with and desire for material things

Kamadhenu: Wish-fulfilling cow

kamakala: A digit of desire

Kamakhya: Famous temple in Assam

kamandalu: Water pot

Kamarupa: Ancient name of Kamakhya

Kanakadara Stotram: Poem by Adi Shankara on Lakshmi

Kanchipuram: City in Tamilnadu

kanda: Egg-shaped junction located just above the *muladhara chakra* that is the source of all *nadis*

kanta: Beautiful

Kapila: Famous sage

kara: Arm

karma: Action; duty

karma yoga: Yoga of action

karmendriyas: Five organs of action: tongue, hands, legs, genitals, and anus

karmic: Pertaining to the law of karma

Kartika: Lunar month, roughly corresponding to mid-October through mid-November

Kaula Marga: Another name for Vama Marga

Kauravas: One hundred princes of the Kuru dynasty; dark forces of the universe

Kaustubham: Ruby on the breast of Lord Vishnu

Kirichakra: One of the chariots of Lalitha's army, driven by Dandanatha

kona: Corner

kosha: Sheath

kri: Denotes *rajas* in *pra-kri-ti*

Krishna Dwaipayana: Name of Vyasa, author of the Puranas

Krishnamayam jagat: World filled with Krishna alone

Krita Yuga: The first epoch; also called Satya Yuga

kriti: Creation

Krittikas: Constellation known as the Pleiades

kriya shakti: Power to create; power of action

kshatriya: Warrior caste

kshobana: Ability to create emotional disturbance

kundala: Coil

kundalini: Psychic power coiled at the bottom of the spine; an aspect of
    Shakti; also the name of the godess who embodies this power

kundalini yoga: Yoga or study of *kundalini*

Kunti: Mother of the Pandavas

Kurukshetra: Battlefield of the Kurus—the race of the Kauravas and Pandavas;
    the field of human consciousness

laasya: Dance with slow movements; Parvati performs this dance to
    counteract Shiva's *thandava*

lakh: Hundred thousand

lam: *Bija mantra* of the earth element

Lanka: Island kingdom of Ravana

lata: Creeper

laya: Dissolution of the individual self; in the spiritual sense, dissolution of the
    individual consciousness into the supreme undifferenetiated consciousness

laya yoga: Synonym for *kundalini yoga* that has the added meaning of
    dissolving in the supreme

lila: Cosmic play

lingam: Sign; phallic symbol of Shiva

linga sarira: Astral or subtle body

loka: Astral world; there are seven upper *lokas* and seven lower *lokas* or
    netherworlds

maarana: Ability to provoke death or destroy the enemy

madhu: Honey; wine; also the name of a demon

madya: Wine

maha: Great; glorious

mahakaarana: The great cause; Shiva

Mahakameswarastra: "Pure divine love"; missile of Kameswara (Shiva) used by Lalitha to kill Bhanda

Mahamoha: "Supreme illusion"; missile of Bhanda

Mahapadmatavi: Place where Lalitha kept her chariots

Maha Pralaya: Dissolution that takes place in the night of Brahma

Maha Puranas: Great Puranas; eighteen in number

Mahar: One of the astral worlds (*lokas*); world of vastness and pure thought and will

maha tattva: One of the five great elements: *akasa* (ether), *vayu* (air), *agni* (fire), *apas* (water), and *prithvi* (earth)

Mahavidyas: Ten ferocious aspects of the goddess: Kaali, Smashan Tara, Bhuvaneswari, Bagala, Dhumavati, Kamala, Matangi, Shodashi, Chinnamasta, and Bhairavi

makara: Crocodile

mala: Garland; necklace

Malati: Mother of Savitri

mamsa: Meat; flesh

manas: Mind

Manasarovar: Lake in the Himalayas; lake of the mind

mana shuddhi: Purification of the mind

mandala: Mystical design

Mandara: Mystical mountain

manes: Ancestors who live on a world of their own

Mani Dwipa: Mystic island on which the Maha Devi resides

Manikkavachakar: Fourteenth-century saint; famous devotee of Lord Shiva

manipura chakra: Stomach chakra

Manoja: A member of Lalitha's army of *shaktis*

manoja: Aspect of love

mantra: Mystical incantation

mantra shastra: Knowledge of mantras; another name for Tantra

Manu: First of the lawgivers

manvantara: Age of one Manu; 4,320,000 human years

Markandeya: Ancient *rishi* who lived for a whole *manvantara*

mathurya bhava: Feeling of intense or ecstatic love

matsya: Fish

maya: Illusion; power of Maha Devi

maya shakti: Power to create illusion

medhas: Discriminative intellect; bone marrow

Medhas: Name of sage

Mena: Mother of Parvati

mithuna: Coitus

mithya: Unreal

mohana: Ability to attract and delude

moksha: Enlightenment; final liberation from mortality

Mount Meru: Celestial mountain; axis of the world

mudra: Mystical sign; in the *panchamakara* ritual also stands for parched
grain

mukti: Liberation

muladhara chakra: First chakra, found at the base of the spine

nad: Motion; movement

nada: Sound of creation

Nada Brahman: *Aum;* pure consciousness manifesting as sound

nadi: Astral tube that carries psychic energy, such as *kundalini*

nadi shuddhi: Purification of the *nadis*

Naimittika Pralaya: Another name for Maha Pralaya

nama: Name

Nandagopa: Foster father of Lord Krishna

Nandi: Bull vehicle of Lord Shiva

Narada: Celestial singing sage

Naraka Chaturdasi: Fourteenth day of the lunar month on which Lord
Krishna kills the demon Naraka

Narayanastra: Missile of Narayana

Nath: Ancient tribe of Aghoris

navadhanyas: Nine types of grains

Navaratri: Nine-day festival dedicated to the Divine Mother

nirakara: Without form

nirguna: Without the three *gunas* or essential qualities of nature

nitya: Eternal

Nitya Pralaya: Dissolution of individual awareness during sleep

Paasupata: Great arrow of Shiva

padmasana: Lotus posture for sitting

panchamakara: Tantric ritual of five offerings, the names of which each begin with the Sanskrit letter *ma*

Pandavas: Sons of Pandu, representing the virtues of the evolved person

Para Brahman: Supreme consciousness, without form or attributes

paramahamsa: Great swan; title given to highly evolved *yogis*

paramanu: Smallest particle of matter

paramanukala: Shortest period of time

Paramatman: The supreme self; Brahman

Parasara: A sage; father of Veda Vyasa

Paraskara-sutra: Vedic hymn

pasha: Rope (of ignorance which binds the soul)

pashu: Animal; a *tamasic* practitioner of Tantra

Patala Ganga: Name of Ganga in the netherworld

peepul: Fig tree (*Ficus religiosa*)

peetha: Seat

pingala: *Nadi* on the right side of *sushumna*

pra: Exalted; superior; denotes *sattva* in *pra-kri-ti*

prajapati: Patriarch

Prakriti: Executive will of the Purusha

Prakritika Pralaya: Complete dissolution, when all the universe reverts to its original cause

pralaya: Cosmic dissolution; flood; period of repose

prana: Life breath or force; associated with Shakti

pranava: The *mantra aum*

prana vayu: Five forces or winds that control all the involuntary actions

pranayama: Science of breath control

prasada: Grace; leftovers of offerings to god

Prayaga: Confluence of the three sacred rivers of the Indian subcontinent: the Ganga, Yamuna, and Saraswati

Preeti: A member of Lalitha's army of *shaktis*

preeti: Highest form of selfless love

prema: Unselfish love

prithvi: Earth

puja: Ritualistic worship of the divine

Punyabhoomi: The blessed land, another name for India

punya thirtha: Especially holy river

Puranas: Hindu scriptures, of which there are eighteen main and eighteen subsidiary

Puranic: Pertaining to the Puranas

purnata: Fullness

Purusha: Supreme soul; witness of the play of Prakriti

Pushkara: Holy city on a lake (the city has taken on the name of the lake) dedicated to Brahma

rajas: One of the three *gunas,* meaning passion, energy, desire, kinesis

rajasic: Having *rajas,* meaning energetic, passionate, active

raja yoga: Yoga of stilling the mind in order to unite with the supreme

rakshasa: Giant of darkness and evil; violently egoistic with uncontrollable passions

ram: *Bija mantra* for the element of *agni*

Ramakrishna: Great Bengali saint of the twentieth century

Ramarajya: Kingdom of Sri Rama, noted for its all-around social perfection

Rasa Lila: Dance of Krishna with the *gopis* in the forest of Vrindavana

rasa mandalam: The circular formation that the *gopis* made suring the performance of Rasa Lila

rasis: Twelve constellations around the earth

Rati: Wife of Kama

rishi: Truth seer; seer-sage; the composers of the Vedic hymns were *rishis*

rita: Truth in action; working of *sat* or reality in the cosmos

Rudra granthi: Knot of Rudra, formed by the junction of the *sushumna, ida,* and *pingala nadis* at the *ajna chakra* between the brows

rupa: Form

Sabda Brahman: Emanation of consciousness or the absolute as sound; *aum*

sadhaka: One who practices spiritual disciplines

sadhana: Spiritual practice or discipline

sadhana shastra: Another name for Tantra

Sagara: Ancient king of the Surya dynasty; ocean

saguna: Having form and all qualities of nature

sahasrara chakra: *Chakra* at the top of the skull; known as the thousand-petaled lotus

sakhya bhava: Attitude of a friend

saligrama: Stone found in the Gantiki River in Nepal that carries the mark or image of Vishnu

samadhi: Superconscious state

samana vayu: One of the five winds that takes care of involuntary actions and controls digestion

Samaya: Conservative path of Tantra

samsara: World of cyclical movement; world of transmigration

samvit: Intelligence

Sanatana Dharma: Eternal law of righteousness; name of Hinduism

Sanat Kumaras: Four boy saints, named Sanaka, Sananda, Sanat Kumara, and Sanatana; they are the eternal powers of the divine, ever youthful, who lead people to the truth

sankalpa: Intention; determination

Sapta Matrikas: "Seven mothers"; the seven fierce forms of Maha Devi: Brahmaani, Maheswari, Kaumari, Vaishnavi, Vaarahi, Indrani, and Nrisimhi

sarabha: Fabled animal that is half bird, half dragon

sarga: Primary creation

sarira: Body

sarva anandamaya chakra: Giver of unending bliss

sarva rakshakara chakra: Giver of all protection

sarva rogahara chakra: Remover of all diseases

sarvartha sadhaka chakra: Accomplisher of all purposes

sarva sankshobhana chakra: Agitator of all

sarva siddhiprada chakra: Giver of all powers

sarva saubhagya chakra: Giver of all auspiciousness

sarvasya paripuraka chakra: Fulfiller of all desires

sat: Being; reality; existence

sattva: One of the three *gunas*, meaning balance, harmony, and equilibrium

sattvic: Having *sattva*, meaning balanced and harmonius

satya: Truth

Satyaloka: The astral world (*loka*) of Brahma; world of highest truth; also Satya *loka*

Satyavan: Prince who married Savitri

Saundaryalahari: Poem in praise of Lalitha's beauty by Adi Shankaracharya

Savarnika: Epoch of the Manu Savarni, in which the story of the Devi Mahatmyam took place

Shaiva: Sect that considers Shiva to be the supreme reality

Shaivite: Follower of Shaiva

Shakta: Sect that considers the goddess to be the supreme reality; also, a follower of this sect

shakti: Power; a particular energy of the goddess that can manifest as another goddess

Shakti Peetha: Place where part of Sati's body had fallen, filled with divine energy

Shaktism: Philosophy of the Shaktas

shanta bhava: Peaceful approach to God

shanta murti: Peaceful aspect of the godhead

shastra: Scripture

Shatagni: Blazing weapon of Agni

shatkona: Six-cornered figure of two intersecting triangles

shava: Corpse

shiva lata mudra: One of the sexual practices in Tantra; mystical gesture in which all traces of animal desire are completely eliminated

shuddha tattva: Purest element

shuddhi: Spiritual purification

Shuka: Son of Vyasa

shunya: Void; zero

Shunyaka: Another name for Sonitapura

siddhi: Spiritual perfection

siddhis: Supernatural powers, eight in number; the eight *siddhis* are (1) the ability to make oneself tiny, (2) the ability to make oneself huge, (3) the ability to become extremely light, (4) the ability to become extremely heavy, (5) the ability to achieve anything and travel anywhere, (6) possession of irresistable will power, (7) mastery over all creatures, (8) having the godlike powers to create and destroy

Sita: Wife of Rama; form of the earth goddess

smashana: Burning ghat

smriti: Vedic truth in a modern setting; collective name for the Puranas

Sonitapura: Bhanda's Capital city

Souryas: Worshippers of Surya, the sun god

spanda: Initial throb of creation; vibration

sraddha: Faith

sri: Auspiciousness or prosperity; also a name for Lakshmi

Sri Chakra: Supreme *yantra* of the goddess

srimad: Excellent; venerated

Srimati Jahnavi: Ganga

Srinagar: Name of Lalitha's city

Sripura: Sanctum sanctorum of Lalitha

sruti: Revealed truth; collective name for the Vedas

stambhana: Ability to induce paralysis

sthuti: Praise

stotram: Hymn

Sudama: Friend of Krishna in Gokula

Sudarshana Chakra: Vishnu's weapon; the wheel of time

Sugriva: Monkey king who helped Rama; also the name of a demon who was Shumbha's minister

Sumeru: Mountain where Mahisha practiced *tapas*

sunyata: Void

Suratha: King mentioned in the Devi Mahatmyam

Suryamandala: The sun and its aura

surya nadi: Another name for the *pingala nadi*

Surya Narayana: Spiritual field of the sun; spiritual aura of the sun god

sushumna: *nadi* that rises up through the spinal column, extending from the *muladhara chakra* at the bottom of the spine to the *brahmarandra* orifice at the crown of the head

Suta: One who recites the scriptures

Swadha: Wife of the *manes*

swadhistana chakra: *Chakra* at the root of the reproductive organs

Swar: One of the astral worlds (*lokas*); the heavenly region or the world of light; a pure psychic state

swarga-sopana-sharani: "Ladder to heaven"; refers to the Ganga

swayambhuva lingam: Representation of the *lingam* of Shiva found in the *muladhara chakra*

tadrupata: Attaining the same form (as the deity)

tamas: One of the three *gunas,* meaning darkness, ignorance, and inertia

tamasic: Having *tamas,* meaning inert, dark, ignorant, sluggish

tanmatras: Five subtle elements: touch, taste, odor, form, and sound

tanmayata: Melting of the devotee's personality into that of the deity

tanoti: Expansion

Tantra: System of worshipping the divine as Shakti or divine energy

Tantric: Pertaining to Tantra

Tantrist: One who practices Tantra

tapas: Meditation; austerity

tapasvin: Male who practices austerities

tapasvini: Female who practices austerities

tapasya: Spiritual force acquired by the practice of austerities, including meditation, for gaining spiritual and material powers

Tapo: One of the astral worlds (*lokas*); world of infinite will; also spelled Tapa

tarpana: Offering of water to the manes and to the sun god

tattva: Element; there are twenty-five *tattvas,* which include the five *bhutas*

tattva shuddhi: Purification of the elements that make up our material body

thandava: Vigorous, violent dance that precedes creation and destruction; dance of Shiva

thirtha: Holy waters

Thirtharaja: King of all *thirthas;* refers to Prayaga

ti: Denotes *tamas* in *pra-kri-ti*

trailokya mohana chakra: "Enchanter of the three worlds"; part of the Sri Chakra

trayati: Liberation

Treta Yuga: Second age or cycle of evolution

trikona: Triangle

Trimurtis: Trinity of Brahma, Vishnu, and Shiva

Trisati: Hymn to the goddess Lalitha

tulasi: The holy basil; also the name of a goddess

turiya: Fourth state of consciousness that underlies all the other states; *samadhi* state

ucchatana: Ability to force a person to stop whatever he or she is doing

udana vayu: Vital breath that directs currents upward; aids spiritual development

Upa Puranas: The eighteen secondary Puranas

Uttama Purusha: The supreme person; Krishna

vac: Power of sound or speech; also a name for Saraswati

Vaikunta: Transcendental abode of Vishnu

Vaishnava: Pertaining to Vishnu

Vaishnavism: Sect that considers Vishnu to be the supreme reality

Vaishnavite: Follower of Vaishnavism

vaisya: Merchant caste

Vaitarini: Name of the Ganga as it circles the city of Yama, god of death, in the netherworld; also refers to the sacrifice of a cow at the time of death

Vaivasvata: Present *manvantara*

vajra nadi: *Nadi* inside the *sushumna nadi*

Valmiki: Author of the Ramayana

vam: *Bija mantra* of the element of water

Vama Marga: Left-hand path of Tantra

vamsa: Lineage

vanamala: Garland of wildflowers; Vishnu and his *avataras* always wear one

Varanasi: Famous temple town of northern India; special to Shiva

varna: Color; one of the fifty articulate sounds; caste

vasana: Inherited or acquired tendencies of the mind

Vasishta: Famous sage; guru of Rama

vatsalya bhava: Love of the parent for a child; one of the modes of approach to God

vayu: Wind

Vedanta: Collective name for the Upanishads

Veda Vyasa: Another name for Vyasa, the sage who compiled the Vedas

Vedic: Pertaining to the Vedas

veena: Indian lute

Videha: Birthplace of Sita

vidya: Knowledge

vidya maya: Power of the goddess to dispel illusion through knowledge

Vidyapati: Midfourteenth- to midfifteenth-century poet who was a devotee of Krishna

vidyarambham: Ceremony to denote the begining of studies for a child

Vijayadasami: Day of victory; last day of the nine-day festival of worship of the Divine Mother

vikritis: Modifications of Prakriti, giving rise to the different emotions that appear in the mind, such as happiness, sorrow, fear, and anger

vilva: Tree whose leaves are used in the worship of Shiva

vimarsha: Seed desire; quality of Maha Devi

Vindhya: Mountains of central India

Vindhyachala: Famous temple town dedicated to the goddess

vira: Heroic; *rajasic* practitioner of Tantra

viraha dukkha: Poignant sorrow of separation

Virini: One of the wives of Daksha

visarga: Secondary creation

Vishnu granthi: Knot of Vishnu, formed by the junction of the *sushumna, ida,* and *pingala nadis* at the *manipura chakra*

Vishnupadi: Another name for the Ganga; "coming from the feet of Vishnu"

vishuddha chakra: *Chakra* located at the throat

vishwarupa: Cosmic form of a deity

Vraja: Village where Krishna grew up

Vrindavana: Forest where Krishna played with the *gopis* and *gopalas*

Vrishabhanu: Radha's father

Vrishadvaja: Tulasi's father

vyana vayu: Life breath that governs circulation

Vyasa: Famous sage; compiler of the Vedas and author of the Puranas

Yadava: Krishna's clan

yajna: Fire sacrifice

yajna kund: Pit where *yajna* is conducted

yajnashala: Hall where *yajna* is held

yakshas: Class of celestial beings that control wealth

yam: *Bija mantra* for the element of wind

Yamuna: Name of the river on whose banks Krishna sported with the *gopis*

yantra: Mystical mathematical figure

Yasoda: Foster mother of Krishna

yoga: Path for discovering the truth underlying the phenomenal world as well as the truth of one's own self; a path that leads to union with the divine

yoga nidra: Spiritual sleep; also the name of the goddess who embodies this state

yogi: Man who practices yoga; saint

yogini: Woman who practices yoga

yoni: Vulva

Yudhistira: Arjuna's eldest brother

yuga: An age; an epoch

Bibliography

Coburn, Thomas B. *Devi-Mahatmyam: The Crystallization of the Goddess Tradition*. Delhi: Motilal Banarsidass Publications, 1984.

Devi Mahatmyam: Glory of the Divine Mother. Translated by Swami Jagadiswarananda. Madras: Sri Ramakrishna Math, 1982.

Dikshitar, V. R. Ramachandra. *The Lalita Cult*. Delhi: Motilal Banarsidass Publications, 1991.

Ghose, Sri Aurobindo. *Savitri*. Pondicherry, India: Sri Aurobindo International Centre of Education, 1962.

Johnson, Linda. *The Living Goddess*. Saint Paul, Minn.: Yes International Publishers, 1999.

Shankaranarayanan, S. *Sri Chakra*. Pondicherry, India: Dipti Publications, 1970.

Sivananda, Swami. *Kundalini Yoga*. Sivanandanagar, India: Divine Life Society, 1971.

Srimad Devi Bhagavatam. Translated by Swami Vijnanananda. Allahabad: Panini Office, 1922–1923.

Svoboda, Robert E. *Aghora*. 3 vols. Albuquerque, N. Mex.: Brotherhood of Life, 1986.

Wilkins, W. J. *Hindu Mythology*. London: Curzon Press, 1973.

Index

puja (ritual), 20
Punyabhoomi, 207–8
Puranas, 22–31, 171–74, 207–8, 222, 258
Purusha, 5, 9, 28–30, 36, 39, 135
Pushkara, 228

Radha, 186, 216–25, 226
Rajarajeshwari, 44–53
rajas, 12, 29–30, 36–37, 38, 118, 267
raja yoga, 311
Raktabija, 122–23, 128
Rama, 233–38
Ramayana, 175, 234
Rambha, 106–7
Ramya, 68
Rasa Lila, 219, 224
Rati, 69–70, 73, 150, 152, 161, 253
Ratktabija, 104, 107, 119
Ravana, 235
religion, 3–4
renunciation, 272
Rig Veda, 1–2, 103, 197, 208
rishi Medhas, 103–4
rishis, 3–4, 51, 199
Rudra, 46–47, 62

Sabda Brahman, 289
sacred water, 208
Sadashiva, 291
sadhakas, 80, 84–85
sadhana, 254, 259, 262, 263–64, 312–13
sadhana shastra, 259
sadness, 222–23
Sagara, 175–76
sahasrara chakra, 84, 141–42, 307–8
sakhya bhava, 221

Samadhi, 100–101, 105, 308–9
Sampatkari, 76
samsara, 97
Sanaka, 258
Sananda, 258
Sanatana, 258
Sanatana Dharma, 38
Sanat Kumara, 258
santanaka trees, 45
Santana Lakshmi, 200
Sapta Matrikas, 47, 123, 250–51
Saraswati, 6, 9–10, 40, 55, 98, 118, 173–74, 201, 205
Sarvaloka. *See* Mani Dwipa
Sarvavidya, 210
Satakshi, 88–89
Sati, 85, 130–39, 140–44, 207–8, 251–52
sattva, 12, 29–30, 36–37, 38, 118, 213, 267
Satyavan, 244–45
Saundaryalahari, 68
Savarni, 100
Savitri, 48, 103, 240–47
science, 3–4, 17–18, 193–94
scriptures, list of, 321–23. *See also* specific scriptures
Sea of Nectar, 92, 202
seven sages, 155, 157
sexuality, 91, 270–82
Shakambari, 89
Shakti, 5–6, 100
    forms of, 6–10
    See also Adi Shakti
shaktis, 14, 68–69, 73–74, 79–80, 89, 89–90, 250

BOOKS OF RELATED INTEREST

Shiva
Stories and Teachings from the Shiva Mahapurana
by Vanamali

Hanuman
The Devotion and Power of the Monkey God
by Vanamali

The Complete Life of Krishna
Based on the Earliest Oral Traditions and the Sacred Scriptures
by Vanamali

The Science of the Rishis
The Spiritual and Material Discoveries of the Ancient Sages of India
by Vanamali

Tantric Kali
Secret Practices and Rituals
by Daniel Odier

The Goddess in India
The Five Faces of the Eternal Feminine
by Devdutt Pattanaik

Sheela na gig
The Dark Goddess of Sacred Power
by Starr Goode

The Great Goddess
Reverence of the Divine Feminine from the Paleolithic to the Present
by Jean Markale

Inner Traditions • Bear & Company
P.O. Box 388
Rochester, VT 05767
1-800-246-8648
www.InnerTraditions.com

Or contact your local bookseller